Trauma and Ethics in the Novels of Graham Swift

For Karen

Trauma and Ethics in the Novels of Graham Swift

No Short-Cuts to Salvation

STEF CRAPS

SUSSEX
ACADEMIC
PRESS

Brighton • Portland

2 4 6 8 10 9 7 5 3 1

First published 2005 in Great Britain by
SUSSEX ACADEMIC PRESS
PO Box 2950
Brighton BN2 5SP

and in the United States of America by
SUSSEX ACADEMIC PRESS
920 NE 58th Ave Suite 300
Portland, Oregon 97213–3786

British Library Cataloguing in Publication Data
A CIP catalogue record for this book is available from the British Library.

Library of Congress Cataloging-in-Publication Data
Craps, Stef.
Trauma and ethics in the novels of Graham Swift : no short-cuts to salvation / Stef Craps.
p. cm.
Includes bibliographical references and index.
ISBN 1-84519-004-1 (hardcover : alk. paper)
1. Swift, Graham, 1949– — Criticism and interpretation. 2. Psychic trauma in literature. 3. Ethics in literature. 4. Memory in literature. I. Title.

PR6069.W47Z64 2005
823′.914—dc22

2004028725
CIP

Uitgegeven met steun van de Universitaire Stichting van België

Typeset and designed by G&G Editorial, Brighton
Printed by The Cromwell Press, Trowbridge, Wiltshire
This book is printed on acid-free paper.

Contents

Acknowledgements

This book started life as a PhD dissertation at the University of Leuven. I am particularly indebted to Ortwin de Graef, who has been everything I could have wished for in a supervisor. It was an honour, a privilege and a pleasure to work under his inspiring guidance. My thanks also go out to Catherine Bernard, Wendy Wheeler, Bart Philipsen and Hedwig Schwall for their valuable criticisms of my dissertation; and to Tim Andrews and Tony Grahame for their judicious editing and helpful advice in the preparation of this volume. The publication of this book was funded by a grant from the Belgian University Foundation, for which I am profoundly grateful. To my parents, Paul Craps and Jeannine Cobbaert, I owe a special debt of gratitude for their unwavering support in this project, as in all of my endeavours. This book is dedicated to Karen Van Holm, light of my life, to whom, try as I might, I cannot give adequate thanks.

The author and publisher gratefully acknowledge the following for permission to reproduce copyright material:

Macmillan, for excerpts from *The Sweet Shop Owner* and *Ever After*. Random House, for excerpts from *Ever After*. A. P. Watt Ltd, on behalf of Graham Swift, for excerpts from *The Sweet Shop Owner*, *Shuttlecock*, *Waterland* and *Out of this World*.

Material from chapter 2 was published as '"As If History Could Be Circumvented": Undying Memories in Graham Swift's *The Sweet Shop Owner*' in *The AnaChronist* (2003): 197–222. A condensed version of chapter 5 appeared as 'Cathartic Fables, Fabled Catharses: Photography, Fiction and Ethics in Graham Swift's *Out of this World*' in *European Journal of English Studies* 7.3 (2003): 293–309. A shortened version of chapter 7 was published as '"All the Same Underneath"? Alterity and

Ethics in Graham Swift's *Last Orders*' in *Critique: Studies in Contemporary Fiction* 44.4 (Summer 2003): 405–20.

Permission to use René Magritte's painting *La lunette d'approche* as a cover image was granted by SABAM on behalf of the Magritte estate. In forcing the viewer to confront the void, to realize the frailty of command, the limits of explanation, *La lunette d'approche* aptly illustrates the title and the overarching argument of this book. A photographic reproduction of the painting was obtained from The Menil Collection in Houston, Texas.

The publishers apologize for any errors or omissions in the above list and would be grateful to be notified of any corrections that should be incorporated in the next edition or reprint of this book.

Abbreviations

The following abbreviations are used to identify quotations from Graham Swift's fictional works:

SSO	*The Sweet Shop Owner*
S	*Shuttlecock*
LS	*Learning to Swim and Other Stories*
W	*Waterland*
OW	*Out of this World*
EA	*Ever After*
LO	*Last Orders*
LD	*The Light of Day*

The abbreviations are not used when the quoted material is from the book that forms the focus of the chapter in question. For example, parenthetical references to *The Sweet Shop Owner* in chapter 2, which concentrates on *The Sweet Shop Owner*, will not contain the abbreviation 'SSO' but only the page number of the quoted passage, whereas any quotations from *Waterland* or any other literary text by Swift will be indicated with the corresponding abbreviation followed by the page number. The same is true, mutatis mutandis, for all succeeding chapters.

Trauma and Ethics in the Novels of Graham Swift

Introduction

Walking Wounded

La place manque, et pourtant il faut parler
des traumatismes swiftiens.
Marc Porée, 'Quelques clefs'[1]

This book offers a critical reading of the novels of Graham Swift. It provides a reappraisal of Swift's work by confronting it with the insights, findings and hypotheses generated by trauma studies, an area of inquiry that emerged on the literary-theoretical and literary-critical scene as one manifestation of the 'ethical turn' affecting the humanities in the 1990s. Using the interpretive wherewithal afforded by trauma theory and the literature-and-ethics movement more widely, this book illuminates hitherto un- or under-explored aspects of Swift's texts and thus contributes to – and, to some extent, reorients – our understanding of what is arguably one of the most significant literary oeuvres of the late twentieth and early twenty-first centuries.

Chapters 2–8 are each devoted to a detailed reading of one of Swift's novels. The order of the chapters follows the chronology of the publication of Swift's work in Britain.[2] Chapter 1 surveys the general literary-theoretical background against which these readings take shape and considers their relationship to the field in which they intervene most directly: that of Swift criticism. These two attempts at contextualization are closely related, as the fault lines between the various types of critical interpretations of Swift's work correspond fairly accurately to divisions apparent in the contemporary literary-theoretical debate on trauma and ethics. These initial remarks are meant to frame the detailed textual analyses that make up the bulk of this book.

The readings of Swift's novels presented here tend to focus on experiences of overwhelming loss that the characters – some of 'the world's walking wounded' (OW 174) – are struggling to come to grips with. Swift's work is haunted by bereavement, both real and symbolic: recurrent motifs are the death or estrangement of a partner, parent or child, the loss of faith, the dissolution of a sense of history and of identity. As Catherine Miquel points out, this fixation has earned Swift the epithet of 'terminal novelist' (131).[3] The reality with which he confronts his characters – typical ingredients of which are murder, war, torture, terrorism, impending nuclear annihilation, suicide, death, madness, incest and rape – is an intensely traumatic one, tripping them up, throwing them off balance, unsettling their comfortable world-views and cutting the ground from under their habitual assumptions. The challenge that is placed before them is to work through this discomforting reality, to establish a relationship with it that would protect them from the brute, destructive force of the trauma without, however, seeking to neutralize or eliminate it.

The prototypical Swiftian protagonist is a humble, unheroic, vulnerable older man who finds himself in a state of acute crisis. The starting point for the story, usually rendered in the first person,[4] is the protagonist's need to account for his current predicament. As Swift has repeatedly stated in interviews, he is interested in story-telling as an existential necessity, a vital urge that manifests itself most poignantly in crisis situations:

> es cuando se está en medio de la crisis que se tiene la urgencia de contar lo que sucede. Uno se pregunta: ¿cómo llegué aquí? ¿Qué hice mal, en qué me equivoqué? Y eso implica mirar hacia atrás, casi de forma automática, para ver lo que ocurrió y poder contar la historia. Así que por eso es que mis narradores están en medio de su crisis de una manera u otra. Están contando la historia de una manera muy urgente, si no para resolver su crisis, para entender cómo llegaron a ese momento.

> it is when one finds oneself in the middle of the crisis that one feels the need to talk about what happens. One asks oneself: how did I get here? What did I do wrong, where did I make a mistake? And this implies looking back, almost automatically, to see what happened and to be able to tell the story. So that is why my narrators are in the middle of their crisis in one way or another. They are telling the story with great urgency, if not to resolve their crisis, then to understand how they arrived at that moment. (quoted in Vásquez 108)

The crisis in the narrative present points to one of Swift's key thematic preoccupations: the insidious hold exerted over the present by a traumatic past. It marks the moment when the ghosts of the past return to haunt a narrator-protagonist who labours under the illusion that he has successfully put the past to rest. As the past catches up with the present,[5] he feels the foundations slipping away upon which he, and the society to which he belongs, have built their existence, and by means of which they have sought to keep the trauma at bay. The question that he now faces is how to respond to this situation of unsettlement and perplexity, whether to hide or flee from it or to try and engage with it in a meaningful way. Negating the radically disorienting impact of trauma, typically through the pursuit of an illusory ideal of wholeness or completion, is shown to have catastrophic personal and political consequences. However, Swift's work also raises the possibility that the process of working through trauma might create the conditions for a viable alternative *modus vivendi* based on openness to and respect for alterity.

Obviously, this very general description of Swift's fictional universe cannot but fail to do justice to the rich variety of his works, even though these do reveal an unusually high degree of continuity – leading one critic to describe Swift's oeuvre as

> a familiar family of novels that resemble one another like siblings who have, perhaps, an odd marital infidelity or two in their heritage. The plots change, the characters are different, but the same patterns recur, the same double time frames, the same use of the past circling around a crucial, half-hidden incident . . . (Harris)

Though the aforementioned concerns are central to Swift's work as a whole, there are significant differences in the way the individual novels articulate them.

In his early works, *The Sweet Shop Owner* and *Shuttlecock*, there is not yet any real engagement with trauma; indeed, the dominant mode of dealing with 'undying memories' (SSO 86) or 'needless painful knowledge' (S 176) is through denial. While this type of treatment is found to be deeply problematic, the texts do not yet put forward any credible alternatives to the strategies of evasion adopted by their respective protagonists. In *Waterland*, *Out of this World* and *Ever After*, by contrast, trauma intrudes with such force that strategies of evasion or containment become altogether untenable. It is in these 'middle-period' novels, which conform most closely to the prototypical model that has just been outlined, that Swift's struggle with trauma is most clearly played out. The texts are quite vocal in their condemnation of redemptive, totalizing narratives, which they expose as dangerous forms of reality-denial. Yet, from the site of trauma, *Waterland* and *Ever After* also intimate more constructive ways of dealing with a shattering experience of loss, the former by promoting the cultivation of a spirit of open-ended inquiry that is to guard us against the potentially murderous consequences of ideological mystification, the latter by tentatively initiating a process of genuine mourning through which its melancholic protagonist may eventually learn to enter into non-totalizing relationships with other people. This theme of personal and social regeneration takes centre stage in Swift's most recent novels, *Last Orders* and *The Light of Day*, which are less directly concerned with the notion of traumatic unsettlement. As Tamás Bényei has remarked about *Last Orders*, 'the text . . . abandons the exploration of trauma and traumatic time, and is therefore exempt from the almost gratuitous proliferation of traumas, which threatened to suffocate the two previous novels' (52). In *Last Orders* and *The Light of Day*, the emphasis shifts from symptomatic acting-out to working-through: the texts' focus is less on the experience of loss itself than on efforts to rebuild community after grief.[6]

This book attempts to chart the entire trajectory of Swift's engagement with the perils, pitfalls and possibilities of navigating a post-traumatic condition. However, it deliberately leaves aside the author's short stories, which, for the most part, date from the very beginning of his writing career,[7] constituting a preamble to the novels.[8] These early texts do not shed any significant new light on Swift's preoccupation with trauma and ethics – which, after all, only becomes truly central to his oeuvre starting with *Waterland*. The remaining texts form a rich enough corpus as it is: an impressive and challenging body of work which requires, and rewards, close attention and careful scrutiny.

What Went Before

1

A Swift Survey

how things of the past aren't things of the past.
Graham Swift, *Waterland*

As Lawrence Buell noted in the 1999 special issue of *PMLA* devoted to ethical criticism, 'Ethics has gained new resonance in literary studies during the past dozen of years' (7). This observation is borne out by, among other things, the numerous special issues of literary and philosophical journals,[1] articles and books on ethics that have seen the light of day since the late 1980s and especially since the middle of the 1990s. The recent nature of the turn to ethics is aptly illustrated by the fact that the original, 1990 edition of Lentricchia and McLaughlin's authoritative *Critical Terms for Literary Study* had no entry titled 'Ethics'; an essay on the subject, written by Geoffrey Galt Harpham, was added for the second edition, which appeared in 1995.[2]

In this essay – which was later included in *Shadows of Ethics* – Harpham points out that for most of the 'Theoretical Era (*c.* 1968–87)' ethics enjoyed 'no respect' (*Shadows* 18). David Parker, another chronicler of the ethical turn in literary studies, concurs that for most of the 1970s and 1980s, 'advanced' (1) literary scholarship[3] had been 'either more or less silent about ethics or deeply suspicious of it' (2). In the 1970s and early 1980s, the heyday of poststructuralism and deconstruction, the profession was predominantly concerned with the linguistic materiality of the literary artefact, which was subjected to rigorous rhetorical analysis. In the 1980s, this textualist paradigm gave way to new historicism/cultural materialism, cultural studies and different types of 'advocacy' criticism (postcolonial, feminist, gay and lesbian, Marxist), approaches indebted to poststructuralism but intent on imbuing it with an attention to history and politics that was felt to be lacking in the previous paradigm. Much of the theoretical and critical work produced during this period shows a strong distaste for ethics, a concept that for many became 'the proper name of power, hypocrisy and unreality' (Harpham, *Shadows* 18). The Marxist critic Fredric Jameson, for instance, accused ethics of serving as 'the ideological vehicle and the legitimation of concrete structures of power and domination' (114), a charge echoed by various postcolonial and feminist critics. Widely regarded as an ideological mask concealing the will to power of dominant groups in society, ethics ended up an object of contempt, ridicule and abuse.

The marked upsurge in interest in ethics that the discipline of literary studies has witnessed since the late 1980s can be attributed to a number of factors. It is often linked to the re-evaluation of the ethics of deconstruction prompted by the discovery of Paul de Man's wartime journalism, which turned out to contain anti-Semitic passages. As Harpham puts it, somewhat hyperbolically: 'On or about December 1, 1987 [the day the *New York Times* broke the news], the nature of literary theory changed' (*Shadows* 20). Other developments that have helped put ethics back on the agenda include the remarkable shift of emphasis in the later work of Michel Foucault, which moved from a concern with the discursive construction of subjects by power/knowledge regimes to a focus on the care of the self conceived as an ethical project, and – perhaps especially – the increasing attention being paid to literature by moral philosophy. Indeed, according to Parker, the turn towards the ethical within literary studies is 'closely connected to', and even 'fuelled primarily by', 'a turn to the literary within ethics' (14).

It is important to underline, however, that the fundamental reorientation of literary theory and criticism which these (and doubtless many other) events and evolutions have set in motion has not led to the establishment of one coherent, homogeneous and easily identifiable ethical paradigm. Buell notes that 'as *ethics* has become a more privileged signifier it has also become an increasingly ductile and thereby potentially confusing one' (11). Marked by a 'disparity of focus', the emerging field of literary-ethical inquiry faces a potential 'problem of cacophony' (Buell 11). Nevertheless, it is possible to distinguish some trends in this 'pluriform discourse' (Buell 7). In his study *Getting It Right*, Harpham divides the various approaches jostling under the umbrella of ethics into two broad groups:

> Those on the right claim that the 'restoration' of ethics to its 'rightful place' in contemporary discourse would produce a return to central or essential 'values,' helping to revitalize a degenerate humanism and reaffirm a battered tradition; while for many on the left, ethics names the obligation to empower the hitherto deprivileged, silenced, or colonized other. (1)

Whereas the latter strand, which is also known as poststructuralist or deconstructive ethical theory, stresses the need to respect alterity and to resist the reduction of the other to the same, the former, neo-humanist strand tends to concentrate on the growth of the self as a moral being. Hence, the distinction between right and left, or neo-humanist and deconstructive ethical theory, can be construed as the opposition between a basically 'self-centred' and an essentially 'other-centred' conception of ethics.

The neo-humanists take their inspiration mainly from Anglo-American moral philosophy and classical, Aristotelian philosophy, which argues for the concrete embeddedness of moral judgements. Among their ranks are philosophers like Martha Nussbaum, Charles Taylor, Richard Rorty, Alasdair McIntyre and Iris Murdoch as well as literary critics like Parker, Wayne Booth and Richard Freadman. The central figure here is arguably Nussbaum, who has set forth an influential case for the importance of the literary imagination in moral philosophy and public life. In 'Exactly and Responsibly: A Defense of Ethical Criticism', Nussbaum usefully summarizes and further elaborates the key findings of her research on literature and ethics as laid out in *Love's Knowledge* and *Poetic Justice*. She begins by approvingly quoting Henry James's statement that the writer engages in ethical activity by cutting through the blur of habit and making us see reality more clearly. It being the case that 'human beings do great damage to themselves and others through obtuseness and refusal of vision' (343–44), the effort to obtain a more truthful picture of reality qualifies as an ethical endeavour. Hence, when we follow the author as attentive readers, Nussbaum continues, 'we ourselves engage in ethical conduct' (344) too. Literature – or at least a particular kind of literature[4] – is said to exert a beneficial moral influence on the reader by exercising his or her imagination and bringing him or her into contact with 'the complexity of our own lives and the lives of others' (348). By 'tak[ing] us into the lives of those who are different in circumstance from ourselves', novels such as those of Dickens allegedly 'enable us to understand how similar hopes and fears are differently realized in different social circumstances' (350). Literature makes us realize, then, that differences between people are only skin-deep: if we but look closely enough, we notice that other people have an inner life very similar to our own. By helping us imaginatively to understand 'the situation of the poor and excluded', Nussbaum contends, literature can make a significant contribution to the struggle to 'improv[e] their lot and ameliorat[e] their suffering' (351).

Proponents of the deconstructive position, on the other hand, align themselves with 'continental' critical philosophy. They tend to focus on the notion of imperativity – the *ought* – as theorized by Immanuel Kant and Emmanuel Levinas. Levinas's work in particular, and the revisions of his thought proposed by the late Jacques Derrida, have turned out to be a major source of inspiration for critics working within this tradition. Their number includes – besides Derrida himself – Harpham, Robert Eaglestone, Derek Attridge, J. Hillis Miller, Simon Critchley, Adam Zachary Newton and Andrew Gibson. The pivot around which their work revolves is the eminently Levinasian notion of responsibility to the otherness of the other. Eluding every attempt to understand, grasp or possess it, the other puts into question the imperialism of the same which insists on reducing the other to the self's horizons of significance. One particular manifestation of this imperialism would be neo-humanist ethical theory, which, from the deconstructive perspective, appears as a totalizing and oppressive moral code. The neo-humanists' presumption to speak for others as if they were exactly like oneself is seen as proof of an ingrained 'obtuseness' to and disregard for alterity. According to Gibson, Nussbaum, Rorty, Parker and Booth promote 'an ethics that cannot allow for radical difference, heterogeneity, the thought of the incommensurable' (11). Indeed, if the task, as Rorty reminds us, is 'to keep trying to expand our sense of "us" as far as we can' (196), there is a real danger that the self ('us'), in its drive to recognize itself in all that is different from it ('them'), will be oblivious, if not altogether hostile, to the needs and wishes of concrete others who exceed the frames of reference by which the self makes sense of the world. Deconstructive ethical theory, in contrast, is concerned with the possibility of a non-appropriative encounter with the other. It conceives ethics as an indispensable bad conscience which continually interrupts the logic of morality lest it produce cruelty and oppression: 'Ethics . . . operates as a kind of play within morality, holds it open, hopes to restrain it from violence or the will to domination, subjects it to a "kind of auto-deconstruction"' (Gibson 15). Indeed, if moral decisions are to represent anything other than 'mere blindness and brutality', they have to pass through the – properly ethical – realm of 'undecidability' (Harpham, *Shadows* 30).

Neo-humanists and deconstructivists also differ widely when it comes to literature and the question of how to approach it. The former hark back to the hermeneutic tradition, which considers the literary text as an object to be interpreted, to be made sense of: the ultimate goal of reading is to arrive at a coherent meaning which is *the* meaning of the text. Nussbaum, for example, regards the literary text as a discourse that can be readily understood by the reader. The reader is constructed as a passive spectator who is watching the unfolding of a fictional reality that seems to require no further interpretive efforts: 'For Nussbaum, texts become no more than glass panes behind which events occur' (Eaglestone 46).[5] Nussbaum's unquestioned acceptance of what is essentially a pre-structuralist methodology has been criticized by literary scholars who accuse her of ignoring 'all the various problematizations of narrative and narrative "form" . . . in novel theory from the 1960s onwards' (Gibson 11). Her 'crucial blindness', according to Eaglestone, lies in the fact that she 'continually passes over the textual nature of a literary work' by treating it as a transparent vehicle for meaning (46). There is no place here for unreadability or undecidability; Nussbaum's reading practice 'cannot accept and, indeed, it must ignore, indeterminate meanings in a literary text' (Eaglestone 47).

For critics of the deconstructive persuasion, such indeterminacies are precisely what reading is all about. Adopting a post-hermeneutic approach (that is, one that is concerned less with meaning than with the production of meaning), they take full account of the materiality of the text which subverts and resists the closure of meaning (the reduction of the text to just one meaning), leaving the reader faced with the experience of the strictly undecidable. Translated in more overtly ethical terms, the difference between the two aforementioned approaches is that the neo-humanists seek to reduce the text to the familiar, to the order of the same, whereas deconstructivists are concerned to preserve a space for an otherness that resists such reduction. As Derek Attridge has remarked, reading – in the specialized sense of attending to the materiality of the text – is 'an attempt to respond to the otherness of the other' which involves 'working against the mind's tendency to assimilate the other to the same' and which brings about 'unexpected reshapings of the familiar' ('Innovation' 25).

An intense preoccupation with the demands of otherness is also a defining feature of trauma theory, an important sub-strand of the ethical turn, whose most prominent representatives include Cathy Caruth, Shoshana Felman, Geoffrey Hartman and Dominick LaCapra. Though theorizing about trauma started as early as the nineteenth century, it gained momentum in the twentieth century, an era saturated with unprecedented violent and wounding events.[6] This evolution culminated, in 1980, in the official acknowledgement of the phenomenon of trauma by the American Psychiatric Association under the title 'Post-Traumatic Stress Disorder' ('PTSD').[7] In *Trauma: Explorations in Memory*, a landmark collection in the formation of what has come to be known as trauma studies,[8] Caruth summarizes the general lines of the psychiatric profession's codification of PTSD as follows:

> there is a response, sometimes delayed, to an overwhelming event or events, which takes the form of repeated, intrusive hallucinations, dreams, thoughts or behaviors stemming from the event, along with numbing that may have begun during or after the experience, and possibly also increased arousal to (and avoidance of) stimuli recalling the event. (4)

Caruth is quick to note the 'very peculiar fact', implicit in this definition, that the pathology in question cannot be defined by 'the event itself' nor in terms of 'a *distortion* of the event'; it consists, rather, solely in 'the *structure of its experience* or reception: the event is not assimilated or experienced fully at the time, but only belatedly, in its repeated *possession* of the one who experiences it' (4). It is the very unassimilated nature of trauma, the way it was not known in the first instance, which returns to haunt the survivor later on. The truth of traumatic experience which forms the centre of its pathology is 'a gap that carries the force of the event and does so precisely at the expense of simple knowledge and memory' (7). In other words, the force of the experience is registered in 'the collapse of its understanding' (7). In Caruth's conceptualization, trauma becomes a figure for the crisis of experience – more particularly, *historical* experience – as modelled on the familiar subject–object dualism. For Caruth, the question raised by trauma, which 'extends beyond the question of individual cure', is 'how we in this era can have access to our own historical experience, to a history that is in its immediacy a crisis to whose truth there is no simple access' (6).[9]

Trauma theory as conceived by Caruth becomes a speaking and listening practice with a clear ethical edge to it. Having construed the transmission of trauma in the testimony of survivors as a 'departure' from the non-experience that they witnessed, Caruth writes that trauma challenges us to 'a new kind of listening', a listening '*to departure*' (10), which is put forward as the key to 'passing out' of the 'isolation', both individual and historical, imposed on us by this, our 'catastrophic age':

> This speaking and this listening – a speaking and a listening *from the site of trauma* – does not rely, I would suggest, on what we simply know of each other, but on what we don't yet know of our own traumatic pasts. In a catastrophic age, that is, trauma itself may provide the very link between cultures: not as a simple understanding of the pasts of others but rather, within the traumas of contemporary history, as our ability to listen through the departures we have all taken from ourselves. (11)

As the appeal to a 'we' that needs to open up and resituate its understanding makes clear, trauma urges us to change not just our notion of history but also our involvement in each other's histories. Caruth returns to this idea in *Unclaimed Experience*, when she argues that it is the 'plea by an other who is asking to be seen and heard' which 'constitutes the new mode of reading and listening that both the language of trauma, and the silence of its mute repetition of suffering, profoundly and imperatively demand' (9).

Though this insistence on the witnessing of suffering and on listening to the plea of the other may create the impression that trauma theory is basically some form of 'collective sympathy therapy' (de Graef 317), the healing exercise of shared suffering, Caruth does not simply join Nussbaum in her defence of the sympathetic imagination. While there is indeed a family resemblance of emotions between Nussbaum's call for an imaginative participation in the lives of others and the listening and speaking articulated in trauma theory, '[t]he proximity of trauma theory to the ideology of sympathy is . . . critical: it marks a measure requiring a critique of sympathy as a sentimental economy restrained by aesthetic ideology' (de Graef 318). Heir to the legacy of 1970s and 1980s textualism,[10] trauma theory continually emphasizes the need to attend to the resistance to understanding that it detects in the language of suffering. In its extension to history, the untranslatable 'literality' of trauma (Caruth, *Trauma* 5), in which 'the force of its affront to understanding' resides (Caruth, *Trauma* 154), assumes 'the non-shape of alterity, an alterity whose transmission amounts to an ethical charge' (de Graef et al. 251–52). With its principled refusal to appropriate or impose closure on that which is addressed to our understanding but can never be reduced to it, trauma theory appears as an indictment of neohumanist complacency and a call for us to rethink our engagement with alterity and to develop new and more just ways of being with others.

However, not all trauma theorists unreservedly subscribe to the critical programme laid out by Caruth – or, for that matter, by Felman, whose seminal 1992 study *Testimony* (which marked another important moment in the emergence of trauma studies) shares many emphases with Caruth's work. Dominick LaCapra, for example, a trauma scholar more directly interested in transformative political practice, has expressed some misgivings about what he perceives as Caruth and Felman's excessive fixation on the symptomatic acting-out of trauma, which threatens to inhibit action in the present oriented to a more desirable future. In *Representing the Holocaust*, LaCapra distinguishes three different ways of dealing with the problem of trauma in historical discourse: denial (or disavowal), acting-out and working-through. Denial – to be understood 'not in its ordinary sense but in its psychoanalytic sense' – may involve 'intricate and subtle modes of evasion' (48 n.6), typically the construction of 'a redemptive, fetishistic narrative that excludes or marginalizes trauma through a teleological story that projectively presents values and wishes as viably realized' (192). In acting-out, by contrast, 'the past is compulsively repeated as if it were fully present, resistances are not confronted, and memory as well as judgment is undercut' (48 n.6). One example of this response, which only 'aggravate[s]' trauma, is the 'construction of all history . . . as trauma', which tends to go hand in hand with 'an insistence that there is no alternative to symptomatic acting-out and the repetition compulsion other than an imaginary, illusory hope for totalization, full closure, and redemptive meaning' (193). Acting-out would thus entail the 'fragmentation or fracturing of all possibilities of bonding and renewal' (195). According to LaCapra, Felman and Caruth's brand of trauma theory succumbs to this pitfall: 'Writing trauma is often seen in terms of enacting it, which may at times be equated with acting (or playing) it out in performative discourse or artistic practice. In significant ways this equation is active in Shoshana Felman's work and has a complicated role in Caruth's' (*Writing* 186–87).

LaCapra stresses the need to create a position that avoids both redemptive narrative and symptomatic acting-out. He sets out to describe a way of working through trauma that does not 'deny the irreducibility of loss or the role of paradox and aporia' but avoids becoming 'compulsively fixated' on it (*Representing* 195). Acting-out and working-through, however, do not simply stand in opposition to one another, for the latter process requires and presupposes the former. LaCapra acknowledges that some acting-out may be 'unavoidable and even necessary' (*Representing* 48) – after all, if there is no acting-out at all, no repetition of the traumatic disruption, the resulting account of the historical trauma will be that teleological, redemptive fetishizing that denies the trauma's reality (*Representing* 59).

If LaCapra charges Felman and Caruth with being obsessively fixated on the destabilizing and fragmenting effects of trauma and insufficiently interested in envisaging concrete possibilities for achieving integration and renewal, Linda Belau's critique can be described as the exact opposite of LaCapra's. In 'Trauma and the Material Signifier', Belau accuses 'the deconstructive school of trauma theory' as a whole – and Felman and Lawrence Langer in particular – of leaving behind 'the ethical dimension of trauma' by positing traumatic experience as an idealized content beyond the limits of the symbolic rather than seeing it as a marker of those very limits. She equates a responsible ethical stance with a radical refusal to understand trauma coupled with an unremitting commitment to acting it out. Such a position is exemplified by Claude Lanzmann, director of the monumental Holocaust documentary *Shoah*, which 'endlessly repeats the impossibility of transmission' (Belau). Belau applauds Lanzmann's refusal of 'the moralizing gesture that embraces the radical negativity of the trauma as something we must understand'. The important point about trauma, according to Belau, is that it is 'necessarily shrouded by an impossible meaning that will not ever function to expand our understanding or develop our interpretive capabilities'.

Felman, who was criticized by LaCapra for overemphasizing acting-out in her analysis of Lanzmann's film, now stands accused of ignoring this very same phenomenon. Belau imputes to Felman and Langer a naive desire to recuperate some meaning out of the experience of trauma, to which they allegedly ascribe a 'miraculous potential to broaden our horizons'. For all their professions of sensitivity to 'the pitfalls of understanding', Belau maintains, their secret ambition is to make the unspeakable meaningful and to achieve an expansion of understanding rather than a recognition of its fundamental obscenity; put briefly, they want 'to put trauma to work': 'Insofar as trauma, as an attainable ideal experience, can teach us new things about ourselves, it can work for us. It can make us better.' According to Belau, these assumptions reveal their work to be implicated in 'a reductive idealism' which 'offers no serious alternative to a recuperative liberalism'. In short, if for LaCapra Felman's version of trauma theory was all too ethical, all too intent on staying within the aporetic space of trauma, for Belau it is not nearly ethical enough as it betrays a residual desire to colonize trauma, to bring it back into the realm of the understandable.

What unites all the aforementioned trauma theorists, despite their disagreements, is a shared concern with the unsettling impact of trauma and with the obligations this imposes. All of them accept the need to confront the challenge that trauma poses to ordinary forms of understanding, and to do so in such a way that the force of its affront to understanding is registered rather than erased. In other words, there is a place, in all these accounts, for disorientation, fragmentation, disruption, confusion and undecidability. The differences between them are largely a matter of emphasis: whereas some theorists (for example, Belau, Caruth and – I would argue – Felman) are primarily concerned with doing justice to the shattering experience of trauma by performatively enacting it, others (for example, LaCapra) seek to drive home the point that one cannot stay within trauma for ever but eventually has to 'reengage life in the interest of bringing about a qualitatively better state of affairs' (LaCapra, *History* 40). This situation can be recast as the tension between a predominant emphasis on ethical purity (the realm of the undecidable) and a focus on desirable moral or political action (the realm of the decision) – a tension that, as Harpham points out, is constitutive of ethics itself (*Shadows* 29–30).

The preceding account of the literary-theoretical context in which this study is embedded can help us identify some dominant currents within existing Swift criticism. The remainder of this chapter will provide an overview of the three main trends that research on Swift's work has tended to follow. The aim here is not to offer an exhaustive analysis of the entire field of Swift criticism, but to highlight some significant tendencies and to clarify general points of divergence and convergence between them. The picture of the current state of Swift criticism that will thus emerge allows the reader to situate this critical inquiry in terms of both its affinities and differences with previous research.

The first category of significant criticism can be classified under the literary-theoretical paradigm of textualism, which, as was noted above, was predominantly concerned with the materiality of the literary artefact and tended to underplay its ethical dimension. This fairly extensive body of critical work takes its inspiration from Linda Hutcheon's analysis of postmodernism, and focuses almost exclusively on *Waterland*, the novel that established Swift's reputation in 1983.[11] In *A Poetics of Postmodernism* and *The Politics of Postmodernism*, Hutcheon named *Waterland* as a major example of 'historiographic metafiction', a phrase she coined to denote postmodern novels that 'are both intensely self-reflexive and yet paradoxically also lay claim to historical events and personages' (*Poetics* 5). Such novels self-consciously play with the boundaries between history and fiction in order to expose the constructed nature of historical discourse, which is revealed as relying on the narrative modes usually associated with literature:

> Historiographic metafiction refutes the natural or common-sense methods of distinguishing between historical fact and fiction. It refuses the view that only history has a truth claim, both by questioning the ground of that claim in historiography and by asserting that both history and fiction are discourses, human constructs, signifying systems, and both derive their major claim to truth from that identity. (*Poetics* 93)

Waterland, a novel that is preoccupied with the exploration of different modes of story-telling and the relationship between history and other forms of narrative, was presented as an obvious example of historiographic metafiction. According to Hutcheon, the central question that *Waterland* raises is 'whether the historian *discovers* or *invents* the totalizing narrative form or model used. . . . It is this distinction that postmodernism problematizes' (*Politics* 64).

It is hardly an exaggeration to say that Hutcheon's treatment of *Waterland* as a paradigmatic example of historiographic metafiction has largely determined the shape and form of academic Swift criticism – which, for the most part, has confined itself exclusively to this celebrated novel.[12] Hutcheon's studies set the tone for a vast number of readings of *Waterland* that have viewed the novel through the prism of historiographic metafiction as a text engaging an essentially epistemological problematic. Alison

Lee, a former student of Hutcheon's, adopts the latter's approach in her book on postmodern British fiction, which offers a reading of *Waterland*, Julian Barnes's *Flaubert's Parrot* and Salman Rushdie's *Midnight's Children* – three novels that had already been identified as examples of historiographic metafiction in *A Poetics of Postmodernism*[13] – that stays safely within the boundaries of the interpretive space opened up by Hutcheon. Indeed, in Lee's view, *Waterland* is a novel in which 'the question of *how* we know history is thematized' (36). Its narrator being principally interested in 'the ways in which history can be structured as narrative' (41), what we take away from our reading is, unsurprisingly, the insight that 'meaning and structure are imposed on history by narrative devices' (44).

In *Writing History as a Prophet*, a perceptive study of the postmodern historical novel, Elisabeth Wesseling similarly follows Hutcheon's lead in subsuming *Waterland* under the rubric of 'self-reflexive' historical fiction, which is that variant of twentieth-century innovations of the historical novel which 'enlarges the generic repertoire of the historical novel with strategies that turn epistemological questions concerning the nature and intelligibility of history into a literary theme' (vii). Again, *Waterland* is seen to bear out the idea that 'teleological continuity is a property of narrative rather than of the object that narrative aims to represent' (133). '[P]rimarily interested in epistemological issues', self-reflexive historical novels like *Waterland* 'explore the constraints on the retrospective retrieval of the past, but ultimately they still search for possibilities for acquiring authentic historical knowledge within the confines of these constraints' (181).

More detailed analyses of *Waterland* that tread the same territory have been put forward by, among others, Catherine Bernard, Pamela Cooper, Andrzej Gasiorek, Robert Irish, George Landow, Sean Murphy, Ansgar Nünning, John Schad and Richard Todd. Their work bears eloquent witness to the pervasive influence of the historiographic-metafictional model. For example, in *Graham Swift: La parole chronique* – one of the few monographs that have been devoted to Swift's work[14] – Bernard emphasizes that *Waterland* foregrounds 'the necessary reassessment of the epistemological link between the world and words' ('Dismembering' 121–22). Cooper, another prominent Swift critic, takes it for granted that '[t]he paradoxes of history – its conceptual overlap with narrative, its tendency both to install and subvert human notions of chronology and development' are 'the obvious focus of *Waterland*'s intellectual endeavor' ('Imperial' 372). '[T]hematically central' to the novel, according to Cooper, is 'the dialectical opposition, elaborated throughout the text, between the discursive practices of narrative and historiography' ('Imperial' 371).

In recent years, however, some academic critics have begun to formulate an alternative to the prevalent historiographic-metafictional approach to Swift's work, an alternative that, in the typology of literary-theoretical inquiry set forth previously, roughly corresponds to the position of trauma theory within the ethical paradigm. In an attempt to recast the terms of the critical debate, Wendy Wheeler, Adrian Poole, Ernst van Alphen and Tamás Bényei have shifted their attention away from epistemological issues to focus on the ethical dimension of Swift's novels, which is typically articulated through an engagement with trauma. The centrality that was formerly accorded to *Waterland*'s problematization of the possibility of historical knowledge is now given to the problematic of mourning and melancholia, which is made out to be the dominant concern not just in *Waterland* but in Swift's other novels as well.[15] Indeed, it is rather striking, considering the almost exclusive focus on *Waterland* in the work of Hutcheon and her followers, to note that ethically-oriented readings mostly take the form of survey articles which address Swift's oeuvre in its entirety. Almost by definition, the format of the survey article favours generalization and abstract analysis at the expense of a close engagement with the texts under discussion, which explains why there has so far been little in the way of detailed textual analysis. It is here that this book, which continues and extends this general line of inquiry, hopes to make a contribution.

Nowhere has this 'paradigm shift' in Swift criticism been more programmatically announced than in a 1994 article on *Waterland* by van Alphen, a literary scholar whose main research interests lie in the – trauma-ridden – field of Holocaust representation. In 'The Performativity of Histories: Graham Swift's *Waterland* as a Theory of History', van Alphen proclaims the need to rescue *Waterland* from the hands of Hutcheon and like-minded critics, whose treatment of the novel he does not hesitate to condemn as plainly misguided. He argues that the epistemological glasses through which Hutcheon recommends we should view postmodern fiction prevent us from seeing that there is a fair amount of postmodern literature, exemplified by *Waterland*, that is not primarily interested in problematizing notions of truth and referentiality: 'some postmodern literature does offer an alternative [to remaining stuck in deconstructing the paradigm of truth]. . . . The novel *Waterland* by Graham Swift offers an illuminating example of a reflection that moves beyond the opposition against the claim to truth' (203). Van Alphen does not mince his words in disputing the relevance of Hutcheon's approach: 'In the case of this novel, Hutcheon's construction of postmodernism as a problematization of the notion of referentiality is clearly beside the point' (204).[16]

If to call *Waterland* an example of historiographic metafiction is a misnomer, according to van Alphen, this is because the novel's principal preoccupation is not with 'truth, truthfulness, plausibility or mimetic success' (206), but with 'the performative, therapeutic and political effect of histories' (209). Given the fact that reality, in *Waterland*, is presented as 'destructive, hardly bearable' (205), history and story-telling serve a 'redemptive function': to '[make] reality tolerable' (206). The essentially traumatic reality with which Swift confronts his characters 'does not need to be presented truthfully or plausibly'; rather, 'it must be *worked through*' (206). In this respect, *Waterland* invites comparisons to Holocaust literature, which, as van Alphen points out, has been approached from this perspective by Felman and others (210 n.5).[17]

Though van Alphen's argument has much to recommend it, in the heat of the polemical moment he tends to be overly dismissive of the historiographic-metafictional line of interpretation. In his zeal to disentangle *Waterland* from the grip of earlier critics, he even goes so far as to claim that the distinction between history and fiction, whose problematization is the hallmark of historiographic metafiction, is essentially left intact in Swift's novel (204–5). However, the passage from the text that he adduces to back up this claim – in which the narrator sings the virtues of 'good dry textbook history', which 'has to be retrieved with empirical fishing lines' from 'the old swamps of myth' (W 86; quoted in van Alphen, 'Performativity' 205) – is dripping with an irony that he inexplicably fails to notice. In fact, one could even argue that ethically-inspired readings of the kind espoused by van Alphen presuppose the insights developed by Hutcheon and others into the constructedness of all discourses through which we apprehend the past. An awareness that historical narratives, for all their claims to empirical accuracy and mimetic verisimilitude, are in fact artificial human products is a precondition for seeing them as attempts to domesticate a terrifying reality that constantly exceeds and eludes our orderings. From this perspective, the trauma-theoretical and the historiographic-metafictional takes on Swift's work appear as related but distinct, rather than as radically opposed approaches.

Other critics exploring Swift's engagement with the all-important question of how to come to terms with trauma have stressed the fact that the various responses to the traumatic situation played out in his work – which Poole and Wheeler have usefully captured under the headings of melancholia and mourning – tend to resonate far beyond the immediate lives of the individual protagonists, even though they are the ostensible focus of attention. Swift's novels present themselves as subtle psychological portraits of one, two or at most a handful of characters living unadventurous lives in suburban London or in some quiet provincial backwater. What is most conspicuous about them is, in fact, their very ordinariness. As one critic has remarked, 'Most of his characters are the kinds of people you might find walking their dogs on the common: office clerks, put-upon schoolteachers, washed-up academics or shop proprietors' (O'Mahony). Through the narratives of this thoroughly unremarkable bunch of characters, however, Swift manages to evoke the cultural pathologies of an entire nation, an empire or even an era. The social dimension of his mourning stories is foregrounded by Poole, who writes that

> Swift is providing much more than individual studies in the psychology of personal loss, bereavement and mourning, persuasive and moving as that is. What attracts readers at a deeper level is their recognition of imagined models of shared reality, something more than the personal possession – and loss – of an individual psyche or consciousness. ('Mourning After' 155)

At one level, Swift's novels can be read as 'condition of England' novels. According to Michael Levenson, his work allegorizes the plight of post-war Britain, a nation struggling to come to terms with its loss of prominence in the world. In a review of *Ever After*, Levenson writes that an encounter with Swift's complete works reveals 'the persistence of a compulsion, a compulsion to invent, again and again, a certain plot. Call it the plot of the Weak Son, the plot that returns through each of the novels and burrows beneath their surface variations.' Swift's novels are all seen to revolve around the opposition between 'Big Pops', who are 'dominating traditionalists', and a weak son, who 'is modern England. This is the connection toward which the books are driven: that in their portraits of individual failure and powerlessness they are also sketching a nation's fate.' This fate is construed as the fall from 'imperial pomposity', from 'the culture of the Great Fathers'. Though, in Levenson's view, Swift accepts Britain's post-lapsarian situation 'with scarcely a hiccup of nostalgia', he is at a loss as to how to proceed from there; indeed, he 'fiercely attacks the old illusions without any idea of what might go in their place'. Though this final point is debatable, what Levenson's discussion brings to light is that there is a problem of inheritance in Swift's work: there is a sense in which a traditional frame of reference, typically associated with the father figure, has lost its credibility and become untenable. For Wheeler, therefore, it is 'the "weak" . . . English father', rather than the weak son, who is a regular theme in Swift's writing, taking on 'an increasingly obvious allegorical weight' ('Melancholic' 66). First and foremost, his novels enact 'the crisis of the "paternal fiction"' (Wheeler, 'After Grief' 80).[18] The failure of the paternal function of transmitting the cultural law may leave the son confused, unsettled and disoriented, but, in Wheeler's judgement, he is not so weak or powerless as to be incapable of mourning his losses and envisaging possibilities for the creation of a viable, radically new future.[19]

In Wheeler's reading, which stands out by its incisiveness and scope, the dysfunctional father represents not just a discredited and obsolete model of Englishness but also 'a divine Father who no longer "works"' ('Melancholic' 66). Thus, she inscribes Swift's work in the wider context of intellectual debate concerning the problematic status of modernity, understood as 'both the unleashing of uncertainties *and* the attempt to sew up this story – of an increasingly Godless, contingent, and meaningless world – with narratives that will give it some kind of meaning' ('Graham' 298). According to Wheeler, modernity and postmodernity are intimately bound up with the phenomena of melancholia and mourning – to be interpreted in the Freudian sense as, on the one hand, a pathological refusal to acknowledge loss and, on the other, the attempt to transform the madness of grief into some accommodation with reality that would allow possibilities of renewal. Insofar as modernity is dependent on narcissistic fantasies of completion, it is an essentially melancholic era; insofar as postmodernity is committed to living with loss and uncertainty as a permanent condition, its dominant mode is mourning.

Wheeler presents a compelling argument that Swift's work seeks to mediate the transition from a melancholic modernity, which has produced terror and strife, to a salutary postmodernity, which would enable the creation of more positive ways of being in the world: 'The task which, over his entire oeuvre, Swift sets himself is that of imagining how the self-destructive melancholias of modernity can be turned into the healthy mournings of something that we might call *post*modernity understood as a precondition for a *new* modernity' ('Graham' 300). His work pursues a viable alternative to the romantic conceptions of meaningfulness whose failure it diagnoses,[20] and it does so by working towards a domestication of the sublime. Indeed, for Wheeler, 'a major organizing thematic' in Swift's work is 'the transformation of the sublime into the domestic' (*From the Sublime* 45). The irreducible excess of the sublime, which is alluded to in various figurations (such as the 'Now' in *The Sweet Shop Owner* and the 'Here and Now' in *Waterland*), is made homely, tamed, brought low and made bearable (*From the Sublime* 45). Though her choice of words – 'taming' and 'domesticating' – would seem to suggest otherwise, this process is emphatically not intent on the repression of alterity. Quite the contrary, in fact: Wheeler insists that

> Taming, or domesticating, is not burying. . . . It is a toleration of otherness which acknowledges difference. It is in this sense . . . that domestication is used here. To tame the sublime thus means to be able to begin to entertain the possibility of alterity as a condition of maturity. It means to be able to initiate a rhetoric of separation and loss and then to mourn properly. (*From the Sublime* 56)

What this process of mourning seeks to achieve, ultimately, is the creation of 'a radically changed future in which both self and world are utterly transformed' ('Melancholic' 65). The stakes at play in Swift's work, then, are nothing less than the possibility of a just, non-violent future, a possibility premised, crucially, on a commitment to working through traumatic loss.

The third and final line of interpretation that needs to be considered here closely resembles the humanist type of ethical criticism practised by Nussbaum and others. Two academic critics who have pursued this approach are Susanne Mecklenburg, who has written a monograph on Swift and Martin Amis, and Alan Hickman, whose doctoral dissertation was the first comprehensive scholarly study devoted to Swift's work. In addition, there is a good deal of journalistic criticism that has viewed his work from a distinctly humanist perspective. In marked contrast to the other two 'schools' of Swift criticism, both of which hailed the author as a pre-eminent exponent of (some version of) postmodernism, these critics tend to treat his novels as traditional realist texts promoting essentially humanist moral values.

Indeed, Swift is regarded by many as a writer working in the realist tradition. Scott Rosenberg, for one, suggests that Swift is 'an anachronistic throwback' who at times seems to 'belong more to the 19th century than to our own'. In the words of another critic, Swift has 'reinstated a solid, traditional approach to fiction' which sets him apart from other novelists writing today:

> Graham Swift seems to have little in common with his literary contemporaries. While most writers these days splash their novels with pop culture references and play with distortions of time and narrative, Swift sets his books in a nineteenth-century context and tells good old-fashioned stories. He is wholly committed to perfecting the art of the novel, developing character with a scrutiny that matches Dickens' and dealing with eternal themes like class struggle and death. ('Graham Swift')

Lord, Lee and Wheeler all concede that Swift's novels can be read as realist texts, and even invite this kind of reading, but they qualify this concession by insisting that this is only one part of the story. While it is true that the focus on matters such as character, narrative, motive, individual and family 'aligns Swift's writing with many of the traditional concerns of the English novel', Lord urges the reader not to lose sight of the fact that the author approaches his subjects with 'a contemporary self-consciousness, revealing their perspectives, and constantly undercutting positions of apparent certainty' ('Graham' 4; 'Mystery' 151). In the same vein, Lee argues that it is naive to ignore *Waterland*'s metafictional strategies, even if, admittedly, Swift does not slap the reader in the face with them:

> Unlike many other metafictional texts, . . . *Waterland* does not at first appear to foreground its structure. It presents itself as what Roland Barthes calls in *S/Z*, a *lisible* (readable) text rather than a *scriptible* (writable) text. The story is so engaging and the manipulation of affect so intense that it can certainly be read (if naively) on this level. (42)

Wheeler, finally, notes the proximity of Swift's work to 'an aesthetics which presupposes human-ness as given (and, therefore, a supposed ease of communication and referentiality)', but adds that it would be misguided simply to reduce the texts to such a programme:

> it would be quite wrong to describe his novels as having any sense of the human as essentially pre-given. Nor do his novels suppose any sense of reference to an unproblematically given world or history. Indeed, his latest novel, *Ever After* (1992) offers, precisely, the image of mourning as the (re)construction of subject and world. (*From the Sublime* 19–20)

Within the humanist camp, predictably, the feeling is that it is the advocates of postmodernism who miss the point about Swift's work. Hickman and Mecklenburg are both very sceptical about postmodern theorizing, which they accuse of being non-committal, defeatist or nihilistic – oblivious, in any case, to the serious moral undercurrents of Swift's work which they make it their business to uncover. For Hickman, who labels Swift a 'morally instructive' (3) writer, postmodernism is simply not a relevant category for discussing his work. Concerned to 'refute those critics who have found his novels to be humorless studies in fatalism' (12), he locates Swift in 'the opposite camp' (6) to postmodernism. With his novels betraying a 'dissatisfaction' with the 'defeatist tone' of 'the post-modern world' (5), Swift is presented as an artist who has 'moved beyond the post-modern posture of evasion and despair to a positive view of 20th century man in relation to his age' (3). The specific moral values that the author is seen to promote have got to do with establishing community, ensuring continuity and connectedness (to be achieved through marriage and childbirth), and fostering communication and understanding among people (6–9).

Mecklenburg objects to Hickman's analysis on the grounds that it distorts Swift's work by enlisting it in the service of the author's own profoundly conservative, if not reactionary, moral agenda:

> Hickmans großes Verdienst einer ersten großen wissenschaftlichen Arbeit über diesen Schriftsteller kann nicht über seine immer wieder völlig unmodifiziert eingebauten eigenen moralisierenden Ausfälle hinwegtäuschen. Stellenweise führt das zu einer Reduzierung von Swifts Werk auf derart fragwürdige Aussagen, wie die uneingeschränkte Aburteilung von Abtreibungen als 'crimes against nature' oder die merkwürdig politisierende Hochhaltung konservativer Familienmodelle.
>
> Hickman's great merit of having produced the first great scholarly work on this writer cannot obscure his invariably in-built moralizing attacks. In places this leads to a reduction of Swift's work to such questionable utterances as the unreserved condemnation of abortions as 'crimes against nature' or the strangely politicizing upholding of conservative family models. (131 n.292)

While Mecklenburg's criticisms of the moral tenor of Hickman's study are undoubtedly justified, similar criticisms can be levelled at her own work. For all her efforts to distance herself from Hickman, she too is concerned to lay bare the essential moral values supposedly undergirding Swift's work. The only significant difference between Mecklenburg and Hickman is that the moral programme to which the former seeks to reduce Swift's writing is more 'politically correct' ('politisch korrekte') than the one put forward by the latter (Mecklenburg 187).

Mecklenburg considers both Swift and Amis as 'didaktisierende zeitgenössische Moralisten mit einer letztlich vorwärtsgewandten Hoffnung auf eine bessere Welt, zu der sie mit ihren Werken beizutragen versuchen' ('didacticizing contemporary moralists with an ultimately forward-looking hope for a better world, to which they attempt to contribute with their works', 3). At the heart of Swift's literary enterprise, she locates an unwavering commitment to a traditional humanist morality; a morality which, the subtitle of her book (*Erfolg durch bodenlosen Moralismus im zeitgenössischen britischen Roman*) notwithstanding, is anything but groundless. She detects an 'immer konstant gleichbleibende humanistische Ethik' ('never-changing humanist ethics', 186) in Swift's work, based on sympathy, communication, understanding and hope, which furnishes the reader with 'feste Maßstäbe' ('fixed standards', 3), 'ewigen, gültigen Anhaltspunkten [sic]' ('eternally valid grounds', 108) and 'zeitenüberdauernde Orientierungswerte' ('timeless reference values', 117) as an antidote to 'zeitgenössischer Entfremdung, Mechanisierung, Aggression und Lieblosigkeit' ('contemporary alienation, mechanization, aggression and lovelessness', 3). Indeed, these 'unverrückbare Werte' ('unshakeable values') are put forward as 'Maxime für eine bessere Gesellschaft' ('maxims for a better society', 115). Mecklenburg insists that the author claims absolute validity for these values ('einen Absolutheitsanspruch', 107): 'Swift stellt aber ein derartiges

Wertesystem nicht nur als bloße Illusion hin, sondern setzt es geradezu als eine Art Lyotardischen "metanarrative" ein' ('Yet Swift does not represent such a value system as a mere illusion, but puts it forward as some sort of Lyotardian "metanarrative"', 115–16).

Though, unlike Hickman, Mecklenburg holds on to the term 'postmodernism' in her reading of Swift's work, the concept becomes an all but empty category in her hands, and does not affect her defiantly traditional analysis in any way. Her critical discussion of Hutcheon's account of Swift (107–12) betrays a clear impatience with key notions such as paradox, contradiction and aporia:

> Mit dieser endlosen Widersprüchlichkeit, die sie hypothetisch als einendes Signum für Postmoderne und historiographische Metafiktion ansetzt, kann sie jedoch Swifts komplexere Grundhaltung nur unvollkommen erfassen.
>
> However, with this endless contradictoriness, which she hypothetically posits as a uniting banner for postmodernism and historiographic metafiction, she cannot fully grasp Swift's more complex basic attitude. (109)

Mecklenburg downplays the importance of the metafictional dimension of Swift's work and rejects the indeterminate political stance that Hutcheon ascribes to postmodern fiction. The metafictional element is reduced to the status of window dressing: it ensures a superficial compliance with fashionable postmodern orthodoxies that has no other purpose than to seduce an incredulous contemporary reading public into imbibing the 'dahinter stehenden ethischen Grundgerüst' ('underlying ethical framework', 111), that is, an unreconstructed humanism which it might otherwise have little taste for.

Fiercely critical of Hutcheon, Mecklenburg has nothing but praise for Wheeler (113–14), though she does not seem to have assimilated any of the latter's insights. While she calls Wheeler's focus on the experience of loss 'hochinteressant' ('most interesting', 113), there is a world of difference between Wheeler's and her respective accounts of the way in which Swift engages with this issue. Wheeler, as we have already seen, stresses the fact that Swift's work attempts to move beyond the redemptive ideologies (or metanarratives) of modernity, which are exposed as melancholic, pathological responses to a situation of traumatic loss. Its specifically postmodern quality resides precisely in its pursuit of an alternative to narcissistic fantasies of completion that cover over the original trauma; an alternative that would consist of finding healthy forms of mourning that allow for the invention of differently constituted selves and communities by inciting respect for otherness and toleration of loss. According to Mecklenburg, however, the way in which Swift's work copes with loss is by promoting a salvific metanarrative; indeed, instead of abandoning romantic conceptions of meaningfulness, it actively encourages such delusions (114).[21] Put briefly, it does not seek to acknowledge or work through loss but simply to overcome it.

Mecklenburg's and Hickman's decision to bury the problem of traumatic loss is poignantly apparent in their idiosyncratic use of the phrase 'Here and Now', the most emblematic figuration of traumatic intrusion in Swift's work. For them, the Here and Now simply designates the site in which the moral values they attribute to the texts are most fully realized: in Mecklenburg's reading, 'das letztlich allein wichtige "Here and Now"' ('the ultimately all-important "Here and Now"') is filled in with inspirational images of 'eines idealen Lebens im Moment durch ein spontanes Aufgehen in Liebe und offenem Miteinander' ('an ideal life in the present moment through a spontaneous immersion in love and open cooperation', 114); Hickman similarly interprets it as 'the solid ground' (187) on which people can meet and connect with one another. Their joint refusal to read the Here and Now for what it most manifestly is – a confrontation with a traumatic reality that opens up an abyss of meaninglessness in which every ideal collapses and seemingly solid ground sinks away – is symptomatic of their refusal seriously to engage with what may well be the single most crucial aspect of Swift's work.

The critical position adopted by this book is indebted in various ways to interpretations of Swift's work that have gone before. In approaching the novels from a predominantly trauma-theoretical and ethical perspective, it obviously reveals great affinity with the second type of criticism discussed above. It is also appreciative, however, of the contribution made by critics working in the historiographic-metafictional tradition, with which it shares a strong focus on matters of textual complexity often elided in overly psychological analyses. With the humanist approach, the present study has little more in common than an interest in the ethical dimension of Swift's work; indeed, it construes Swift's engagement with ethics in a radically different way, which is why humanist accounts will figure mostly as foils for the more theoretically informed interpretations that make up the remainder of this book.

Burying 'Undying Memories' 2

Traumatic Denial in The Sweet Shop Owner

No, it doesn't burn, it doesn't perish.
Undying memories.
Graham Swift, *The Sweet Shop Owner*

In a 1993 interview with Marc Porée, Graham Swift speaks of his dedication to the business of debunking the 'glorious myths' which dominated his childhood years:

> Je suis né peu de temps après la fin de la deuxième guerre mondiale, et mes romans portent la marque de ces glorieux mythes que l'on agitait beaucoup autour de moi, dans les années 50 qui furent celles de mon enfance. Il nous est revenu, à nous romanciers, de faire exploser ces mythes.
>
> I was born shortly after the end of the Second World War, and my novels bear the mark of those glorious myths people around me were spreading in the 1950s, when I was a child. It falls to us, novelists, to explode these myths. (quoted in Porée, 'Entretien' 10)

The typical Swiftian narrative features one or more contemporary characters – mostly frail, unimpressive elderly men – whose world has collapsed around them. A crisis situation in the protagonists' personal lives forces them to face up to an often traumatic individual and collective past which their way of life had been specifically designed to repress or deny. Almost without exception, Swift's novels diagnose the failure of a 'mythical' conception of the individual and the world in which he or she moves, and explore the possibility of inventing a viable way out of the impasse in the narrative present, which usually involves a renewed and sustained engagement with the demands of a catastrophic history.

This novelistic programme finds its first articulation in *The Sweet Shop Owner*, Swift's debut novel and in many ways the founding text of his oeuvre. Paying quiet homage to Joyce's *Ulysses* and Woolf's *Mrs. Dalloway*,[1] *The Sweet Shop Owner* depicts the final day in the life of Willy Chapman, the owner of a sweet shop in South London, interspersed with flashbacks to earlier events from his schoolboy days in 1931 to the fictional present, a sunny Friday in June 1974. As he goes about his daily routine, Willy's mind is cast back to his courtship of and marriage to Irene Harrison, a beautiful and wealthy woman who bought him his shop and bore him a daughter on condition that he would never seek nor offer love. About a year after Irene's death from a heart disorder, Willy receives a letter from Dorothy, his estranged daughter, thanking him for sending her £15,000 from her mother's estate and apparently ruling out any prospect of a reunion. Four days later, lonely and deserted, he commits suicide by bringing on a fatal angina attack through undue physical exertion during the day.

While *The Sweet Shop Owner* establishes many of the themes and techniques that will dominate Swift's later fictions, it is unique among his novels for several reasons. To begin with, unlike Swift's other protagonists, Willy is singularly unaware of the source of all – or most of – his troubles. Right until the end, the traumatic sexual assault which his wife suffered as a teenager at the hands of a family friend remains hidden from him. This crucial incident, which Irene struggled to repress as best she could, has left an indelible mark on every aspect of their married life. It is related in a brief portion of the narrative given over to a deposition from Irene, a ghost testimony which serves to acquaint the reader with the relevant facts of Irene's life before she met Willy. Whereas Swift's later protagonists are all in a position which allows them to account for the mess they are in and to find a measure of redemption, Willy has no idea as to what has hit him. Unable to figure out where things went wrong, he appears unable also to do anything about his predicament.

Moreover, whereas *Waterland*'s Tom Crick and *Ever After*'s Bill Unwin, for instance, achieve some form of relief by actively recalling the past and recounting their experiences, no such commitment is apparent on the part of the protagonist of *The Sweet Shop Owner*. Indeed, Willy's paralysis and passivity are reflected by the text's peculiar narrative situation: unlike Swift's other novels, all of which employ first-person narrators, *The Sweet Shop Owner* is primarily related in the third person, with the protagonist acting as the main focalizer.[2] While his prominence as a focalizer does of course imply that some form of mental activity is going on in Willy's mind, it is hardly the same level of engagement which could have been expected of a narrative agent.[3] Rather than critically reassessing the way of life responsible for his current state of desolation and abandonment, Willy continues to uphold the values and beliefs by which he has always been guided.[4] The notion of transformation or renewal is quite beyond him; in fact, the only possibility of genuine change which he can conceive lies in ending it all.[5] In *The Sweet Shop Owner*, it falls to Willy's daughter – who, born in 1949, is the author's exact contemporary – to unravel the glorious myths proliferated by her parents' generation and to envisage a different future. The odds, however, are stacked against her in this, Swift's most despairing novel.

Critics have tended to overlook the extent to which the lives of the characters in *The Sweet Shop Owner* are determined by the background of trauma, both personal and national, against which the narrative is set. This critical oversight has caused a great deal of interpretative confusion, not least regarding the characters' motivation for behaving the way they do. Michael Gorra, in his review for the *New York Times Book Review*, identifies 'the novel's main weakness' as 'its defective analysis of the emotional web within Willy's family, which leaves Irene and Dorry's motives obscure'. Much of the fog will clear, however, once we read the characters' actions as responses to a traumatic situation. Irene's maniacal obsession with stasis, control and predictability, for example, can be explained as a reaction formation to the trauma of her rape by Frank Hancock, a brash young estate agent whose attentions were encouraged by her parents and brothers, and – insofar as these preoccupations are shared by the wider community – as a response to the collective trauma of the First World War, which left an entire nation reeling.

Born in 1915, Irene remembers being told as a young girl about her three maternal uncles who were killed in the Great War. In her mind, she pictured them like 'skittles' which had been 'suddenly knocked down (it said in the Book of Remembrance they were "fallen")' (50). Only later did she become aware of the full scale of the disaster: 'And later I learnt – it was a common fact so nobody mentioned it – that everywhere there had been knocking down, great gaps and holes everywhere, families with only one or two skittles left standing' (50). Nobody mentioned it – possibly because loss was indeed a very common experience at the time, but more likely, perhaps, because the nation was actively engaged in a process of collective denial. Indeed, Irene goes on: 'But that was in the past. They talked of Trade and Opportunity, Recovery, the Fruits of Peace. They wanted to forget history. They wanted new life' (50). New life – a recurring concern in Swift's work – is not to be bought, however, by covering over the disquieting reality of a death-ridden past. This attitude is epitomized by the Harrison family, who established a laundry business with the fortune Irene's mother inherited, her brothers all having died during the war. Anxious to put the past behind them, they devote themselves to the task of whitewashing history. Irene's beauty is used by her family as evidence vindicating their way of life: 'They set me up into a little emblem, carried me before them like a banner, so they could say, Look, even beauty is on our side' (50). Irene makes the picture complete for them – literally, during a family photo shoot in Aunt Madeleine's garden, but figuratively as well. However, the viability of this collective cover-up operation is put into question by the unpunished rape suffered by Irene, which may be seen as symptomatic of the contradictions embedded in the social order – contradictions which, in the aftermath of the First World War, remained fundamentally unchallenged.

The senseless death of hundreds of thousands of young men in the trenches of the First World War revealed that a political system which promises safety, security and meaning can actually produce the worst forms of abuse, control and coercion. If the violence inherent in the system which the war has exposed is deliberately ignored rather than confronted head-on, this can only lead to a resumption or continuation of practices of oppression, subjection and victimization – as evidenced in the novel by the sexual assault upon Irene.[6] Irene finds that what has happened to her is beyond the possibility of communication, in the sense that there is no language for it. Trying to talk about the rape, all Irene manages to bring out is that Hancock 'was not good to [her]' (52), a statement which is immediately dismissed as 'nonsense' (52, 53) by her family, who are anxious to strengthen their ties with an up-and-coming estate agent who could help further their business interests. No infusion of non-sense is allowed to disturb the carefully orchestrated patterns of meaning through which the Harrisons have resolved to keep history at bay. When Irene smashes her bedroom mirror to signal her rejection of the fraudulent notion which she has been made to represent – namely, that all is well with the post-war world of denial – she is carted off to a mental institution, as if to be disabused of this scandalous suggestion.

When Willy appears upon the scene, Irene's family are relieved to see her go: 'She has let us down once, she may let us down again; we cannot afford that embarrassment' (55). Though under normal circumstances they might have been expected to object to the marriage on account of Willy's lowly background, they now jump at this opportunity to wash their hands of a renegade scioness. Willy is said to be 'as simple as she's cracked', which makes their union seem 'the perfect solution' (55). Indeed, the Harrisons are quick to turn their back when they see 'cracks' appear in their symbolic universe which threaten to expose its claim to being a closed, self-contained structure as a sham. After all, the glorious myth of Trade and Opportunity sustaining their sense of reality was designed precisely to cover up the 'great gaps and holes everywhere' which the war had left. The fatal cracks in the system which the war had brought to light were repressed rather than acknowledged.

In 1945, however, plenty of new gaps and holes are in evidence, leading Willy to suspect that the appearance of fixity and security produced by the pre-Second World War social order had always been just that: an appearance. Surveying the damage done to shops and other buildings during the Second World War, Willy reflects that 'you seemed to walk (but perhaps you always had) through a world in which holes might open, surfaces prove unsolid – like the paving-stones over which the children picked their way, returning to re-opened classrooms, dodging the fatal cracks' (96–97). However, Willy also notices that, along the bomb-scarred High Street, his fellow shopkeepers are 'resuming their old ploys as if history could be circumvented and the war (what war?) veiled by the allurements of their windows' (98). In fact, he had already sensed that another cover-up was under way while witnessing the victory celebrations. The cathartic message which the bonfire around which people were dancing was meant to convey was neatly captured in a comment by Hancock: 'Well – there goes the war. . . . There it goes, there it goes. All over. Forgive and forget, eh?' (86). Willy's thoughts, however, were drawn to the dead soldiers, whose memory could not simply be consumed by the fire:

> Burn it all. Burn away the memories of five years, the 'sacrifice' and 'endeavour', the headlines, the photographs, the odour of barrack huts, the names of foreign battlefields, the 39,000 helmets, the 81,000 packs. But it wouldn't burn. For, look, behind the flames, objects immune to fire, heroes of bronze and stone, too rigid and fixed ever to dance, and black names on marble, gold names on bronze, 'undying memory', 'their name liveth'; and one of the names under the chestnut trees by the railings, on the white school memorial, where boys born after the war would be herded on Remembrance Day, was Harrison. No, it doesn't burn, it doesn't perish. Undying memories. (85–86)

The 'undying memories' at the centre of *The Sweet Shop Owner* can be redescribed as instances of trauma, involving 'the direct imposition on the mind of the unavoidable reality of horrific events, the taking over of the mind . . . by an event that it cannot control' (Caruth, *Unclaimed* 58). The reason why traumatic memories cannot die or be forgotten is that they were never fully known in the first place. Constituted, in part, by their lack of integration into consciousness, traumatic memories are not a possessed knowledge, but themselves repeatedly possess the one they inhabit.

The haunting nature of trauma is clearly evinced by another undying memory – besides the massive loss of life inflicted by the two world wars – which will turn out to play a crucial role in the novel: that of Irene's rape. Irene recalls the incident in the following way:

> And when he pulled me into the hedge on the way back from a drive to Brighton (how sickly the grass smelt and the stems of cow-parsley) I did not assume it was wickedness at first. He looked at me as if I should have expected this. He pulled up my clothes like a man unwrapping a parcel. 'All right,' he said, 'all right, now', as if we had both been anticipating. I struggled. The sun was in my face. This was like a performance in which people were really stabbed and wounded. He needed his victory. . . . I only knew I wasn't prepared. Life, life. (52)

Throughout her life, Irene suffers severe and frequent asthma attacks during which she seems to relive the assault, which, in its unexpectedness and horror, she could not fully assimilate as it occurred.[7] These attacks are triggered by stimuli such as grass and blazing sunlight which recall the original event: 'I couldn't go near the grass or lounge in the sunlight without suffering' (52). The element of struggle is apparent in a vision which Willy has of his wife on their honeymoon in Dorset. During an evening walk along the cliff tops, Willy suddenly sees Irene 'flailing in the current', 'struggling in the gold water, beating her arms to be free of it, though her face was as golden as the waves' (31). This vision becomes reality (or just about) later the same evening, when Irene is seized with a fit of asthma, brought on, it seems, by the fatal combination of grass, cow-parsley and sunlight: 'her chest was heaving, long jagged breaths came from her throat, and she tore at the stem he held out to her, as if she were really drowning, clutching the straw, as if it were closing in to suffocate her, that golden summer-time' (32–33). Willy will never be able to shake off the vision of 'arms lifted in a golden sea' (39), his wife's 'drowning expression' and 'the silent cry on her lips – Save me, save me' (102), which, many years later, he realizes '[he]'d never stopped hearing' (183). At some point, he is struck by the possibility that, contrary to what he had initially assumed to be the case, Irene is not so much drowning and reaching out for help during her asthma attacks as frantically fending off some forcible intrusion from without: 'Was it to be saved she gasped and clawed, or to be left alone? For sometimes she clutched with those flailing hands, sometimes fended. And it was never, it seemed, against the illness she struggled but against something else' (128).[8] This 'something else' is the closest Willy will ever come to understanding his wife's predicament. Unlike the reader, he has hardly any knowledge of Irene's past: 'She never did say much about the time before we met' (150).[9] Deprived of this vital information, he remains in the dark as to the exact nature of her symptoms, which the reader, however, has no difficulty recognizing as traumatic re-enactments of the rape incident which Irene experienced as a young woman.

Irene's way of handling the trauma of her rape closely resembles the survival strategy which her family adopted in the face of the terrible losses sustained during the First World War. At the home in Surrey to which her parents had sent her, Irene devises a coping mechanism – 'I had found my balance, struck my bargain' – which bows to the family tradition of evasion and denial: 'I was a skittle, Willy, but I wouldn't fall' (54). The plan for stabilizing her life which she conceives there, and which she will never veer from, invests heavily in a fictitious sense of fixity and security. Irene dedicates herself to the pursuit of peace – 'That was Irene's word: Peace' (88) – or, at least, a particular version thereof. The novel presents Irene's conception of peace by setting it in opposition to notions such as 'action', 'excitement', 'change', 'newness', 'things happening', 'nonsense', 'falling', 'touching', encountering 'the real thing' and, ultimately, to life itself. As Willy points out, peace, for Irene, amounts to 'a kind of not acting' (77). She seeks to bring life to a halt, to achieve an ideal steady state in which everything would be fixed so that a skittle would run no risk of falling. What seems to have given her this idea is a scene at the home in which she imagined, sitting in an easy chair by the window, that by 'concentrating hard' she could somehow ensure that 'the orderly wouldn't sink through his shiny floor and the gardener wouldn't slip from his ladder. I was responsible' (54). Just as she was made to feel responsible for upholding her family's mythical vision of the world after the First World War, so Irene, after her rape, assumes responsibility for maintaining all things in a perpetual state of balance. The ambition to create a zero-risk environment, in which the self would be immune to anything that might adversely affect its supposed integrity, inspires the various pieces of advice which Irene dispenses to Willy, and which resonate throughout the text: 'Don't move, keep still' (72); 'Nothing must be touched, nothing must be changed' (55); 'Let nothing happen' (43).[10] Unsurprisingly, Irene sets great store by 'unmoving objects', filling her house with 'frozen items of stock' (220), mostly crystal and porcelain. After all, such 'lifeless, lasting things' (221), which not only 'remain' (218) or 'endure' (83) but also 'keep their value' (148), fully exemplify the ideal of immobility and permanent stasis to which she aspires.

If the world cannot be brought to a standstill altogether, its movement must at least be seen to conform to general rules or predictable patterns. Irene's yearning for pattern[11] manifests itself both in the way in which she organizes her domestic life and in the attitude which she adopts towards world-historical events. In both areas, she can rely on the support of her husband, who has always been attracted to the notion of 'regularity and order' (24). As a printer's apprentice, Willy 'liked the daily routine, the taking of orders' (25). His predisposition to docility and passivity goes hand in hand with a deterministic conception of history, leading him to believe that history is 'only a pattern' which leaves no room for individual agency or 'action' (197). He remembers thinking, as a schoolboy sitting in a history class, that 'Henry VIII and his wives were like characters in costume. They weren't real, but they didn't know it. History fitted them into patterns' (44). In the same vein, he once wrote a contentious essay arguing that 'Henry VIII dissolved the monasteries because he'd have done so anyway' (190). History, for Willy, is something that 'came to meet you' (32): 'things would come to you anyway, and when they did they would already be turned into history' (189). The course of his own life he believes to have been similarly predetermined, 'set out like a map' (189), so that as a young man he might in principle already have known his older self: 'Perhaps I knew him then, perhaps I was already his memory . . .' (189). Seen from this perspective, making plans for the future appears as a rather pointless occupation: 'He had planned nothing. Not for himself. And yet he knew: plans emerged. You stepped into them' (24). This outlook on life makes him an ideal partner for Irene, who, 'meant to command, not obey' (25), is eager enough to give him new patterns, first the predictable formulas of courtship, then the routine of the shopkeeper: 'Yes, that was pattern. That was not adventuring. She had said, Why don't you? And he did. And afterwards it was precisely the predictable formula that pleased him' (28). Life becomes a series of patterns for Irene and Willy; patterns, moreover, which are perfectly in line with social norms and expectations. A shopkeeper in a nation of shopkeepers, Willy easily blends in with the crowd, as does his wife, who 'sheltered behind that same disguise' (99). Always and only doing 'the thing to do' (47), and doing it 'properly' (12), Irene and Willy conspire to lead a neatly arranged life of respectable conventionality.

Moreover, they expect to see the sheer uneventfulness and predictability of their own lives reflected in the world at large. One way in which grand history enters the novel is through the medium of newspapers, which both Willy and Irene have a peculiar fascination with. Willy only ever scans the headlines of the papers which he sells at his shop, so as not to appear totally ignorant in front of his customers, but he does take genuine pleasure in them: 'He didn't read them, but he liked them. Their columns, captions and neat gradations of print. The world's events were gathered into those patterns' (17). What appeals to Willy, then, is not so much the actual 'content' of the newspapers, which he dismisses as 'unimportant', but the reassuring sense of order and direction which their particular 'layout' (24) creates. Irene, who, unlike her husband, is a voracious newspaper reader, is interested ultimately in the same effect. Keeping up with the papers is a way for her to 'keep abreast of the facts' (31), to 'tak[e] note of the facts, as if the course of things was predictable and she had only to observe its fulfilment' (60). It even seems to Willy that Irene has a way of speaking 'as if she'd already arranged for what she said to happen' (78). More than her husband, however, Irene is aware that adherence to pattern and form does not come naturally to the world but has to be forcefully imposed upon it. Indeed, by reading the papers she attempts to 'hold sway over the array of facts and regard them all with cold passivity. And sometimes, indeed, it was as if she didn't read at all, her head hidden behind the outspread page, but peered through it, as through a veil, at a world which might default or run amok if it once suspected her gaze was not upon it' (17). Irene's self-assumed responsibility for establishing stability thus appears to extend far beyond the bounds of her domestic life to include the world of public affairs and international politics.

The precarious balance of the interbellum period is thoroughly upset, however, by the onset of the Second World War. While the entire world runs amok, Irene and Willy manage to remain essentially untouched by the upheaval. Having incurred an injury in trying to fix a sign above his shop, Willy is exempted from active service, and works instead in the Royal Engineer Stores. The duty which he is required to perform as a quartermaster's clerk, namely the issue of equipment to new recruits who will face combat overseas, is merely an extension of his work at the sweet shop. Indeed, his new job actually allows him to carry on in much the same manner as before. Just as he used to keep track of the stock in his own shop, so he now keeps a running count of the helmets and side-packs he hands out. He duly records these numbers in his letters to Irene, who, having found employment at the Food Office, replies by quoting the number of ration books that she has counted. Willy is struck, for the very first time, by the discrepancy which he perceives to exist between the soothing routine that thus establishes itself and the rampant chaos of the war to which it is supposed to bear some relationship: 'And here suddenly was the real thing. And yet how did it express itself? In barrack huts and wire fencing, in numbers, inventories, lists? 360 capes, 360 helmets, 720 side-packs. What was the connection?' (59). Willy is haunted by this question as he ponders the strictly regulated environment of the camp in Hampshire where he carries out his counting and accounting tasks. There appears to yawn a gulf between the reality of war and the careless 'pattern making' (57) in which both he and the soldiers whom he sees marching in drill formation are engaged: 'Left, right. The patterns shifted, the figures grouped, regrouped over the gravel. '42, '43, '44: while the headlines spoke (what was the connection?) of faraway action' (78). Once taken for granted, the connection between reality and the various patterns in which it is framed comes under strain during the war.

There is a clear suggestion, at this point, that the practice of pattern-making amounts to a strategy of reality-denial which works to keep the self in a state of aloofness and disengagement. For one thing, the obsessive phrase 'What was the connection?' becomes associated with the words 'What war?' (79), which are repeatedly used in regard of people's attempts, in the wake of the Second World War, to turn their back on a traumatic past by reverting to business as usual. Not only do they crop up in the description of the shopkeepers 'resuming their old ploys as if history could be circumvented and the war (what war?) veiled by the allurements of their windows' (98), but they are also invoked to denounce the anaesthetization of society through the commodification of history as entertainment:

> John Mills and Kenneth More in cheerful re-enactments of the war. History enshrined in make-believe. Like the lurid stories in the boys' comics he sold in the shop: grim-jawed fighter-pilots and ogreish Germans. What war? A packet of gum please, and another card in the series 'Great Battles of World War Two'. (131)

That fitting the world into patterns carries similar connotations of detachment and disinvolvement is also implied by Willy's reflection that the drive to absorb an unsettling event into an existing scheme, such as the annals of history, can be linked to an underlying desire not to become implicated in it: 'So Private Rees said, smacking his lips over a newspaper bearing the news of the occupation of Paris: "History, that's what it is." As if the statement would save him, immune as a rock, from an invasion of Germans and all the outrages of war' (59). The immunity of a rock is, of course, exactly the condition aspired to by Irene, the master pattern-maker.

Willy's awareness of cracks in the system is never of such a kind, though, as to pose any real threat to the hard-fought stability of his married life. Whenever he has any doubts or misgivings concerning the viability of the principles by which he and his wife have chosen to live their lives, Irene's commanding gaze stops him from putting these into words, let alone acting upon them and disturbing the balance: 'But such mutinies could never have occurred, for her glance would have caught him before he slipped and fell: "Play your part"' (136). The power of Irene's gaze is mobilized, then, not only to prevent an impetuous world from running amok, but also – and more successfully – to hold an occasionally unruly husband in check. Another aspect of their marital arrangement which Willy sometimes seems to want to reconsider – though again to no avail – is its lovelessness. Besides reducing the outside world to a set of predictable patterns, Irene also conceives human relationships according to a strictly controllable economic model within which there is no place for any kind of emotional involvement. Intersubjectivity is reduced to a simple trade-off in this novel, crammed as it is with references to exchange, deals, bargains, agreements, prices, investments, return, debts, forfeits, rewards and bribes. Irene's marriage to Willy in particular is presented throughout the text as a bargain whose terms Irene established right from the beginning. It is a contractual agreement which excludes conjugal love from the marital equation for the 'gifts' of the shop and a daughter: 'And all I ask in return for this is that there be no question of love' (22); 'No, that was not included, not part of the bargain. Wasn't the rest enough?' (31). A typical example of the economic dynamic on which their marriage is based can be found in the following passage, which shows Irene and Willy striving to pay off the respective debts they feel they owe each other:

> Her face showed only the pinched look of someone labouring to pay a debt. So that he felt, through that lean winter of '48, while her womb swelled, that he'd inflicted some penalty upon her for which he, in turn, must make amends by never showing gladness; taking her hint, leaving the house at six, standing obediently behind his counter: counting, counting the endless change so as to pay his own debt. (101)

The reason why Irene is so anxious to keep love out of the picture is that such an uncontrollable force would disrupt the strict economy of exchange, of give and take and of settling scores. Indeed, in Willy's mind, love is closely associated with the notion of 'action', which is, of course, complete anathema to Irene: 'But he didn't add – perhaps that was only for the heroes, writing from the field of action – "I love you"' (62). Willy realizes all too well that a declaration of love 'would alarm her, more than war, more than bombs and blackness. No, she would say, that wouldn't be a good plan' (65).

Despite occasional reservations about the businesslike nature of his marriage, Willy ends up conducting his relations with other people according to the same economic logic. 'They were paid' (16) is his silent farewell to his shop assistants and paper boys as he slips them generous bonuses on the last day of his life. Even his relationship with Smithy the barber, the closest thing he has to a friend, Willy fails to conceive as anything other than a commercial transaction: 'It was a bargain: he got his shave, Smithy got a pinch of tobacco and free magazines for his customers' (36). In fact, almost all forms of interaction between any two characters in the novel turn out to be governed by economic principles. The friendship between Irene's brother Paul and Hancock, which leads the latter to offer the former a job, is ultimately a matter of business interests: 'the two friends struck their terms, made their bargain' (150). Mrs Cooper secretly hopes that her attempts to ingratiate herself with Willy will earn her the 'reward' (93) of a life of leisure. She wants Willy to marry her, not (primarily) because she loves him, but in order that '[she] will no longer have to work' (33).[12] Yet another character who lives by the principle of '[s]ervice rendered; reward given' is Sandra Pearce, an attractive sixteen-year-old whose dealings with the other sex are described in starkly economic terms: 'she had something to offer. And she'd calculate in return *his* assets and give, or not give (though, usually, she gave) the appropriate favour. But all this had become a kind of business. All predictable; nothing new' (105).

The novel subtly but unmistakably intimates that the rigid immobility and monotonous predictability of the characters' lives amounts to a kind of death-in-life, a condition of sterile stagnation but little removed from death. An adherence to a strictly regulated economy of exchange which reduces all relations to questions of barter appears to turn people into lifeless objects. Reading *The Sweet Shop Owner*, one is struck by the frequency with which the novel's characters – and especially its protagonist – are compared to toys, puppets, pins, skittles, statues, machines and dummies. Willy's body even seems to undergo a literal stiffening process over the course of the narrative. The accident with the ladder leaves him with a stiff leg, and in the following years and decades the stiffness gradually spreads to the rest of his body: 'And in the shop I felt my face, over the counter, go hard like a shell. I thought, this is what happens: you harden, you set in your mould' (187). The climax of this development is reached when Willy is finally transfixed into 'a cold, stone statue' (10) by death. In fact, his marriage had already been placed under the sign of death by the remarkable simile in the following sentence: 'The sun shone at both their funerals, making the white graves in the cemetery sparkle like wedding cakes' (46). The novel also sets up a revealing parallel between Willy and the lilac tree in the garden which he is repeatedly said to be watching intently from the chair by the living-room window. While Willy sits waiting for life to end and death to come, the lilac tree, the only part of the garden to catch some sun, is gradually enveloped in shade: 'The shadow had crept further up the lilac tree' (220). Significantly, however, the lilac's sunlit crown, with which Willy's life becomes identified, is described as being dead already: 'The lilac was half within the shadow of the house, but its upper leaves, where the mauve cones had already bloomed and died, fluttered in the sunshine' (218). The implication is that Willy has been in a state of lifelessness all along: death has already caught up with him long before his heart actually stops beating.

Willy dies when he is forced to confront the illusory nature of the fantasy of a reunion with his daughter which has sustained him ever since his wife passed away. The realization that Dorothy will not return home despite the money which he has sent her – 'She will not come' (222) – disrupts the symbolic universe in which he lives. The old economic logic of exchange, according to which a gift is always expected to be reciprocated (in this case, by the daughter's return), appears to have lost its validity. Seeing his long-held beliefs contradicted, Willy hastens towards death.[13] In fact, the situation in which Willy finds himself at the end of his life is structurally analogous to that of Irene's father, who dies on the eve of victory in the Second World War. A workaholic like Willy, who also came into money through marriage, suffers from a heart condition[14] and ignores doctor's orders to take it easy, Mr Harrison is crushed by the death of his son Jack – or, more likely, by the realization that 'Money won't bring Jack back' (81). Money having always been his guiding principle, Mr Harrison breaks down when faced with the incontrovertible fact of a loss which no amount of money can compensate. Like Willy, who becomes aware that money will not bring Dorothy back, Mr Harrison can no longer connect his mythical, utilitarian way of life with the distressing reality at hand: 'His face was grey and dumb and held in suspense as if he couldn't make some connection' (80). For Willy, too, the purportedly self-evident connection between pattern and reality, whose precariousness he had already sensed during the Second World War, has become altogether untenable.

Even so, his death appears to be specifically intended as a punishment to his daughter for violating the terms of the agreement which he believes her to be inescapably bound by. As such, it constitutes an attempt posthumously to reinstate the rules of exchange which Dorothy has transgressed by accepting his money and yet refusing to honour the obligation that came with it. Indeed, the circumstances of Willy's suicide are carefully orchestrated to inflict maximum devastation on his daughter's life. For one thing, he has planned his death-day to coincide with Dorothy's twenty-fifth birthday: 'And today, Dorry, is your birthday. He could almost smile at the neatness of it' (11). What is more, Willy makes sure that he will be found sitting in the chair by the window in the exact same pose in which his daughter last saw him when, two months earlier, she had come back unannounced to rob her parents' house. As Catherine Miquel points out,

> En faisant en sorte que sa fille le trouve mort dans l'exacte position où elle l'avait quitté et 'trahi', deux mois auparavant, Chapman l'accuse implicitement de l'avoir tué, et la condamne à rester hantée par le souvenir du Père

> symboliquement assassiné, transformé en 'cold statue', c'est-à-dire en Commandeur accusateur, plein de reproches amers envers l'Ingrate, sinon l'Impie.
>
> By ensuring that his daughter finds him in the exact position in which she had left and 'betrayed' him two months earlier, Chapman implicitly accuses her of having killed him and condemns her to remain haunted by the memory of the Father who has been symbolically murdered, transformed into a 'cold statue', that is, into an accusing Commander, full of bitter reproaches to the Ungrateful – if not the Infidel – Daughter. (143)

Willy's apparent vindictiveness towards his daughter finds a counterpart in Mr Harrison's fanaticism about the war, which boils down to a perverse attempt to reinstall a compensatory mechanism allowing him to make at least some sense of the loss of his son. Though he realizes all too well that money will not bring Jack back, Mr Harrison yet insists on the need to make the enemy pay for his son's death: 'Jack's killed, we must win and wipe all the Germans off the map' (82). Defeated by a situation of irredeemable loss which gives the lie to their utilitarian principles, both Willy and Mr Harrison in the final stage of their life resort to a vicious fantasy of retribution which only reiterates the discredited logic of exchange.

The only character in the novel to show any serious determination to challenge the pervasive economy of exchange governing the world of the text is Dorothy, whose very name connotes resistance to the hegemony of economic idolatry. Whereas names such as 'Chapman' and 'Irene', meaning 'merchant' and 'peace', have an obvious relationship to their respective bearers, Dorothy's name cannot be so readily explained from inside the novelistic universe. Yet it is the only name whose meaning is made explicit in the text: '"Dorothy": we called you "Dorothy". . . . But it was only years later that you yourself, coming home from school (how quick you were to learn things) explained what it meant. Dorothea: God's gift' (112). In her parents' scheme of things, however, Dorothy is Irene's 'gift' to Willy, '[her] side of the bargain' (10): 'You were her gift' (186). Like all other gifts in the novel, Dorothy is made to serve a function in a narrowly contractual relationship governed by a principle of self-interest.[15] Indeed, the only type of gift thinkable within the utilitarian discourse prevalent in the novel reduces to a form of calculation: it obligates the recipient to offer some counter-gift in return.[16] However, apparently unbeknownst to her parents, Dorothy's name exceeds this limited and limiting vision by introducing a transcendent principle into the text which interrupts the immanent logic of reciprocal and symmetrical exchange.

Interestingly, the notion of 'God's gift' is central to Derrida's recent inquiry into the nature of responsibility and justice, which presents itself as a deliberate attempt to formulate an alternative to dominant conceptualizations steeped in an economy of exchange. Derrida finds inspiration in the Christian tradition, which, in his reading, announces a new way of acceding to responsibility that 'comes from a gift received from the other, from the one who, in absolute transcendence, sees me without my seeing, holds me in his hands while remaining inaccessible' (*Gift* 40). The *mysterium tremendum*, as this experience is called, rouses one to the responsibility of making a gift of death, of sacrificing oneself for the wholly other – which Christianity represents by the name of God – without any hope of return:

> The gift made to me by God as he holds me in his gaze and in his hand while remaining inaccessible to me, the terribly dissymmetrical gift of the *mysterium tremendum* only allows me to respond and only rouses me to the responsibility it gives me by making a gift of death [*en me donnant la mort*], giving the secret of death, a new experience of death. (*Gift* 33)

Such a sacrificial self-offering, which expects no benefit in return, would be a true, '*aneconomic*' gift, that is, a gift which 'interrupts economy' in that it 'suspend[s] economic calculation' and hence 'no longer gives rise to exchange' (Derrida, 'Given' 166). The notion of 'God's gift' thus becomes associated, in Derrida's thinking, with a conception of ethics as radical non-reciprocal generosity which represents a decisive break with the hegemonic system of economic circularity.

Dorothy is a dissenter not only in name but also in character and in deed. In many respects, she is the exact antithesis of her parents, especially her mother. Whereas Irene is frequently depicted as being in a state of drowning, Dorothy surprises Willy by not being afraid of water (119). As a young child, she does not 'flail [her] arms' (108) while being baptized, nor does she 'scream and struggle' (114) when her father gives her a bath – all this in marked contrast to her mother, who displays such behaviour during her asthma attacks. Later, Dorothy even becomes 'a good swimmer' (119), with a particular talent for back-stroke, diving and – significantly – life-saving. While her parents 'don't dance' (75, 87), preferring to remain static and immobile, Dorothy 'had that lightness and deftness of step as if [she]'d have liked to dance – if only someone had let [her]' (117). She challenges the status quo maintained by her parents on the family holidays, which are invariably spent in Dorset, a town Irene and Willy are familiar with from their honeymoon: 'We might have gone elsewhere, to Wales, to Norfolk, but (since we had to go) she was against anywhere new. Nothing new' (117). However, Dorothy makes Willy realize that Irene's stipulation cannot possibly be fulfilled: 'Yet (how could you defy her?) everything was eternally new; the old cry of the sea-gulls, the old tingle of the breeze, the old mystery of the rock-pools – how you loved to squat and explore those delicate little worlds' (117). From Irene's point of view, the choice of Dorset as holiday destination is particularly apt. Very set in her ways herself, Irene hopes to impose the same fate upon her daughter: 'Dor-set', Dorothy set in her mother's ways. Willy appears to confirm this derivation when he wonders: 'And did you sense how that scene in which you stood for the first time had already been encountered before and its limits fixed?' (117).[17] However, Dorothy refuses to be boxed in by her mother's expectations.[18] One such summer, knowing her parents' eyes to be upon her and her head 'set in defiance' (191), she walks along the top of the breakwater, not on the horizontal planks, but on the narrow, seven or eight feet high uprights, leaping from one to the next. Her willingness to take risks – 'how you needed to run risks' (119), Willy muses – scares her mother witless but is secretly admired by her father, who watches her progress with an open mouth.

Dorothy has little patience with the patterns established by her parents. After school, she sometimes drops in on Willy at the shop, disrupting his daily routine and rekindling his long-suppressed desire for excitement rather than peace: 'Why did you have to come into the shop? To disturb those patterns? To see my look of disguised excitement, faint apology, as I greeted you from behind the counter?' (138). Moreover, she defies her parents' motto 'Nothing touches you, you touch nothing' (44) not only with her adolescent determination to 'make [her] mark' (140) but even with her sleeping pose: 'Hair tumbled, one arm raised on the pillow, as though to touch someone' (13). Irene's yearning for uneventfulness – 'Let nothing happen' (43) – is also completely alien to Dorothy, who takes a keen interest in things happening in the world around her, both locally and globally. Sitting at the dinner table with her parents, she insists on bringing up for discussion momentous events which upset some long-maintained balance, much to the consternation of her mother. For example, Dorothy announces, with an offence-giving 'note of adventure' in her voice, that her uncle Paul has run off with Hancock's wife: 'Something has happened' (152). On another occasion, having read the papers, she provokes Irene's anger by raising the subject of the Cuban missile crisis, then in full swing: 'Doesn't it bother you – that there might be a war?' (140). However, Irene 'refused to be drawn': 'All this excitement, this nonsense. I won't have it. I won't suffer it' (17).[19] The 1962 missile crisis, the climax of the Cold War and the closest the world ever came to nuclear Armageddon, represents an eruption of nonsense which exposes the fragility of the equilibrium established by Irene and Willy's generation. Dorothy accuses her parents of irresponsibly repressing this unsettling event, which not only threatens to disturb the meaningful patterns into which Irene habitually fits world events, but might well spell the end of the world as such: 'Neither of you care! What do you read the papers for if you don't care what happens? It's not something you can just ignore –' (141).[20]

Her desire to break with the stifling and oppressive milieu of her family is apparent from her ominous decision, against her teachers' wishes, to play the part of Shylock's daughter Jessica rather than that of Portia in her school's staging of *The Merchant of Venice*. Jessica has, of course, a very different relationship with her father than Portia with hers. Whereas the latter obeys her father's commands to the letter, the former runs away from her father's house with her lover, taking some bags of ducats and precious stones, and converts to another religion, namely Christianity. The Shakespearean intertext thus anticipates both Dorothy's desertion of Willy and the brief return visit on which she loots her father's house.[21] Moreover, *The Merchant of Venice* is commonly seen to celebrate the triumph of the Christian concepts of mercy, love and self-sacrifice over the narrowly materialist worldview and the unyielding, legalistic conception of justice associated with Jewishness. The reference to Shakespeare thus seems to afford further proof of the aspiration to a different, aneconomic ethics implicit in Dorothy's name.[22] Modern accounts of the play, however, tend to focus on the issue of anti-Semitism and draw attention to the way in which values like mercy and charity are abused by the play's Christian characters, who are exposed as power-hungry, unscrupulous and vengeful hypocrites.[23] Jessica's position is thus rendered deeply ambiguous, the apparent success of her escape from the restrictive parental regime of relentless commercialism, self-interest and vindictiveness being compromised by the duplicity and expedience of her fellow Christians, who are revealed to be no strangers to these supposedly Jewish vices.

In *The Sweet Shop Owner*, too, the daughter's escape is surrounded by question marks. Like Jessica, Dorothy clearly succeeds in physically transcending the 'narrow bounds' (184) of her parents' humdrum existence. Her decision to move to Bristol with her boyfriend even manages to catch her mother off guard: 'She raised her face and said – she who'd always seemed able to predict things – "What now? What happens now?"' (183). However, there are several indications in the text that Dorothy has absorbed her parents' values more thoroughly than she would presumably care to admit; mentally, at least, she has not quite broken free from the world of her upbringing. For example, the double-edged letter of thanks with which the novel opens is so steeped in Irene's trademark rhetoric that it subtly belies its stated aim of establishing a definitive break with the past: 'I should have thought you'd be glad to be finished with me at last' (9). Just like her mother, Dorothy reduces her relationship with Willy to a business transaction, which, to her mind, has been successfully concluded with his payment of £15,000: 'I think we can call everything settled now' (9). This phrase recalls Irene's obsession with the settling of accounts: 'Good. Then it's settled' (21); 'I want things to be settled' (182). Dorothy also asserts her superior vision in her letter to Willy: 'I'm sure this is for the best and how Mother would have wanted it. You will see in the end' (9). Again, she is only echoing a claim made by Irene: 'And you will see, you will see it is for the best in the end' (103).[24] Dorothy's insistence on predictability and exchange thus shows the extent to which her thinking is still implicated in her parents' discourse.

Dorothy's letter thus seems to bear out Willy's assessment that his daughter's struggle 'to escape history, to put it all behind you – me, her, those twenty-odd years in that house' is doomed to failure: 'And have you escaped history, down there in Bristol? Found new life? Encumbered with all those things of hers, encumbered with the money I sent you (that money which was only converted history). Don't you see, you're no freer than before, no freer than I am?' (216–17). Throughout the narrative, Willy is at pains to stress that Dorothy is subject to the utter inevitability of historical patterns just like everyone else. In his view, the 'new life' which awaits her as she leaves school to go to university – 'Did you step away from it all, as you stepped out of your uniform, as if a new life beckoned?' (161) – is nothing but a continuation of her old life: 'And why did it seem to me . . . that you wore your student's outfit as if it were only another uniform?' (161). Moreover, by continually drawing attention to the physical likeness which he observes between Dorothy and Irene, Willy seems to suggest that Dorothy has no choice but to become her mother. She is said to '[have] her looks' (116), to move her hands 'just like her' (139) and to be equally uncomfortable with her own beauty: 'Dorry, at seventeen, had not known what to do with her beauty – she'd buried herself in books, as though to disown it' (95); 'Other people noticed her [Irene], other people admired. Though she'd never known how to deal with their glances except by lowering her own eyes' (118).

Dorothy's chances of escape are further compromised by the analogy which the text sets up between Willy's home life and his life at the sweet shop, where, as John Marsden points out, Mrs Cooper and Sandra are 'ironic doubles' of Irene and Dorothy (*After Modernism* 72). Though in physical appearance Mrs Cooper could not be more unlike Irene – having 'never been beautiful, with that bird's face' (35) – she turns out to share the latter's outlook on life: 'she didn't want action any more, only peace' (81). A similar relationship exists between Sandra and Dorothy. Whereas Dorothy did not know how to deal with her own beauty, Sandra 'traded so much on her attractions . . . that they sometimes seemed to him [Willy] not to belong to her' (95). On a more fundamental level, however, Sandra, like Dorothy, is desperate to escape the economic logic in which she has become caught up. Bored with trading sex for cheap thrills, 'She'd give anything for something new' (105, 107). However, the text gives us no reason to believe that Sandra will ever find the newness she craves. On the contrary, we are told that 'She'd try anything. . . . But it seemed she'd already tried everything' (105). Moreover, the formulation of her desire for release from the economic order in which she is stuck betrays its inescapability, depending as it does on the very notion of exchange which is supposed to be transcended: as the proper payment which Sandra hopes to receive in return for the 'anything' she is willing to offer, 'something new' has already been reduced to another commodity, absorbed into the old economic cycle.

Envisaging the possibility of genuine renewal appears to be a deeply problematic undertaking in *The Sweet Shop Owner*. The novel diagnoses the demise of a way of life based on the principles of predictability, arrested motion and economic circularity, but it is extremely wary of endorsing a viable alternative. Though tantalizing flashes of a truly new future are offered through the character of Dorothy, the suggestion that there is no possibility of achieving real change is at least equally prominent in the text. The apparent impasse in the narrative present is largely accounted for by the succession of traumas with which the characters have failed seriously to engage, taking recourse instead to coping mechanisms which, in the long run, prove inimical to life and whose pernicious effects threaten to be transmitted across the generations. In exposing the ravages wreaked by a determined evasion of a catastrophic history, *The Sweet Shop Owner* inaugurates Swift's search for a way of coming to terms with trauma that would help bring about the conditions for the creation of a more humane, just and less destructive future. Never fully assumed in this text, this crucial quest becomes a central concern in the author's later novels.

3 Getting Rid of 'Needless Painful Knowledge'

Problem Dissolving *in* Shuttlecock

They say you only recall what is pleasant and you only forget what you choose not to remember. Perhaps. But do I say 'remember'? This was not so much a memory as a pang . . .
Graham Swift, *Shuttlecock*

In his second novel, *Shuttlecock*, Graham Swift rewrites the defeat with which *The Sweet Shop Owner* ends as an apparent triumph, while remaining true to the basic set-up established in his first novel. Whereas *The Sweet Shop Owner* is the story of an ageing shopkeeper who commits suicide to free himself from the desolation and abandonment in which a sustained investment in reality-denial has landed him, *Shuttlecock* presents us with a distressed thirty-something police archivist – by far the youngest of all Swift's male protagonists – who seems to find redemption through the very strategies of denial responsible for Willy Chapman's predicament. The novel bears witness to a protracted attempt on the part of the narrator-protagonist, who sings the virtues of suppressing traumatic knowledge, to *dis*solve – rather than to solve – the problems diagnosed by the earlier novel. The validity of this distinction is borne out by Swift's later work, starting with *Waterland*, which reveals all attempts to exorcize the problem of trauma to be doomed to backfire and takes up the search for alternative, more fruitful ways of dealing with the issue.

Flirting with the genre of the *Bildungsroman*, advocating a return to nature, appealing to the power of the imagination and making explicit reference to the notion of the pathetic fallacy, *Shuttlecock* clearly demands to be read against the background of Romanticism. In fact, according to Wendy Wheeler, both *The Sweet Shop Owner* and *Shuttlecock* are centrally concerned with the problem of 'Romantic symbolism' (*From the Sublime* 106). In the former novel, which tells a story of 'Romantic "failure"' (*From the Sublime* 114), this engagement takes the form of a critique. The protagonist's fantasy of achieving 'symbolic unity' is rudely shattered by his estranged daughter's refusal to return home: 'Willy's search for a final Romantic patterning – a final symbolic concordance between objective world and subjective Idea – comes to nothing' (*From the Sublime* 114–15). This failure is redeemed, however, in *Shuttlecock*, one of Swift's most 'closed' novels, in which '[s]ymbolic unity ("love") is achieved' through 'the healing power of nostalgic memory' (*From the Sublime* 118, 123, 122). While Wheeler appears to take the novel's idyllic happy ending on its own terms, interpreting it as the triumph it purports to be,[1] this chapter focuses on textual elements which allow it to be seen as a disturbing cop-out from the problem of coming to terms with life in a disenchanted world.

Shuttlecock is the story of a man identified only as 'Prentis' who works as a senior clerk in the 'dead crimes' department of the London police archives. He is a family man in his early thirties, with a wife, Marian, and two sons, Martin and Peter. Two years prior to the novel's action, Prentis's father ('Dad') suffered a breakdown which left him speechless and confined to a mental institution, where his son pays him regular visits. Prentis is engaged in three separate, though not unrelated struggles. On the home front, he tries to assert his mastery over his wife and kids by acting the family tyrant. At work, he is hoping to gain the upper hand over his inscrutable boss Quinn, who appears to take sadistic delight in assigning him complicated cases which are impossible to resolve on the basis of the limited information at his disposal. Finally, as the son of a Second World War hero, Prentis is tormented by feelings of inferiority and inadequacy. During the war, his father – a handsome, successful, happily married, highly regarded and socially well-connected engineer – had been active as a secret agent in France. Dad later wrote about his war experiences in a book entitled Shuttlecock (after his spy code-name), which for the best part of the novel Prentis is busy rereading.[2]

Shuttlecock's plot is based on the model of the traditional *Bildungsroman*, which charts a young person's transition to maturity and harmony. This generic affiliation is inscribed in the protagonist's name: he is an *apprentice* who has to undergo a learning process to attain mastership. Prentis announces this ambition at an early stage in the narrative, which is rendered in the form of a diary. The novel opens with Prentis's memories of the way in which as a child he used to torture Sammy, his pet hamster. His recollection of the unfortunate animal's attempt to escape its tormentor's grasp by digging a tunnel in the garden – 'Needless to say, I punished it severely' – leads to the following reflection: 'Now let me tell you something. We are all looking for a space where we can be free, where we cannot be reached, where we are masters' (36). Recurring several times at key moments in the text, the image of the burrowing animal which has found protection from persecution in nature accurately captures the ideal of freedom to which the novel's protagonist aspires.

At the start of the narrative, however, Prentis experiences his own condition as one of bondage, alienation and unfreedom. Feeling put upon and oppressed by two domineering paternal presences – Dad and Quinn – he finds himself in much the same position as Sammy, a captive at the complete mercy of a powerful master. His abusive behaviour towards his family is explained as a pathetic attempt to compensate for his powerlessness in the office and his nagging sense of unworthiness and weakness *vis-à-vis* his father's apparent heroism and strength: 'Underneath everything, they know that I am essentially a weak man. That's just the trouble. . . . So all this show of strength means nothing' (11). Prentis is a man who lives in discord with the world. Describing himself as being in a state of 'constant dissatisfaction' (72), he clearly finds his own situation deeply problematic. He is alienated from his wife – 'My wife is afraid of me, she does not know me' (100) – and his relations with his sons, which are characterized by 'non-communication' (211), 'aren't exactly harmonious' (53) either. Haunted by a sense of personal inauthenticity, Prentis also feels alienated from himself. He regrets being unable ever to 'act simply or straightforwardly' (8), and describes his actions in terms of scenes in a 'performance' which he 'can't do anything about' (10). As if reduced to an instrument of forces outside of himself, he cannot seem to help acting against his own wishes: 'And these days it seems that I too, for some inexplicable reason, for some spiteful reason, because what I really want to do is precisely the opposite, am choosing to stay indoors when we could go out' (54).[3]

Not only is Prentis alienated from his family and from himself, but he also feels estranged from nature. There is a strong sense in the novel that contemporary society has become so far removed from nature that nature itself seems 'something foreign' (153). It is a matter of some concern to Prentis that the subject of Nature Study has been dropped from the curriculum at his sons' school (33). He disapproves of his sons' alleged appetite for the unnatural, which he infers from their fascination with the Bionic Man, a robotic hero who 'bears no relation to anything natural' (10), and from their preference for watching TV over playing 'healthy games' on the common: 'All this simply isn't natural' (54). Even during his own schooldays, however, when Nature Study was still on the curriculum, Prentis perceived nature as 'a rare and mysterious commodity' (33), 'some precious lost treasure': 'Above all, it was something quite separate and distinct from me' (34).

This theme of exile from nature also pervades those passages in which Prentis contemplates his sexual relationship with his wife. He informs the reader that 'it's a long time since I've experienced with Marian that thing called "ecstasy" or "fulfilment"' (72). It emerges that their love-making is a far cry from the simple, spontaneous sexual pleasures which in Prentis's mind are associated with proximity to nature and which he claims to have enjoyed in the early years of his marriage to Marian. He envies the 'easy contentment' (73) of the sparrows and the ducks whom he observes copulating, with natural simplicity, on the guttering and on the common. He regrets having fallen away from this primordial natural state, and goes to great lengths to recapture it:

> And sometimes that is just how I see it with Marian and me: a little careless, unadorned instant, like the sparrows; a little flutter of wings and hearts: at one with nature. Perhaps it was like that once, long ago. For Marian and me. For all of us. But now we have to go through the most elaborate charades, the most strenuous performances to receive enlightenment. Because that is the goal, don't mistake me – enlightenment. All nature's creatures join to express nature's purpose. Somewhere in their mounting and mating, rutting and butting is the very secret of nature itself. And when, night after night, I conduct my sexual experiments with Marian, for ever modifying the formula, it's with the yearning that one day it won't just be sex, but enlightenment. (73)

In his quest for 'enlightenment', Prentis subjects his wife to strenuous, contorted bedroom gymnastics involving the use of 'certain "manuals"' and articles from sex shops and mail-order catalogues (73). All this artificial paraphernalia is meant to help him achieve 'some ultimate thing that always seemed elusive' (73), that is, enlightenment conceived as a redemptive return to the state of nature.

By the end of the novel, alienation appears to have ceased. Prentis closes his narrative with an evocation of an idyllic family outing to Camber Sands, a beach on the English Channel, one bright spring Sunday. The entire scene seems designed to convince the reader that Prentis is (once again) a man at one with himself and his surroundings. For one thing, Prentis claims to have undergone a 'transformation', as a result of which his family allegedly no longer 'doubt or disbelieve what they see' (209) when he comes home from the office. No longer the 'complete sham' (95) he used to be, he purports to coincide with his true self again. As a result, family harmony appears to have been restored. In marked contrast to the former 'days of non-communication' (211) with his sons, Prentis establishes what looks like a harmonious relationship with them. He even enjoys a 'deadly-earnest' (219) cricket match with Martin and Peter, who in the past did not show 'the slightest interest' in cricket and 'stubbornly refused to enter the spirit of the game' (53) when Prentis forced them to come out and play with him.

To his wife, Prentis imagines coming across as 'a reformed man: the man I was, years ago, before Mum's death and Dad's breakdown, before the kids grew up' (210) – that is, in the idealized, supposedly non-alienated first years of his marriage to Marian. In fact, the trip to the seaside on which Prentis takes his family explicitly commemorates their early married life. While their sons frolic in the sea, Prentis and Marian make happily spontaneous love in the dunes at Camber Sands, just as they used to do when Martin was still a baby.[4] Renouncing the 'pointless sophistication' (219) which had reduced their sex-life to '[a] sham, a mockery' (75), they have uncomplicated sex in the sand, 'quick as sparrows' (219) in case someone might appear over the crest of the dunes. Another significant natural image – besides that of the copulating sparrows – which is reinvoked in this connection is that of the burrowing animal: 'All those laborious bedroom antics, to return at last to burrowing in the sand' (219). By the end of the novel, Prentis seems to have successfully overcome alienation and achieved the longed-for state of freedom which was unavailable to him at the outset. As if to underscore his attunement with his surroundings, he sees his own nakedness reflected in the dune-landscape, which he describes as 'naked' like 'human flesh' (220). The 'soft-gold hues and gentle contours' of the dunes in turn remind him of his hamster and of his original reason for wanting it. The novel ends with Prentis's recollection of 'the magical words Mr Forster had spoken when I was a boy (Peter's age): "a piece of nature"' (220).[5]

The communion with nature evoked in *Shuttlecock*'s final pages is anticipated in the penultimate chapter, consisting of only two sentences, which are thus given special significance. Prentis asks Marian, who has a habit of talking to her plants, whether she believes in the pathetic fallacy: 'That it's really a fallacy, I mean?' (215). As Wheeler points out, 'Like his wife's behaviour, the question suggests Prentis's dawning sense of the possibility of continuity between things which seem divided (here the human and the natural worlds and, by implication, Prentis and his wife)' (*From the Sublime* 121) – a possibility which is actualized in the novel's concluding chapter. The notion of the pathetic fallacy, which is explicitly invoked at three key points in the text, constitutes a useful starting point for a critical reflection on the redemptive trajectory governing Prentis's narrative. The term 'pathetic fallacy' was originally coined by John Ruskin in his book *Modern Painters* to decry the tendency of certain literary artists to ascribe human characteristics, traits, feelings and dispositions to non-human organisms or inanimate objects. Such ascriptions, Ruskin argues, 'produce in us a falseness in all our impressions of external things' (1278). An 'error' which the mind admits when 'affected strongly by emotion', the pathetic fallacy distorts our perception of things as they are in reality (1278). The first example of this practice which Ruskin mentions – only to condemn it as 'very untrue' (1278) – is taken from an unnamed poem by Oliver Wendell Holmes: 'The spendthrift crocus, bursting through the mold / Naked and shivering, with his cup of gold' (1278). The attributes of nakedness and gold imputed to the crocus – 'its yellow is not gold, but saffron', Ruskin objects (1278) – both recur in Prentis's anthropomorphized description of the dunes at Camber, which is itself a blatant case of the pathetic fallacy.

Though, *pace* Ruskin, the pathetic fallacy is arguably endemic to literature as such, it is generally associated with the work of the Romantic poets, who used it extensively to indicate a feeling of oneness with nature and a sense of the unity of being. To gain further insight into the specific use to which this notion is put in *Shuttlecock*, we should turn to Stanley Cavell's discussion of the pathetic fallacy as being integral to the project of Romanticism, which he conceives as essentially a response to the 'Kantian settlement'. Kant had described his philosophical settlement as limiting knowledge by making room for faith. Moreover, in limiting knowledge, he effectively secured it against the threat of scepticism and the powers of dogmatism. In Kant's scheme, the only thing that can be known with certainty is the phenomenal world, the world as we perceive and understand it. That which causes these phenomena, the thing-in-itself or noumenon, lies beyond the bounds of perception and so is unknowable and incomprehensible. As Cavell points out, Kant introduced the irreducible dualism between phenomenon and noumenon in an effort to 'strike a bargain between the respective claims upon human nature of knowledge or science and of morality and religion' (31). For Kant, the human being lives in two worlds at once, 'in one of them determined, in the other one free, one of which is necessary to the satisfaction of human Understanding, the other to the satisfaction of human Reason' (Cavell 31–32). As phenomenon, the human being is subject to causal laws; as noumenon, he or she is free. According to Cavell, one 'romantic use' for this idea of two worlds lies in its accounting for 'the human being's dissatisfaction with, as it were, itself' (32). Indeed, it appreciates 'the ambivalence in Kant's central idea of limitation, that we simultaneously crave its comfort and crave escape from its comfort, that we want unappeasably to be lawfully wedded to the world and at the same time illicitly intimate with it' (Cavell 32). Kant's ambivalent settlement offers up the insight that 'the human being now lives in *neither* world, that we are, as it is said, between worlds' – a condition which Cavell characterizes as the endemic 'worldlessness' or 'homelessness' that is of a piece with the modern condition (32).

Disappointed with the Kantian settlement, Romanticism sets itself the task of 'bringing the world back, as to life' (Cavell 53). The assumption is that the world made available to us by Kant's faculty of the understanding is dead. Cavell quotes Coleridge's *Biographia Literaria*: 'all the products of the mere *reflective* faculty partook of DEATH' (44). The Romantics' quest for 'the recovery of the world', which may present itself as 'a new creation of our habitat' (in Wordsworth and Coleridge) or as 'the creation of a new inhabitation' (in Blake and Shelley), hinges on an acceptance of 'animism, represented by what seems still to be called, when it is called, the pathetic fallacy' (Cavell 45, 53). Thus, Romantic poetry seeks to recuperate 'the intimacy with the world' which we are denied under the Kantian regime (Cavell 65). If the Kantian bargain with scepticism can be described as 'buying back the knowledge of objects by giving up things in themselves', then Romanticism's bargain with the Kantian amounts to 'buying back the thing in itself by taking on animism' (Cavell 65).

The Romantic recourse to the pathetic fallacy is inspired, then, by the idea – which, according to Cavell, Romantics 'would be lost without' – 'that the world could be – or could have been – so remade, or I in it, that I could *want* it, as it would be, or I in it' (35). As a matter of fact, the gulf between the world of determinism and the world of freedom postulated by Kant's critical philosophy was a matter of great concern to Kant himself as well. In the *Critique of Judgement*, which completes the trilogy of the great *Critiques*, Kant looks into the possibility of an ultimate union of the two realms. The general aim of the third *Critique* is to construct a bridge which would unify the heteronomous faculties of the understanding and reason and thus restore the unity of philosophy and, consequently, the unity of the subject who is the bearer of these faculties. Having claimed, in the introduction, that the realm of freedom is meant to influence the realm of nature, Kant goes on to suggest that the experience of beauty can bridge the gulf which separates them. In Section 59, he famously declares that 'the beautiful is the symbol of the morally good' (quoted in White 179). The central faculty through which the sensible and the supersensible can be reconciled would be the imagination. As David White comments in 'On Bridging the Gulf between Nature and Morality in the *Critique of Judgment*',

> the imagination – in a manner which, again, Kant does not discuss in any further detail – somehow allows an individual when judging aesthetically to enter that distinctively Kantian supersensible ground which underlies the freedom essential to morality and is also an essential factor in the nature of beauty. (186)

The pathetic fallacy, of course, is one way in which the imagination manifests itself in literature, a privileged medium for the exercise of this faculty. However, as White's obvious vexation with the lack of argumentative clarity in the third *Critique* would seem to suggest, the imagination's ability to mediate successfully between nature and morality remains at the level of a hypothesis rather than an established fact in Kant.[6]

Vastly less cautious than the *Critique of Judgement* in its affirmation of the power of aesthetic judgement to underwrite the harmony of the faculties, however, is Friedrich Schiller's *On the Aesthetic Education of Man*, which draws on Kant's work to develop a concept of aesthetic education that has proved massively influential. As Marc Redfield points out,

> In Schiller the aesthetic becomes a supremely synthetic moment, an instant of freedom balanced between the binary oppositions of the empirical and the ideal – the 'sensuous drive' and the 'formal drive' of the *Aesthetic Education* – a synthesis that provides man with 'a complete intuition of his human nature' and 'a symbol of his accomplished destiny'. (20–21)

This destiny unfolds as the progress from a 'naive', sensual aesthetic to a 'sentimental' interiority, defined – in Schiller's essay 'Naive and Sentimental Poetry' – as the self-conscious quest for a return to the naive, and thus as the motion towards an ideal state of aesthetic synthesis: 'We were nature . . . and our culture, by means of reason and freedom, should lead us back to nature' (quoted in Redfield 21). According to Schiller, the evolution of poetry or aesthetic form is by definition also that of humanity: 'This path taken by the modern poets is, moreover, that along which man in general, the individual as well as the race, must pass' (quoted in Redfield 21).

Aesthetic education plays a pivotal role in this process, which is meant to heal 'the split within man' and to restore 'the totality of our nature' (Schiller 45, 43). The itinerary which this education is to follow is described by Schiller in the following passage:

> Every individual human being, one may say, carries within him, potentially and prescriptively, an ideal man, the archetype of a human being, and it is his life's task to be, through all his changing manifestations, in harmony with the unchanging unity of this ideal. This archetype, which is to be discerned more or less clearly in every individual, is represented by the State, the objective and, as it were, canonical form in which all the diversity of individual subjects strive to unite. (17, 19)

Thus, by definition, the acculturation or *Bildung* of an individual models a political process. The full realization of Schiller's 'ideal man' would take place as the emergence of the notorious 'Aesthetic State' evoked in the final pages of the *Aesthetic Education*. Though the state, like the individual, will forever journey towards full self-realization, *Bildung*, as an aesthetic event, demands phenomenal manifestation: 'this is to say that it requires a figure, a *Bild*, exemplifying and prefiguring the identity underlying *Bildung*'s difference and deferral. In the concordant discord of history, then, certain subjects and states can, indeed must, become exemplary' (Redfield 50). It is thus inherent in the logic of aesthetic education that Schiller's treatise should regress from 'the universalist promise of its title' to 'the less democratic model of history' suggested in the text's conclusion, which talks of the Aesthetic State existing as 'a realized fact' only in 'some few chosen circles' (Redfield 50–51).

It is this aspect of Schiller's work which led Paul de Man to argue that Schiller's aesthetic humanism is in fact latently authoritarian and thoroughly sinister. In his lecture entitled 'Kant and Schiller', de Man suggests a direct link between Schiller's notion of the Aesthetic State as the telos of *Bildung* and the fascist state as envisaged by Joseph Goebbels. Schiller's alleged misreading of Kant and his consequent inordinate investment in the aesthetic as a way of bridging the gap between nature and morality thus seems to lead to serious political consequences. In 'Aesthetic Formalization: Kleist's *Über das Marionettentheater*', de Man argues that the trajectory of Schiller's aesthetic theory, which exemplifies the idea 'of innocence recovered at the far side and by way of experience, of paradise consciously regained after the fall into consciousness', represents 'one of the most seductive, powerful, and deluded topoi of the idealist and romantic period' (267). De Man's critique of what he calls 'aesthetic ideology' seeks to expose the ominous political tendencies with which the kind of aesthetic thought set forth by Schiller is seen to be infected. Interestingly, the notion that modern alienation can in any way be 'overcome' or abolished is also dismissed as a dangerous fantasy by Slavoj Žižek, who argues, in *The Sublime Object of Ideology*, that man has to 'come to terms' with his separation from nature if the worst is to be avoided:

> man as such is 'the wound of nature', there is no return to the natural balance; to accord with his milieu, the only thing man can do is accept fully this cleft, this fissure, this structural rooting-out, and to try as far as possible to patch things up afterwards; all other solutions – the illusion of a possible return to nature, the idea of the total socialization of nature – are a direct path to totalitarianism. (5)

As a *Bildungsroman*, *Shuttlecock* is inevitably embroiled in the problematic of the aesthetic. Indeed, as a literary genre 'defined by the aesthetic project of *Bildung*', the *Bildungsroman* can be said to 'symbolize the possibility of aesthetics itself' (Redfield 63). Redfield shows how the prototypical *Bildungsroman*, Goethe's *Wilhelm Meister's Apprenticeship*, can be read as a 'fictional counterpart' (66) of Schiller's *Aesthetic Education*, which was written concurrently with it. In this reading, the character Wilhelm stands for 'the subject of aesthetics, representative of universal humanity', and the Society of the Tower into whose ranks Wilhelm is eventually initiated represents the Aesthetic State (Redfield 67). However, Redfield goes on to demonstrate that Goethe's novel, while closely following the path sketched by Schiller's aesthetic theory, at the same time deconstructs it through the use of irony, which 'disarticulates the aesthetic and naturalizing illusion that composes all ideologies, thus opening them to critique by accounting for their occurrence' (93). A similar tension is evident in *Shuttlecock*, which relates how Prentis breaks with the world of determinism and gains his freedom through the power of his imagination. Although *Shuttlecock* does not mount a full-fledged critique of aesthetic ideology – a task reserved for *Waterland* – it nevertheless shows clear signs of unease with the project of aesthetic totalization into whose service it finds itself pressed.

The joyous affirmation of symbolic unity at the end of the novel is rendered possible by Prentis's having realized a double ambition in the course of the narrative. As he announces early on, there are 'two promotions' (71) that he wants. Firstly, he wants to become equal to his father: 'I wanted to step into Dad's shoes. Now his mind was gone, now Dad was no more: I wanted what he had had. To be even with him' (71). If Prentis rereads his father's memoir after the latter's breakdown, it is to know exactly what this involves. His father having retreated into silence, he turns to his book in the hope of finding an answer to the obsessive question 'What was it like, what was it really like?' (52). Convinced that 'Dad is *in* that book', or even that 'the book *is* Dad' (52), Prentis opens its covers 'hoping Dad would come out; hoping to hear his voice' (199). Secondly, he wants to be promoted to head of his department at the office, the position currently occupied by Quinn: 'I wanted his job. I wanted to sit in his leather chair. I wanted to look down, like him, through his glass panel, at the underlings I had once worked beside' (71). In this sphere of life too, however, his overriding desire is for enlightenment: 'And yet it seemed (and I still feel this now) that what I wanted was not so much the promotion itself, but to be in a position where I would *know*; where I would no longer be the victim, the dupe, no longer be in the dark' (71). In fact, the same desire underlies Prentis's frantic reading of Shuttlecock, which is expected to provide him with knowledge that his father can no longer impart himself: 'Tell me, Dad. Enlighten me' (76).

By the end of the novel, Prentis has achieved both promotions, which turn out to be intricately related. The two strands of the plot come together in 'C9', a mysterious case on which Prentis has been set to work by Quinn and which he finds impossible to solve due to crucial information missing from the files. Carrying out investigations of his own so as to be able to shed some light on the matter, Prentis comes to suspect that the case bears directly on his father's past. This suspicion only reinforces his feeling that he is being tested in some obscure way by Quinn, an impression which his boss later confirms. Anxious not to jeopardize his promotion chances, he hesitates for a long time between challenging Quinn about the missing files and keeping silent. When he finally decides to confront Quinn, the latter confesses that he has been deliberately withholding and destroying files, with a view to protecting unknown people from the potentially damaging information held within them. C9 is a case in point: according to Quinn, it could mar the reputation of Prentis's father, suggesting as it does that Dad had made no heroic escape from Nazi imprisonment, as he asserts in his memoir, but had succumbed to torture and sent three fellow agents to their deaths. In this case, Quinn has been withholding the crucial 'File E', whose contents may lead to conclusive proof of Dad's guilt or innocence. However, struck by doubts regarding the morals of his 'little enterprise for the good of mankind', he could not bring himself to destroy it:

> It was all right, you see, doing good turns for people who were only names in files. I didn't have any qualms, then, that what I was doing was keeping from them the truth. I thought, they can do without the truth. But when it suddenly became a case of keeping the truth from someone I knew, then it was a different matter. I began to waver. . . . What do you do? Let the truth out, always, no matter how painful? I began to get conscience-stricken. (179–80)

We learn that the tests to which Quinn had subjected Prentis were meant firstly to find out whether he was the sort of person who would want the truth regardless of the cost, and secondly, with Quinn's retirement beckoning, to determine whether Prentis would make a suitable successor. In the end, Quinn leaves it to Prentis to decide if File E should be destroyed. In a surprise move, Prentis renounces his desire for enlightenment – which is what File 'E' presumably stands for – and agrees to let Quinn burn the documents in a garden incinerator, having never even read them: 'And then suddenly I knew I wanted to be uncertain, I wanted to be in the dark' (199). Afterwards, Quinn informs Prentis that he will shortly receive official notification of his promotion. Prentis does indeed replace Quinn after the latter's retirement, and takes over what Quinn calls his 'little half-baked scheme to save the world' (181). Following his promotion, Prentis no longer bullies his family, but he replicates Quinn's position in the office, lording it over his former colleague Eric and giving him incomplete files to work on.

Not only does Prentis eventually gain the upper hand over Quinn, but he also realizes his ambition of getting even with his father. The demystification of his father effected by the news of his possible breakdown under torture has a liberating effect on Prentis: 'Something had collapsed around me; so I couldn't help, in the middle of the ruins, this strange feeling of release. I had escaped; I was free' (183). The idea that his father had cracked under torture like an ordinary human being enables Prentis to conceive his relations with Dad as being in a state of 'perfect balance': 'with the knowledge I have but don't show Dad, and the knowledge Dad perhaps has and believes I don't, our relations could not be more finely tuned than they are' (213). That Prentis comes to regard himself as his father's equal is signalled by his use of epithets normally associated with his father's war-time heroics to describe his newly adopted stance of willed ignorance and uncertainty: '"I don't know", I said, resolutely. It seemed to me this was the answer I would give, boldly, over and over again for the rest of my life' (200). Adverbs such as 'resolutely' and 'boldly' confer on Prentis himself the qualities of bravery and courage on which Dad had always seemed to have a monopoly. Prentis's identification with his father is further underscored by his fantasy of a reunion with Quinn, whom he has not seen again since taking over from him: 'I think, one day Quinn and I will meet, like secret agents at some seemingly innocent rendezvous . . .' (206). The simile clearly implies that Prentis sees a connection between his own clandestine business in the office and Dad's spying activities during the war. Having settled his account with his father – whom he feels has 'spoken again' (204) through Quinn's revelations – Prentis stops reading his book. The novel ends with Prentis forgoing one of his visits to Dad to take his family on an outing to the seaside.

In celebrating Prentis's new-found harmony with himself and his surroundings, *Shuttlecock*'s closing chapter defers to the *Bildungsroman* tradition. As Franco Moretti points out in *The Way of the World*, the classical *Bildungsroman* ends with the hero reaching 'the conclusive synthesis of maturity' (19).[7] As *Bildung* is 'truly such' only if, at a certain point, 'it can be seen as concluded', the novel has to end with a 'merging' of the protagonist with the world: 'when the "merging" has occurred the journey can end, and the classical *Bildungsroman* is over – it has achieved its function' (26, 27). This 'perfect, and perfectly meaningful conclusion' (28) is described by Moretti in terms which call to mind the device of the pathetic fallacy and the fusion with nature to which it aspires: 'Ultimate symbolic gratification: the world speaks our language' (71). In following this convention, *Shuttlecock*'s ending appears to offer definitive proof of the successful *Bildung* of the novel's protagonist.

In fact, the great majority of critics seem to agree that *Shuttlecock* may indeed be read as the story of a fairly straightforward journey towards maturity. Del Ivan Janik, for example, regards Prentis's crucial decision to destroy File E – which he describes as unequivocally 'liberating, enabling, and even redeeming' ('History' 81) – as the triumphant outcome of a comprehensive learning process which reconciles Prentis to the human condition and equips him for life 'in the present':

> Now, in the acceptance of uncertainty, of the ambiguity that comes with being human, Prentis has found that space ['where we can be free, where we cannot be reached, where we are masters']. He no longer badgers his mute father with unanswerable questions, having found 'the perfect balance' of mutual ignorance. He no longer bullies his children, having learned to accept their need for space in which they can mature. He returns to his wife with affection instead of domination and 'pointless sophistication.' He is able now to live in the present, not because he has conquered history but because he has learned to live with its ambiguities. ('History' 82)

The narrator's abandonment of his epistemological quest is interpreted along the same lines by John Marsden, who states that 'Prentis has come to terms with the fragmented, disconnected, epistemologically uncertain world that he inhabits' (*After Modernism* 104). According to Susanne Mecklenburg, the novel strikes a distinctly hopeful note in envisaging the possibility of overcoming the cycle of violence in which its protagonist is enmeshed at the outset:

> Doch beläßt Graham Swift es nicht bei der Sezierung eines Teufelkreises der Gewalt, sondern nutzt die Perspektive des Ich-Erzählers, um die Möglichkeit der Bewältigung persönlicher Erfahrungen und eines aufbrechens [sic] aus jenen Strukturen der Gewalt aufzuzeigen.
>
> Yet Graham Swift does not stop at the analysis of a devilish cycle of violence, but uses the perspective of the I-narrator to point to the possibility of overcoming personal experiences and breaking out of those structures of violence. (138)

These reactions reflect a widely shared feeling among critics that the transition to maturity and harmony which *Shuttlecock* lays out is both persuasive and instructive.

And yet, several of these commentators seem to be ill at ease with such a positive conclusion. Alan Hickman, for example, who contends that Prentis has 'surely done something right to have been so rewarded' (98), is troubled by the fact that 'the bargain he has struck with Quinn – the fount of all this bounty in his life – is based on a lie, the denial of information' (99). Marsden is discomforted by the following passage, in which Prentis advises the reader to refrain from probing under the surface of his text:

> I stopped reading Dad's book. I inquired no further. How much of a book is in the words and how much is behind or in between the lines? Perhaps it is best not to probe too deeply into those invisible regions, but to accept on trust what is there on the page as the best showing the author could make. And the same is true perhaps of this book (for it has grown into a book) which I have resumed now after a six-months' lapse, only to bring to its conclusion. Once you have read it, it may be better not to peer too hard beneath the surface of what it says – or (who knows if you may not be one of those happily left in peace of mind by my 'work' at the department?) what it doesn't say. (214)

In fact, this admonition to forgo a critical reading of the book – which Hickman, incidentally, considers to be 'wise counsel' (98) – makes explicit a central feature of the *Bildungsroman*. As Moretti points out, 'the symbolic totality of the *Bildungsroman* does not allow for interpretation. To do so would be to recognize that an alterity continues to exist between the subject and his world, and that it has established its own *culture*: and this must not be' (63). In other words, the 'beautiful harmony of the symbol' serves to obscure the irredeemable split between the subject and the world which the act of interpretation has the power to expose (Moretti 63). In urging the reader to refrain from delving too deeply into his text, *Shuttlecock*'s narrator shows his concern to safeguard the precarious symbolic unity which it establishes. Though Marsden finds Prentis's 'metacritical commentary' admirably 'postmodernist', he hesitates to grant him his request: 'given what we know of the narrator, we should be wary of taking his advice' (*After Modernism* 105). However, he quickly settles his doubts by appealing to authorial intention: 'his sentiments are apparently those of Graham Swift himself' (*After Modernism* 105). Yet, the passage from the interview with the author which he adduces to back up this claim does not bear this out: instead of choosing any one side, Swift, as is his wont, talks about wanting to present the full 'complexity' of the moral issues surrounding knowledge and ignorance without 'resolv[ing]' the matter in any way (quoted in Marsden, *After Modernism* 105).

Another critic with mixed feelings about *Shuttlecock* is Marc Porée. In a survey article on Swift, he appears to go along with the redemptive return to nature which the novel stages: the text being concerned to 'restituer l'acuité primitive ressentie au contact de la réalité massive de la matière' ('restore the primitive intensity experienced in contact with the massive reality of matter'), Prentis's final tribute to his pet hamster – 'un retour attendrissant, touchant – après tout son poids de cruauté – à ce qui touche, à ce qui émeut' ('a moving, touching return – after all the cruelty – to that which touches, to that which affects') – is felt to bring the novel to a moving and fitting conclusion ('Quelques clefs' 64). In an earlier review of *Shuttlecock*, however, Porée puts a question mark over this reading, describing the novel as a *Bildungsroman* ('un roman d'éducation') fraught with ambiguities ('[a]vec ses ambiguïtés propres'):

> Education à une forme de santé mentale arrachée à la folie, ce mal anglais. Recherche d'un équilibre précaire, à redéfinir contre l'emprise traumatisante d'un père dominateur. Education à rebours, vers l'enfance perdue, au terme de laquelle une libération s'opère et le temps d'avant l'aliénation paraît (?) se retrouver.
>
> Education to a form of mental sanity detached from madness, that English malady. The search for a precarious balance, to be defined against the traumatizing authority of a dominant father. Reverse education, to a lost childhood, by virtue of which liberation is effected and the time before alienation seems (?) to be rediscovered. ('Au non dit' 21)

The novel's perceived ambivalence, which – if at all – is only referred to in passing by the aforementioned critics, is brought out in the open by Patrick O'Donnell. While acknowledging that Prentis can be seen to have 'grown up' and to have been 'successfully initiated into a form of adulthood' by the end of the novel, O'Donnell points out that 'Swift leaves open . . . the possibility of a quite different reading, wherein existence is seen as a form of repression'. After all, 'Prentis' success and happiness are ultimately based on a suppression of knowledge'. According to O'Donnell, there are 'sinister undertones' to Prentis becoming 'another Quinn', that is, 'a disseminator and destroyer of information, a dictator of fact'. Unlike Janik and most other critics, who accept the complete integrity and objectivity of Prentis's story – 'Prentis seems to be a reliable narrator' (Janik, 'History' 80) – O'Donnell has grave doubts about the narrator's reliability:

> in the final scene, where he romps with his wife and children on the beach, one senses that Prentis, the narrator, is hiding something from the reader in this artificial portrait of the nuclear family reunited. Playing the role of narrator, Prentis is unreliable precisely when he becomes chief of information, a job that requires the judicious suppression of the truth: The reader is left with the question, What form and quantity of truth does one receive in this cold confession?[8]

This question also informs Donald Kaczvinsky's article on *Shuttlecock*, the only substantial reading of the novel to date to give pride of place to the issue of narratorial unreliability. However, Kaczvinsky not only raises the question, as O'Donnell does, but goes on to frame a concrete answer to it. Speculating that the narrator lies about how he got promoted, Kaczvinsky concocts an elaborate theory in which Prentis ruthlessly blackmails Quinn into appointing him as his successor:

> Perhaps Quinn promoted Prentis not because he saw a lot of himself in his underling, but because Prentis knew or discovered Quinn's cowardice and dereliction of duty and threatened to expose Quinn to the authorities. . . . Perhaps that is why Prentis leaves the conversation in the office between himself and his boss so elliptical and why, curiously, Prentis does not tell his family about his promotion until well after his initial conversation with Quinn. (8)

Prentis's motive for writing his story would be to 'exculpate' (7) himself in the eyes of the world and especially in the eyes of his family. According to Kacvinsky, the narrator's apparent transformation, 'from family tyrant to loving father and devoted husband', 'cannot simply be explained as an education or a maturation process. He has not "progressed" into a more humane and sympathetic character . . . but "created" or "invented" a self, through a textual strategy that at the same time broadens and secures his power base' (12). Indeed, the one thing Prentis has learnt is how to achieve power over others with a more subtle technique than physical force: 'he establishes a textual power over them [his family] through the writing of his own history that, unlike the torture and physical punishment he used earlier, breeds not resentment and rebellion but love and admiration' (11).

Kaczvinsky's interpretation is impaired, however, by the rashness with which he seeks to solve the issue of Prentis's unreliability. The blackmail story which he puts forward as being the hidden truth of Prentis's narrative appears far-fetched and unwarranted in terms of the available textual evidence. Even on a second reading, there does not seem to be anything remotely suspicious about the first conversation between Quinn and Prentis in the office, and the fact that Prentis does not immediately mention his promotion prospects to his wife is more plausibly accounted for by the general lack of communication between them. Nevertheless, Kaczvinsky does deserve credit for giving due consideration to the narrator's unreliability and self-invention, a dimension of the novel often ignored by its critics – which is all the more remarkable given the text's emphatic foregrounding of the very performance of narration. While no one fails to note the paranoid quality of the novel – which establishes an elaborate network of connections linking together the malicious exercise of authority to which Prentis is subject at work, Prentis's cruel treatment of his hamster, his domination of his family and the Gestapo's imprisonment and torture of his father – the relationship between the identically titled Shuttlecock and *Shuttlecock* – which, moreover, are written by identically named authors (after all, we never find out the first name of either Prentis senior or Prentis junior) – has rarely been discussed at any length. It deserves closer scrutiny, though, for several reasons. Not only is there a clear thematic link between the two narratives, both of which 'focus on the hero's escape from a prison' (Kaczvinsky 7),[9] but the *mise en abyme* structure suggests that the questions which are raised inside the text about the truthfulness of Dad's version of events should also be addressed to Prentis's story: 'If Prentis learned to question the "objectivity" and "integrity" of his father's story, to see it as a narrative with significant "gaps" of information, so we too, as "apprentice" readers, must learn to question the "objectivity" of Prentis's story' (Kaczvinsky 5). Indeed, if we are to arrive at a critical understanding of Prentis's self-professed transformation, it seems imperative that we take on this task.

Clearly, the interpretation of Shuttlecock is a major concern in the novel. Prentis claims that his father's memoir, which he has read 'a dozen times' (51), seems to get 'not more familiar but more elusive and remote' (52) each time he reads it. He is left with 'a thousand questions' about 'things which aren't actually stated in the book' (52). In particular, he is bemused by the fact that Dad provides an almost purely descriptive account of his exploits. He hardly mentions how he felt at the time, and when he does convey his feelings, he does so 'in a bluff, almost light-hearted way', giving his narrative the air of 'some made-up adventure story' (52). As a result, Dad's book, which is 'all fact', sometimes seems to Prentis 'like fiction, like something that never really took place' (52). The final chapters of Shuttlecock, however, which contain the story of Dad's capture, torture and escape, make a very different impression on him: 'These pages are more vivid, more real, more believable than any other part of the book. And yet, strangely enough, this is because the style of Dad's writing becomes – how shall I put it? – more imaginative, more literary, more speculative' (106–7). If, in the main body of the book, there is only 'the occasional brief passage of reflection, of emotion', in these final chapters it is as though 'the philosophic note is always there' and Dad's words seem ever ready to take on 'a quieter, sadder, even eloquent tone' (107).

Another reason which Prentis gives for the fact that the last two chapters have 'more of the flavour of reality' than the rest of the book is that they contain 'more mystery – and more misery' (146). He is intrigued by the 'gaps' or 'hazy areas' in Dad's narrative, that is, the scenes of torture which are described in the scantiest detail if not omitted altogether: 'it is about the goings-on in that interrogation room, and other, sinister rooms, that Dad is silent, or circumspect' (105). To account for this fact, he considers two different explanations, the first of which is the presence of 'gaping holes in the memory' (105). In other words, the reason why Dad neglects to write about these dreadful experiences would be that he has blissfully forgotten about them. The other explanation Prentis offers is 'the reverse' of the first one: 'The memory not in the least impaired, still vivid-sharp; but the memory of something so terrible that it cannot be repeated, cannot be spoken or written of' (105–6).[10] This theory accords well with Bessel van der Kolk's conception of trauma as a literal imprint on the psyche. '[E]tched' or 'engraved' on the mind with 'unparalleled vividness and accuracy', traumatic memory, for van der Kolk, is 'radically dissociated from symbolization, meaning, and the usual processes of integration' (Leys 239). From the fact that Prentis later refers to the treatment Dad received at the hands of his captors as 'this experience beyond words' (106), we may infer that he settles on this second explanation.

The traumatic nature of the events recounted in the final chapters of Shuttlecock may go some way towards explaining the 'more imaginative, more literary, more speculative' quality of these pages, which sets them apart from the preceding chapters of the book. Indeed, many trauma theorists agree that literature is, in Dominick LaCapra's words, 'a prime, if not the privileged, place for giving voice to trauma' (*Writing* 190). Trauma, which exceeds the frameworks by which we normally make sense of the world, demands a vocabulary and syntax in some sense incommensurable with what went before. It is felt that literature, as an imaginative creative enterprise, is eminently suited for this task of addressing and transmitting trauma. As Geoffrey Hartman puts it, 'the "unclaimed experience" can only be reclaimed by literary knowledge' (545). The frequent appeal to the imagination in the final chapters of Shuttlecock may thus be viewed as necessitated by the specific nature of the disconcerting experiences Dad is struggling to convey.

As he tells the story of how he escaped from the Château Martine and fled through the surrounding forests trying to shake off his pursuers, Dad's account assumes Wordsworthian overtones in its invocation of nature as a benign force responsive to man's needs and desires. Dad describes the shock he felt at the destruction of a wood which, having skirted it many times on bicycle or on foot, he had come to regard as 'an emblem of things that would continue unchanged, regardless of the war' (107): 'I felt the loss of that wood like few human losses. The thing that most embodies the evil of war, is not, it seems to me, its human violence (for humans cause wars), but its wilful disregard for nature' (108). His subsequent escape from the Château becomes an attempt to re-establish the harmonious relationship with nature which the war has disrupted. On crawling out of his cell through a carved-out hole in the wall, Dad is met by what he perceives as a benevolent nature: 'The darkened vegetable patches and fruit bushes in the kitchen garden and the fresh night air seemed to welcome me like conspiring friends' (163). As he makes his way through the forest like 'a hunted animal', he feels 'a strange rush of gratitude' (164) for the branches and the thick tangles of foliage which, though they scratch and snare him, seem to assist him in his flight. His mentioning of the pathetic fallacy, which he openly embraces, is the first explicit allusion to this notion in the text: 'Since then I have come to believe – a blatant case of the pathetic fallacy, no doubt – that woods and the trees are always on the side of the fugitive and the victim, never on the side of the oppressor' (164). This feeling of affinity leads on to a desire for oneness with nature:

> I was trying to turn myself into an anonymous creature of the woods. In this irrational idea hope seemed to lie. . . . Through all the agonies of my flight, I did not lose the sense that the trees, the leaf-strewn ground I trod were my friends. In fact, it grew. . . . Even as I blundered on, I thought: nocturnal animals are fleeing from me, just as I am fleeing my hunters. If only I could follow their example, disappear into holes and roots. Merge with the forest . . . (169)

In fact, this is exactly what happens. There comes a time when Dad can no longer remain on his feet and has to make 'the decision that the hunted rabbit or the cornered mouse has to make as the dogs draw in or the cat prepares to leap: to crouch, to huddle, offering no token of defence, waiting either to be pounced on and destroyed or for some miraculous intervention of destiny' (170). He makes a hollow in the undergrowth and, having covered himself with leaves, curls up in it like 'some burrowing animal' (170) awaiting its fate. And destiny does intervene, miraculously, in the form of the American Seventh Army: Dad's nightmare is over when, on awakening after a desperate night in hiding, he discovers, through the trees, not the Gestapo but the advancing Americans.

Prentis's private investigations into C9 lead him to read Dad's memoir with a critical eye. Having ascertained that another British agent was held at the same prisoners-of-war camp around the same time as his father, he is puzzled by Dad's claim that he was 'the only Britisher at the Château' (146). He notes down textual inconsistencies which render Dad's account problematic, for example the assertion that 'I made a mental note of everything' versus 'I only recall . . . there is much I simply do not remember. Memory provides its own censorship' (147). The veracity of Dad's narrative is called more radically into question at the climactic meeting between Prentis and Quinn in the latter's garden, during which Quinn raises the possibility that the story of Dad's heroic escape may be a lie designed to cover up an act of treachery. Prentis initially rejects this theory on the grounds that the last pages of the book are 'too convincing not to be real. He couldn't have written those things, if they never happened' (186). In support of this claim, he points to 'the authentic detail' – Barthes's reality effect – and 'the tone' of Dad's text: 'In the rest of the book you hardly sense Dad's feelings, you don't sense Dad himself. But in the last paragraphs you –' (186). He goes on to argue that, if Dad had indeed struck a deal with the Germans and betrayed his friends in return for his release, he would surely not have 'put himself at risk' by writing a false story when he could 'have just kept quiet' (187). However, Quinn takes the edge off this argument by pointing out that Dad needed to justify how he got out of the Château: 'He couldn't just say, They let me go' (187). To be at all credible, Dad's final adventure had to measure up to the expectations created by his earlier acts of heroism: 'His war record up till then had been pretty remarkable – the grand finale had to live up to it' (187). If the last two chapters are 'more convincing, more heartfelt' than the rest, Quinn continues, this is because

> it's here the real issue lies. The *true* exploits, all the brave and daring deeds, what do they matter? They can be treated almost like fiction, but the part of the book that's really a lie – that's where all the urgency is. It's here that he's trying to save himself. Why does it read like a real escape? Because it is an escape, a quite real escape, of a kind. (187)

Quinn further surmises that, 'torn between the desire to construct this saving lie and an instinct not to falsify himself completely – to be, somehow, honest', Dad put down 'little hints, little clues' (188) allowing the discerning reader to see through the pretence.

Though Quinn stresses that he is only 'speaking hypothetically' (187), his alternative reading of Shuttlecock obviously casts serious doubt on the veracity of Dad's account. In fact, there was already a hint of deviousness in Dad's handwriting: the personal dedication in one of the two copies of the book which Prentis owns is said to be inscribed in a 'bold and slanting' (51) hand. Implicit here is the suggestion that Dad's assertions are not to be trusted, as he may be rigging or falsifying – 'slanting' – the facts. If we accept Quinn's version of what happened, we are forced to conclude that the imagination serves another purpose altogether in Dad's account than that which we had originally ascribed to it. It is used, apparently, not in an effort to gain access to a traumatic reality but as an instrument of deception and bad faith. Far from contributing to a faithful representation of a shattering reality, it seems to lead in the opposite direction of denial and disavowal. Dad's act of self-representation becomes an exercise in self-invention which finds him straining his imaginative powers to create an unblemished image of himself as a superhuman hero. This idealized self-image conveniently and disingenuously covers over the actual facts of human frailty, weakness and betrayal.

Prentis's narrative imitates his father's in several respects. For example, if the final chapters of Shuttlecock were unusually reflective and speculative, the same tendency is apparent in Prentis's own account. He alerts the reader to this fact in the parenthesis in the following sentence: 'But all these observations and reflections (you are wrong if you think I am normally a thoughtful man – it is just something brought on by this urge to write things down) I do not make at all about Dad' (127). Moreover, Prentis's narrative, like Dad's, is strewn with little (and not so little) hints and clues which create doubts about the narrator's reliability. Initially, the truthfulness of the narrative had seemed to be guaranteed by the sheer fact that it is written in the form of a diary, a genre which carries the promise of immediate access to truth: 'you will have gathered by now that I am writing all this as thoughts come to me and as things happen' (39). It does become an issue, however, when Prentis casually admits to having told the reader lies and half-truths:

> Did I mention, by the way, a little while back, something about taking my kids out on the common at weekends to play healthy games with bats and frisbees? It doesn't really happen, of course. You will have gathered that my relations with Martin and Peter aren't exactly harmonious. Not that we don't go out on the common. But that picture – the exuberant father, the frisky children – it's quite wrong. (53)

A little further on in the text, Prentis retracts another claim which he has just made: 'You see, when I said I didn't mind if it was just I who was the obstacle, that was a lie' (56). On another occasion, he owns up to having exaggerated the harshness of Quinn's manner:

> I have said already that the first time I have known Quinn to be pleasant to me was last Monday when he mentioned my promotion. That was something of an exaggeration, I admit – though that's not to say that pleasantness from Quinn isn't a rarity. However, there was one brief occasion when Quinn was not only pleasant but positively sympathetic – and that was over the business of Dad. (66)

The narrative also features some inconsistencies which, unlike the ones mentioned above, are not openly acknowledged by the narrator. One of these concerns the frequency of Prentis's visits to Dad. At the beginning of the narrative, Prentis declares: 'I go to see Dad most Wednesday evenings, and often on Sundays too' (40). By the end of the narrative, however, 'often' seems to have become 'always': 'And today – a Sunday – I forwent for the first time one of my visits to Dad' (215). Occurring right after the narrator's appeal not to read his book too attentively, this conflicting statement only deepens the reader's suspicions about Prentis's sincerity and credibility. These suspicions are hardly assuaged by the narrator's apparent disregard for citation conventions: a particular passage from Dad's memoir is quoted twice over the course of the narrative, once excluding (108) and once including the following parenthetical remark: 'I should have eaten when food was offered me' (170). The fact that the ellipsis in the first instance is not indicated typographically shows that Prentis is manipulating not just his own text but also that of his father.

Like Shuttlecock, Prentis's narrative becomes increasingly imaginative and ends with the realization of a fantasy of total communion with nature. That Prentis has a rich imagination is revealed early on in the text. We are told that Quinn repeatedly censures his assistant's 'lurid' imagination, which hampers his work in the office by causing him to make hasty assumptions and to jump to conclusions: 'You've got a rich imagination, haven't you, Prentis? A lurid imagination. That doesn't help, you know, in this job' (22–23); 'Lurid imagination, Prentis, lurid imagination. No good in this job' (30). Outside the office, however, Prentis can give free rein to his imagination. Sitting home reading Dad's book one sunny Saturday afternoon, he tries to picture what his wife and sons, who have gone out for a walk, are doing at that same instant. He finds his imaginative efforts to be singularly successful: 'I can see all this almost more vividly than if I were there myself' (63); 'All of this touches me more than if I were really there to see it happen' (64). The sheer power of Prentis's imagination is further underscored by his insistence on the ease with which he can identify with his father's experience: 'because I believe in these passages, I can put myself into them, I can imagine myself in that dark cell, in those passage-ways, that courtyard. Why does it seem that I *know* that Château? So that sometimes in my mind – it is like this tonight – it almost seems that Dad and I are one too' (146). This impression is reinforced by the fact that Prentis echoes Dad's discourse on several occasions. For example, the words which he cries out in his sleep – 'Is there anyone there?' (156) – are the ones which Dad reports having shouted (albeit in French) after being left alone in his cell at the Château Martine: '*Il n'y a personne?*' (134). The observation that 'They say you only recall what is pleasant' (5), which stands at the beginning of Prentis's narrative, is another literal echo of Dad's memoir (139). The most conspicuous borrowing, however, is the embrace of the pathetic fallacy and the redemptive identification with a burrowing animal in the closing paragraphs, which marks the culmination of the imaginative endeavour undertaken in the preceding pages.

In a further parallel, Prentis buys into the logic of erasure embraced (or so it seems) by his father. Indeed, his critical decision to destroy File E, which appears to foreclose the possibility of ever exposing Dad's deception (if deception it is) and publicly demystifying his heroic self-image, is the first in a long series of decisions specifically aimed to suppress potentially explosive information. Assuming the inheritance of Quinn's 'little enterprise for the good of mankind' (179), Prentis sets himself with gusto to the task of erasing traumatic knowledge as it is inscribed in the records of the dead crimes department. The underlying idea, spelled out by Quinn, is that by getting rid of such 'ruinous' information, one is actually 'ridding the world of trouble' (178): 'I thought, perhaps one can wipe out certain harms simply by erasing the record of those harms' (120). Prentis continues along the path which Quinn has opened up to him: 'All these little bits of poisoned paper I am slowly dropping into oblivion. What people don't know, can't hurt them. . . .' (212). Having succeeded Quinn, Prentis finds himself in a position where he can let loose his lurid imagination to create a congenial image of himself and of the world blissfully forgetful of the 'nefarious and inflammatory' (15) information preserved in the police archives. The envisaged imaginative reconstruction of self and world is predicated on the erasure or denial of a traumatic reality documented by the records of the dead crimes department. This is confirmed by the third appearance of the notion of the pathetic fallacy in the novel. On the way home from his meeting with Quinn, Prentis stops off at a pub to have a drink. As he watches the other customers, who are sitting outside because of the warm weather, he wonders why they seem to be having such a good time: 'Perhaps the people were happy because of the warm summer twilight wrapping round them and making the world grow soft and dim. Perhaps it was all a case of the pathetic fallacy. Then I thought: these people are happy because of what they don't know' (203). Personal happiness and, by extension, social well-being are equated with a flight of the imagination which allows one to view the world as sympathetic to one's needs and desires, and to blank out any unpalatable facts which threaten to disrupt this sense of harmony.

In repressing the impact of trauma, the imagination serves the same self-protective purpose as the attachment to routine which had allowed Prentis to carry out his job without being affected by the horrendous nature of some of the cases that landed on his desk:

> Most of the time is spent in mundane chores like cataloguing and indexing. . . . No matter how extraordinary the material you work with, it becomes, when it's your daily business to deal with it – unextraordinary.
>
> But then again, I'm wrong. It isn't like that. I'm trying to say something perhaps, that I don't really feel at all. It's in the nature of routine not so much to make things ordinary as to numb you against recognizing how remarkable they are. And you'd be surprised at some of the things contained in our files. You'd be appalled at the black and desperate picture of the world they sometimes offer. (23)

If routine immunizes or anaesthetizes the archivist against this black and desperate picture of the world, the imagination shelters him from it by over-painting it with a gentle and appealing one. It is worth noting that Prentis shares his adherence to routine with the protagonist of Swift's previous novel, whose yearning for predictable patterns was prompted by a desire to keep history at bay and to avoid becoming implicated in it. The similarity between Prentis and Willy Chapman is underlined by the recurrence of a scene from *The Sweet Shop Owner* in *Shuttlecock*. This scene involves the protagonist being urged by a doctor to assist in the cure of a relative suffering from a mysterious illness, presumably connected to the repression of some past traumatic event. In *The Sweet Shop Owner*, Willy is taken aside by the doctor who is treating his wife's asthma – a psychosomatic illness apparently linked to the rape which she endured as a young woman – and asked to impart any information he possesses about his wife's past which might shed some light on the cause of her disease and thus contribute to finding a cure: 'A lot might depend – I get this impression from her – on the sort of help you're able to give her' (SSO 126). However, averse to breaking the bargain he has struck with Irene and upsetting the balance of their lives, Willy resolves never to talk to Doctor Cunningham again and thus to perpetuate the safe (but doomed) routine of his marriage. In *Shuttlecock*, Prentis is informed by one of the doctors at the hospital to which Dad has been admitted following his enigmatic breakdown that, over the course of several months, 'virtually no progress' (66) has been made in his father's treatment. He is urged, however, not to give up hope: '"There's always a possibility – a remote one – that something you may say may succeed . . . Don't give up, Mr Prentis," – he twisted the corner of his mouth into a smile – "the key might lie with you"' (66). The text suggests that Dad's muteness may be understood as an attempt to isolate himself from a long-repressed traumatic past; a past that re-emerged two years before

Prentis begins his diary, when Dad is thought to have received a letter from a blackmailer threatening to make his supposed deceit public: 'The perfect defence: impenetrable silence' (184). When Prentis at last hits upon the key which might awaken Dad out of his catatonic stupor – that is, the question 'Did you betray your comrades?' (193) – his reaction mirrors Willy's in that he too decides to remain silent and thereby to maintain the status quo.

By taking this decision, Prentis effectively silences the question which 'all the time . . . kept repeating itself, like a little wave inside my skull: Why? Why?' (67). This question, asked here in relation to Dad's breakdown, looks forward to the crucial question 'Whywhywhy' in *Waterland*, which is 'like a siren wailing in our heads' (W 107). In marked contrast to Prentis, however, the narrator of *Waterland* considers it imperative to 'accept the burden of our need to ask why' and never to 'turn off that wretched siren' (W 108). *Waterland*'s Tom Crick sets great store by the faculty of curiosity, which incites human beings never to take for granted so-called final answers or ultimate explanations, but to keep asking ever more questions. The cultivation of our innate curiosity is put forward as a salutary alternative to the fatal pursuit of finality, definitive knowledge and total control of reality, which is seen to involve the repression of curiosity. The belief that the human imagination can shape reality at will, strip it of its violence and transform it once and for all into an ideal, utopian environment is exposed as a form of reality-denial which can lead to murderous consequences. If, as the narrator claims, reality is fundamentally traumatic and therefore unbearable, the embrace of ideological fictions with absolutist pretensions is a way of obfuscating this state of affairs which is likely to result in catastrophe.

To drive home these points, *Waterland*'s narrator fully exploits the metaphorical potential of the marshy Fens landscape which forms the backdrop for much of the novel's action. This particular setting is prefigured in *Shuttlecock* by Camber Sands, the liminal zone between land and water in which the novel's denouement is played out. However, the purposes which these respective settings are made to serve could hardly be more different. Prentis uses the Camber Sands episode to impose closure on his story; to 'bring to its conclusion' (214) the book which he has resumed six months after his promotion. Enacting a redemptive fantasy of restored harmony, it is meant to convince the reader of the solidity and viability of the way of life on which the narrator has embarked. However, the dune landscape in which the final scene is set seems to be somewhat ill-suited for the grounding function which it is expected to perform. Not only is the region littered with 'the relics of the war' (216), which act as a constant reminder of an undeniable, indelible reality defying all attempts at imaginative erasure or transformation, but, forever threatened by the 'enemy invader' of 'the incoming tide' (216), it is also profoundly marked by topographical instability. This feature of the landscape is not dwelt upon at any great length in *Shuttlecock*, but assumes central importance in *Waterland*. Indeed, it is repeatedly stated in the latter text that the Fens are reclaimed land which, appearances notwithstanding, remains liable to flooding. As the narrator points out, the Fens are 'not quite solid' (W 8) even today. Land reclamation, he maintains, is to be conceived not as an accomplished fact but as a never-ending process requiring constant vigilance: 'Strictly speaking, they [the Fens] are never reclaimed, only being reclaimed' (W 10). Thus, the Fenland setting lends metaphorical support to the narrator's claim that the pursuit of totalizing meaning – the desire definitively to reclaim a traumatic reality – is a dangerous delusion: the soothing imaginative constructions by which we make sense of a terrifying and absurd reality must be subjected to continuous scrutiny, revision and adjustment lest they invite the dreaded waters of disaster to return. Though *Shuttlecock* never quite arrives at such an affirmation, the novel's manifest discomfort with the relentless pursuit of full meaning – which it is often held unequivocally to endorse – sets the stage for the profound engagement with the demands of trauma that characterizes Swift's 'middle-period' novels.

4 'To Be Realistic'

Close Encounters of a Traumatic Kind in Waterland

Write in order not simply to destroy, in order not simply to conserve, in order not to transmit; write in the thrall of the impossible real, that share of disaster wherein every reality, safe and sound, sinks.
Maurice Blanchot, *The Writing of the Disaster*

Waterland, Graham Swift's most celebrated novel, is almost invariably discussed in relation to the academic debate over the epistemological status of history conducted between, on the one hand, narrativist philosophers of history like Hayden White, Frank Ankersmit and Hans Kellner and, on the other, traditional historians struggling against the contamination of their field by postmodernism.[1] *Waterland* is a multi-narrative, first-person account by history teacher Tom Crick, whose life is in a state of crisis. Tom abandons the official school curriculum to tell stories and to speculate self-consciously about the uses and abuses of history. This reflection is prompted by his forced retirement and the closure of the history department at his school, by his wife Mary's arrest and subsequent commitment to a mental institution for abducting a baby (an event reaching far back into family history), and in the last instance by the challenging remarks made to him by his star pupil Price. In deliberately blurring the boundaries between history and fiction, Tom positions himself against the tradition, which draws a categorical distinction between the two realms. He appears to side with the postmodernist camp, which stresses the essential similarity of history and fiction as discursive practices.

However, despite its obvious sympathy for the narrativist critique of traditional history, *Waterland* does not – as is often thought to be the case – reflect the extreme relativism and the radical scepticism in relation to the referentiality of language and narrative that are commonly imputed to post-modernist historiography. The novel insists on the possibility and the necessity of maintaining some form of contact with the real, which it reconceptualizes in terms of trauma. A determination to bear witness to a traumatic reality, a reality that resists integration into familiar narratives, is promoted as a precondition for a new, post-humanist ethics that opens up the prospect of a different, more benign future.

At the outset of his narrative, Tom presents a theory of reality as a series of catastrophic moments, of traumatic encounters with the 'Here and Now', which usually comes 'dressed in terror' and which 'we seldom glimpse unscathed' (51). The Here and Now, which 'comes but rarely – does not come even when we call it' (61) and 'is never what we imagine' (60), is said to deliver 'surprise attacks' (61) and pictured as a 'knife blade' 'punctur[ing]' the 'thin garment' of history (36): 'the reality of things – be thankful – only visits us for a brief while' (33). Tom puts forward this view of reality partly in response to his headmaster's self-declared commitment to the 'real world' (22), which is belied, however, by his evident desire not to know anything about the tragedy of Tom's wife Mary: 'He'd rather pretend it isn't real. . . . He doesn't want to discuss it' (25). Tom's suggestion is that the real world is made up of just such bewildering and disastrous occurrences as his headmaster seeks to exclude from it. On the other hand, this conception of reality as essentially traumatic is meant as a corrective to the simplistic notion of the here and now posited by Price. Price calls into question the relevance of history by arguing that 'What matters . . . is the here and now. Not the past. The here and now – and the future' (6). Tom complicates this notion of an unproblematic and readily accessible here and now, which is supposed to make the study of history superfluous, by recasting it as an unbearable reality unavailable to direct experience and comprehension.

Further on in the narrative, however, Tom subscribes to a seemingly opposite view: 'Reality's not strange, not unexpected. Reality doesn't reside in the sudden hallucination of events. Reality is uneventfulness, vacancy, flatness. Reality is that nothing happens' (40). This nothingness makes itself felt most acutely in the English Fenlands, the waterland of the novel's title, where Tom and Mary were born and where most of the action unfolds: 'For what is water, which seeks to make all things level, which has no taste or colour of its own, but a liquid form of Nothing? And what are the Fens, which so imitate in their levelness the natural disposition of water, but a landscape which, of all landscapes, most approximates to Nothing?' (13). Hence, 'To live in the Fens is to receive strong doses of reality' (17). Tom puts forward this conception of reality as nothing happening as part of his polemic against official history, understood as a chronicle of great events and extraordinary feats. In Tom's view, such grand narratives, which purport to capture the essence of reality, are just as many pathetic attempts to deny its fundamental emptiness: 'I present to you History, the fabrication, the diversion, the reality-obscuring drama. History, and its near relative, Histrionics . . .' (40).

Though in the text they are presented as irreconcilable opposites between which one must choose, these two theories of reality are actually two sides of the same coin. The Here and Now, which tears asunder the veil of history, disrupting all dramas, is after all 'the impossible, oxymoronic occasion of nothing happening' (Boughner 71). *Waterland*'s fictional universe is profoundly marked by the disturbing visitations of this Here and Now, the 'invasion by Nothing of the fragile islands of life' (341). The shadow of two world wars looms large over the novel, as does the spectre of imminent nuclear destruction which haunted the Cold War era. *Waterland* abounds with characters who have suffered some kind of trauma, either at the hands of history or in private tragedies. They are only too familiar with 'the old, old feeling, that everything might amount to nothing' (269).

Tom's father Henry, for example, comes home after serving in the First World War, saying 'I remember nothing' (20). It soon becomes apparent that this statement should not be taken at face value. The nothing-landscape of the Fens to which Henry returns after the war does not so much stimulate forgetfulness as recall a nothingness which he is trying to escape from:

> this flat, bare, washed-out Fenland, which ought to be the perfect home of oblivion, the perfect place for getting used to forgetting, has quite the opposite effect on our limping veteran. And maybe that's just the point: it's oblivion he'd like to forget, it's that sense of the dizzy void he can't get away from. He could do without this feeling of nothing. (223)

Remembering nothing, it turns out, is not a matter of simply forgetting something that happened in the past and that one fully experienced at the time, but rather of remembering the occasion of nothing happening: one's obliviousness to events which one could not grasp or make sense of as they occurred. It is precisely this unassimilability which accounts for their traumatic impact. It will come as no surprise, then, that Henry shows clear symptoms of what is now known as post-traumatic stress disorder: 'Henry Crick comes home from a long walk one October afternoon, a mass of twitches, trembles, shakes and jitters, unable to speak a sensible word' (223). Overwhelmed by events that fail to settle into understanding or remembrance, Henry is condemned to repeat them: 'For poor Henry things couldn't be worse. He's back where he came from all right – in the old, old mud [of Flanders]' (223).

Another instance of nothing happening can be found in Tom's account of the history of Jack Parr's alcoholism. As keeper of a level-crossing, Jack once came close to causing a terrible accident. Due to a lapse in attention, he forgot to close the gates when two trains were approaching at full speed from opposite directions. If he had not awoken to this dreadful omission just in time to take the appropriate action, the results would have been disastrous. As it was, however, catastrophe was averted in the nick of time:

> No one is scathed. Jack Parr's professional record remains unblackened. But so great was the shock, so terrible was the thought of what *might* have happened and so unendurable was the possibility that at some time another lapse might occur, that Freddie Parr's father took to earnest drinking, thus forestalling any future forgetfulness through regular alcoholic oblivion. (113)

Again, the source of distress is not the memory of events which one (might have) directly experienced, but rather the awareness of one's forgetfulness to events which (might have) happened but which one somehow (would have) missed owing to some sort of non-vigilance.

This description accords well with the theory of trauma as articulated by Cathy Caruth and other deconstructive theorists. Caruth defines trauma as 'the response to an unexpected or overwhelming violent event or events that are not fully grasped as they occur, but return later in repeated flashbacks, nightmares, and other repetitive phenomena' (*Unclaimed* 91). Hence, trauma 'is not locatable in the simple violent or original event in an individual's past, but rather in the way that its very unassimilated nature – the way it was precisely *not known* in the first instance – returns to haunt the survivor later on' (*Unclaimed* 4). Caruth is concerned with the question of how, in this era, we can gain access to a traumatic history, to a historical experience whose force resides precisely in the collapse of its understanding. Raising the possibility of 'a history that is no longer straightforwardly referential (that is, no longer based on simple models of experience and reference)', she calls for a rethinking of reference which would be aimed 'not at eliminating history but at resituating it in our understanding, that is, at precisely permitting *history* to arise where *immediate understanding* may not' (*Unclaimed* 11). In her view, only a speech which 'exceeds simple understanding' 'opens up the possibility of what could be called a truly historical transmission' (*Trauma* 156). *Waterland* takes up this challenge: the novel aims to offer a history true to the impossible experience of nothing happening. It treads what it calls 'the minefield of the past', charting its many 'no-go areas and emergency zones' in an attempt to respect their essential incomprehensibility and not to reduce the force of their affront to understanding (330).[2]

The prime example of an encounter with the Here and Now in the novel is arguably Tom's nightmarish evocation of the brutal abortion which Mary undergoes as a teenager and which leaves her infertile. This horrific episode, spread over two chapters towards the end of the novel, exerts a lasting influence on Tom and Mary's lives. Mary decides on the abortion out of a sense of guilt about the death of their friend Freddie Parr, who was reportedly killed in a jealous rage by Tom's brother Dick after Mary had told him that Freddie was the father of her unborn child (in fact, it is Tom's, or so she later claims). The abortion is carried out in primitive circumstances by Martha Clay, a quack doctor whom Tom and Mary have gone to see in her cottage on the far side of Wash Fen Mere.

Tom introduces this encounter with the real as a fairy-tale about the local '[w]itch' (298). However, the inadequacy of the fairy-tale form is signalled by his subsequent admission that Martha lacks any of the attributes which this description of her calls to mind: 'No pointed hat, no broomstick, no grinning black cat on shoulder . . .' (301). The traumatic history that Tom is struggling to convey resists integration into a preconceived narrative. In an attempt to give his student audience some idea of Martha's cottage and the events that took place there, he refers to 'a full-scale mock-up of an old Fen cottage' (303) exhibited in a Gildsey museum that they could go and visit. However, he drops the analogy when he realizes that this bland reproduction cannot but fail to give access to the excessive experience he is seeking to transmit: 'But it won't begin to tell you, it won't begin to convey in the slightest . . .' (303).

By Tom's account, the abortion takes place not simply in a hut in the Fens, but in some sort of parallel universe: 'we've already stepped into a different world. The one where things come to a stop; the one where the past will go on happening' (304). This paradoxical description of things coming to a stop yet going on happening is an accurate representation of the impact of trauma. As Lawrence Langer points out, traumatic events take on a timeless quality in the mind of the survivor: '[Trauma] stops the chronological clock and fixes the moment permanently in memory and imagination, immune to the vicissitudes of time' (quoted in van der Kolk and van der Hart 177).[3] Thus, trauma can effectively launch people into a different world: 'Many traumatized persons . . . experience long periods of time in which they live, as it were, in two different worlds: the realm of the trauma and the realm of their current, ordinary life. Very often, it is impossible to bridge these worlds' (van der Kolk and van der Hart 176). The unassimilated event, which brings time to a halt, goes on happening in the world of the trauma: it continually returns, in its exactness, at a later time. Possessed by the past, the trauma victim compulsively repeats it as if it were fully present. As Tom remarks with respect to Mary's breakdown much later in life: 'sometimes the happening won't stop and let itself be turned into memory. So she's still in the midst of events . . . which haven't ceased' (329). Living in the unremembered past, Mary re-enacts past traumatic experiences in contemporary reality.

Trying to get his bearings in Martha's otherworldly cottage, Tom begins to describe in meticulous detail every household object and every piece of furniture known to him. However, he soon finds himself at the end of his tether: 'And that's all. Because the rest – it's not like a home at all. It's full of things people wouldn't keep inside a home – or that people wouldn't keep at all' (303). Martha's dwelling-place is littered with uncanny things, 'incongruous items' and 'stray objects' which resist Tom's classificatory impulse (304). His capacity for naming and knowing reaches a limit as he directs his gaze towards the ceiling:

> Hanging from a ceiling beam, like amputated, mummified legs, a pair of long leather waders. But take a look at that ceiling! Look what else it's hung with. It's hung with dead birds. Mallard – a duck and drake – teal, plover, snipe. It's hung with strips of fur and eel-skin, a bloody-mouthed water-rat dangling by its hairy tail. It's hung with nameable and unnameable bunches of leaves, grasses, roots, seed-pods, in every stage of freshness and desiccation. With misshapen things blackened with smoke that you don't like to ask what they are. With all manner of bags and pouches that you don't like to ask what's inside. (304)

The precision of the catalogue gives way as Tom is overcome by the horror of unnamable things and of things about whose exact nature he would rather remain in the dark. As Catherine Bernard argues, the movement from what is known to what is beyond knowledge enacted in this descriptive passage can be regarded as emblematic of the novel as a whole:

> la conclusion de cette description ('things you don't like to ask what they are... You don't like to ask what's inside') renvoie, sur le mode de la prétérition, au chapitre dans son ensemble – moment d'exploration cauchemardesque de l'être – mais aussi à la logique même du texte, tendu vers l'exhumation d'une part cachée du réel.
>
> the conclusion of this description ('things you don't like to ask what they are . . . You don't like to ask what's inside') refers, by paralipsis, to the chapter as a whole – moment of nightmarish exploration of being – but also to the very logic of the text, directed towards the exhumation of a hidden part of the real. (*La parole chronique* 57)

Driven by a desire to gain access to the traumatic kernel of reality, *Waterland* seeks to penetrate to that which cannot be construed as knowledge nor assimilated into full cognition. Thus, Tom insists that the actual truth of what went on in Martha's cottage that fateful night has never entered 'the communal gossip-pool of Hockwell' (316):

> Yes, it's common knowledge. But only I know about that night in Martha's cottage. What I saw through the window. And that dawn. That dawn. I carried the pail, down to the Ouse. Because Martha said: 'You gotta do it, bor. Only you. No one else. In the river, mind. An' when you throws it, don't you look. Nothin' but bad luck if you looks.' So I carried the pail across the mist-wrapped, dew-soaked meadows. Larks were trilling somewhere above the mist, but I was stumbling through a mist of tears. I climbed the river wall, descended to the water's edge. I turned my head away. But then I looked. I howled. A farewell glance. A red spittle, floating, frothing, slowly sinking. Borne on the slow Ouse currents. Borne downstream. Borne all the way (but for the Ouse eels . . .) to the Wash. Where it all comes out. (316–17)

This passage testifies to Tom's resolve not to blind himself to the true horror of the abortion, which the common knowledge of Hockwell's gossip-mongers will not and cannot convey. Ignoring Martha's prohibition to look at the aborted foetus while emptying the pail in the river (a course of action that would have spared him a painful confrontation with an unspeakable reality), Tom chooses to face up to the full horror of the situation.[4]

Interestingly, the passage recalls the Orpheus myth, whose famous reinterpretation by Maurice Blanchot is particularly relevant in this context. Blanchot's major insight, succinctly captured in his recasting of this myth in *The Space of Literature* but reiterated throughout his entire work, is that literature is governed by an impossible and insatiable desire for that which is denied to the movement of comprehension. Orpheus disregards the prohibition against looking Eurydice in the face that is imposed upon him by the gods of the Underworld, thereby losing his beloved. Though his work is 'to bring it [Eurydice, that is, 'the profoundly obscure point toward which art and desire, death and night, seem to tend'] back to the light of day and to give it form, shape, and reality in the day', his desire is rather to '[look] at the center of night in the night' (171). Orpheus is not satisfied with bringing Eurydice into the daylight, negating the night, but rather wants to gaze at her in the night. He does not want to make the invisible visible, but rather (and impossibly) to see the invisible as invisible. Day being the negation of night, the accomplishment of Orpheus's work would be the betrayal of both Eurydice and his desire for her. Pure exteriority cannot fall within the horizon of the day without losing its alterity. By turning around to look at Eurydice, Orpheus is able at least to intimate the experience of an absence which is in excess of any act of negation. His gaze may therefore be seen as the trace of the interruption of the totality of the work by its involvement with excess.

In writing, the writer is caught and suspended between two forces that are both necessary and impossible. In his essay 'Literature and the Right to Death', Blanchot describes this radical ambiguity in terms of two slopes between which literature is said to be divided. If one side of literature is 'turned toward the movement of negation by which things are separated from themselves and destroyed in order to be known, subjugated, communicated', its other side is 'a concern for the reality of things, for their unknown, free, and silence [sic] existence' (330). On the first slope is a literature of realism, which seeks its realization through 'meaningful prose', that is, by means of a language that 'designates things according to what they mean' (332). The second slope, however, is concerned with things 'prior to the day' (329), that is, with things prior to their negation by language and human systems of order. It 'sympathizes with darkness' and 'protests against revelation' (330). On this second slope is poetical language, which is concerned not with negation and meaning but with the materiality of language. Though these two slopes may seem to be utterly incompatible, Blanchot insists on the impossibility of realizing either of them in their purity. The first slope is unavoidably contaminated by the second, and vice versa: 'an art which purports to follow one slope is already on the other' (332). No cancellation of one slope by the other can occur, as each slope inevitably veers away from itself to the other:

> if you choose exactly where your place in it [literature] is, if you convince yourself that you really are where you wanted to be, you risk becoming very confused, because literature has already insidiously caused you to pass from one slope to the other and changed you into something you were not before. This is its treachery; this is also its cunning version of the truth. (333)

Blanchot's arguments about literature will be used here critically to frame Bernard's perceptive analysis of *Waterland* in *Graham Swift: La parole chronique*. The aim of this exercise is twofold: to shed more light on the exact manner in which the text attempts to gain access to the nothingness which it takes to be at the core of reality, and to point out a limitation of Bernard's approach which stems from its failure to address issues of ethics explicitly raised by the text.

This is how Bernard sums up the gist of her reading of Swift's work:

> En déconstruisant un ordre romanesque, Swift déconstruit une conception normée et conventionnelle du monde et tente, dans les déchirures ouvertes par les mots, de faire surgir une réalité plus sauvage face à laquelle seule peut se dresser la force d'une écriture métaphorique.

> In deconstructing a novelistic order, Swift deconstructs a normative and conventional conception of the world and attempts, in the tears opened by the words, to bring forth a more savage reality in the face of which only the force of a metaphorical writing can maintain itself. (6)

The text's movement is said to go 'de la déconstruction des conventions réalistes à l'émergence d'une logique, plus poétique, de l'écriture' ('from the deconstruction of realist conventions to the emergence of a more poetic logic of writing', 7); or, in other words, from a deconstruction of the first, realistic slope of literature to an embrace of the second, poetic slope.

Bernard astutely analyses *Waterland*'s dealings with the first slope of literature, that is, the pursuit of meaning. She demonstrates how the novel subverts the realist project by radicalizing the conventions of the realist tradition:

> La subversion de la représentation naîtra donc tout d'abord du sein même de ses codes, par une application systématique de leurs principes esthétiques et une exploration opiniâtre de leurs implications structurelles.
>
> Hence, the subversion of the representation will originate first of all from inside its own codes, by a systematic application of their aesthetic principles and a persistent exploration of their structural implications. (9)

Rather than elucidating the meaning of reality, *Waterland* insistently points to a radical absence of meaning by carrying traditional narrative codes to an extreme. In particular, the novel subverts organicist and contextualist models of historical explanation, which, as Hayden White points out in *Metahistory*, are two well-worn strategies by means of which historians (and novelists, for that matter) have habitually attempted to make sense of the past.

By establishing emblematic links between the characters and their historical background, the realist novelist aims to forge organic ties between the text and the world: the characters become synecdoches of society. There is indeed a strong sense in *Waterland* that individuals 'imitate' the 'grand repertoire' of collective history 'in miniature' (41), and that 'all private interest is subsumed by the National Interest' (92). Parallelisms between individual and collective experience abound, especially in the chapters 'About the Rise of the Atkinsons', 'About my Grandfather' and 'About Coronation Ale', which establish a close relationship between the history of the expansion and decline of the industrial empire of Tom's maternal ancestors and the destiny of the British Empire and of Europe at large in the nineteenth and early twentieth centuries. In these chapters, Bernard argues, the organicist vision of the world is parodically radicalized, as the Atkinsons come to exemplify 'the paradigm of the microcosmic-macrocosmic relationship' just a little too perfectly (Hayden White, quoted in Bernard, *La parole chronique* 19). Events in the lives of Tom's ancestors are continually juxtaposed with and related to significant simultaneous happenings in national or European history. To quote just one passage from the novel in which the synecdochic relationship between the Atkinson empire and the Empire of Great Britain is cultivated:

> How many times does the Union Jack flutter above the arched and motto-inscribed entrance to the New Brewery to mark some occasion of patriotic pride? How many times do George and Alfred and Arthur pause in their boardroom addresses, hands on lapels, to allude to some new instance of imperial prowess? And how often do those barrels and bottles of Atkinson Ale find new wonders to celebrate? 'The Grand '51'; 'The Empress of India'; 'The Golden Jubilee'; 'The Diamond Jubilee' . . . ? (93)

The correspondences between the Atkinsons' destiny and the course of the world surrounding them become so systematic that the artificiality and conventionality of these ties stands revealed, for example in the following passage: 'While on the continent the millennium arrives, while the Bastille tumbles, Jacobins oust Girondins and there is widespread draining away of blood, Thomas Atkinson studies the principles of land drainage, of river velocity and siltation' (69). As Bernard points out, such arbitrary parallelisms stretch the metonymic coherence established in the text to the breaking point: 'La mimésis, pour vouloir être maximum, atteint un seuil presque négatif et le système analogique censé fonder la représentation confine à l'immotivé' ('The mimesis, by wanting to be maximal, attains an almost negative threshold and the analogical system deemed to support the representation borders on the unmotivated', 26). The organicist vision is definitively shattered in the twentieth century. The chapters relating the adolescence of the narrator during the Second World War emphasize the absence of any metonymic link whatsoever between the individual and the collective: the characters 'engaged in matters little affected by (and little affecting) the muffled noises-off of world events' (181).

An excessive concern with coherence, which eventually backfires, also motivates the novel's adoption of the contextualist point of view, which seeks to explain events by setting them within the context of their occurrence. Tom's narrative is propelled by an insatiable desire for knowledge, which aims to understand events by looking for causes ever further back in time. The fundamental question guiding Tom in his inquiry is 'why', a question which can never be definitively answered, as all possible answers only lead to renewed questioning:

> Whywhywhy has become like a siren wailing in our heads and a further question begins to loom: when – where – how do we stop asking why? How far back? When are we satisfied that we possess an Explanation (knowing it is not a complete explanation)? How – if only for a moment's peace – do we turn off that wretched siren? (107–8)

Though Tom finds himself forced to concede that 'there is never any end to that question' (108), he carries on contextualizing undeterred, driven by a passion for exhaustivity which can never be satisfied. More specifically, he tries to make sense of the catastrophe that has recently befallen him – his wife's abduction of a child from a Safeways supermarket – by tracing its origins back to Mary and his adolescence (their relationship, Mary's teenage pregnancy and abortion, Freddie's death and Dick's disappearance), and further still, to the remote depths of family history (the story of the Cricks and the Atkinsons and the development of the Fens). The three main currents of the novel's intricate plot are thus placed in a causal chain. The entire narrative structure is governed by an unrelenting quest to find the reasons behind things, setting off a movement of infinite regress which, for all its ambition to encompass the whole of reality, results in utter fragmentation. The desire to probe the true nature of things by framing and contextualizing them ever more precisely leads to all sorts of digressions about all manner of things, the joint effect of which is to leave the reader utterly bemused and at a complete loss. In Bernard's words:

> Logique contextualiste et souci d'explication se combinent dans *Waterland* pour créer une narration versatile, faite de récits enchâssés, de trames multiples qui visent une impossible exhaustivité. L'émiettement du continuum diégétique défait la cohérence d'ensemble des faits comme de la narration. Chaque écart semble dresser un écran narratif devant le référent, dissimule les faits autant qu'il veut s'en rapprocher. Alors que ces décrochements narratifs sont introduits afin de préciser l'action, d'éclairer un arrière-plan, ils rendent la représentation plus opaque, plus contradictoire.
>
> Contextualist logic and concern with explanation combine in *Waterland* to create a versatile narration, made up of inserted narratives, multiple strands aiming at an impossible exhaustivity. The fragmentation of the diegetic continuum destroys the coherence of the facts as well as of the narration. Each diversion seems to erect a narrative screen before the referent, hides the facts however much it wants to get closer to them. While these narrative departures are introduced to clarify the action, to illuminate the backdrop, they render the representation more opaque, more contradictory. (38)

What Bernard's dogged examination of the pursuit of meaning in *Waterland* brings to the fore, then, is that the first slope of literature inadvertently lapses into its opposite. Paradoxically, the attempt to express reality in meaningful prose can only be successful to the extent that it ends in failure. If carried through to its ultimate conclusion, realist representation comes up against the materiality of language. Becoming opaque, it loses its capacity to communicate, and instead offers intimations of an incommunicable reality which precedes and exceeds language. As Bernard puts it:

> Les codes trop cohérents qui figent les modèles représentatifs et interprétatifs préconçus se déchirent en effet sous la présence d'un référent qui toujours excède les limites de la représentation et met le langage au défi.
>
> Overly coherent codes that fix preconceived representational and interpretative models break up in the presence of a referent that always exceeds the limits of representation and defies language. (41)

Bernard goes on to claim that the violence of an unnamable referent, which Swift substitutes for the chimera of a coherent and readily available reality, can best be approached through poetical language. In *Waterland*, she discerns 'une écriture feuilletée, faite de répétitions et de métaphores' ('layered writing, made up of repetitions and metaphors', 68), which she holds responsible for 'une irrépressible désorganisation narrative . . . qui mêle inextricablement les fils du temps, disloque le cours du récit et fait de l'illogisme un principe' ('an irrepressible narrative disorganization . . . which inextricably mixes time lines, dislocates the flow of the narrative and makes a principle of illogicality', 69). The novel is indeed marked by sudden temporal and narrative breaks and shifts which continually disrupt the logic of linear progression and the stability of narrative point of view characteristic of the realist method. Different time strata are intertwined, so that the narration of particular episodes is often divided over several chapters placed at various points in the text. The abrupt shifts resulting from this fragmentation tend to be obscured by the conjunctions used to introduce many chapters, such as 'and', 'but' and 'so', which create a false effect of continuity, suggesting logical and causal relations where in reality there are none to be found. The fact that some chapters begin with a pronoun whose antecedent is either to be looked for in a previous chapter or simply non-existent only exacerbates the reader's disorientation.

Confusion also reigns supreme when it comes to narrative perspective. The narrative wavers uneasily between the past and the present tense, undermining the distinction between the different time levels. The irruptions of the present tense, which subvert the reassuring vision of a coherent, retrospectively reconstructed past, are often (though by no means always[5]) occasioned by the brutality of the Here and Now, which, as Tom reminds us, 'launch[es] us into the present tense' (61). Bernard associates such incursions with the repetition compulsion which forces victims of trauma to act out a traumatic situation that refuses to settle into understanding and remembrance as if it were fully present:

> Un présent insistant fait souvent irruption dans le cours du récit comme une blessure refusant de se refermer, et restant ouverte dans une mémoire meurtrie qui revit inlassablement les événements traumatisants du passé. Cet écrasement de la perspective réactualise sans fin, bien que sur un mode mineur, la déchirure du 'here and now'. En perturbant le cours du récit, chaque inflexion répète la cassure, rouvre la brèche.
>
> An insistent present often interrupts the flow of the narrative like a wound that refuses to heal and stays open in a bruised memory that relentlessly relives the traumatizing events of the past. This shattering of the perspective endlessly re-enacts, albeit in a minor key, the irruption of the 'here and now'. In disturbing the flow of the narrative, every inflection repeats the fracture, reopens the breach. (82)

The shift to the present tense is frequently accompanied by a transition from homodiegetic to heterodiegetic narration, which might be interpreted as a symptom of traumatic dissociation on the part of the narrator. When recalling disturbing events, Tom shows a tendency to slip into third-person narration, thus distancing himself from the person who undergoes them as if this were someone else. To give but one example, the scene in which Tom comes home from school to find that Mary has stolen a baby is recounted in the present tense and the first person. In the following passage, Tom describes how he desperately tries to recover the baby from his wife: 'The wife pulls. The husband pulls. Baby blankets unravel. The dog barks, wanting to join the game. The wife's face contorts – like a baby's. As the husband pulls he cannot suppress the sensation that he is pulling away part of his wife. He is tearing the life out of her' (267).

According to Bernard, the disjointed nature of the narrative can be accounted for by the fact that the incongruous bits and pieces making up the novel are held together by a different, essentially poetic logic, which sets little store by linearity or narrative consistency, but proceeds by association: 'A la logique strictement temporelle s'oppose donc constamment celle des mots, des associations d'idées, des glissements conceptuels' ('Hence, the strictly temporal logic is constantly opposed by that of the words, of the association of ideas, of conceptual slides', 80).[6] The novel gives itself over to 'une modélisation métaphorique des faits' ('a metaphorical modelling of the facts', 69), a form of textual organization which casts 'un réseau métaphorique étroitement serré' ('a tightly drawn metaphorical network', 70) that ends up being the text's only 'échelle référentielle' ('referential ladder', 86). Bernard carefully examines *Waterland*'s repetitive and metaphorical structure, detailing numerous factual repetitions and echoes and exposing the novel's intricate metaphorical paradigms. These paradigms – revolving, for example, around land reclamation, salvation, revolution and circularity – not only link the geographical background and the narrator's reflection on historical representation, but also generate coherence by connecting seemingly unrelated occurrences and by yoking together the destinies of successive generations: '*Waterland* . . . est en effet sous-tendu par une armature répétitive et métaphorique qui confère sa réelle unité au texte' ('*Waterland* . . . is in fact propped up by a repetitive and metaphorical armature that confers its real unity on the text', 86).

The materiality of language foregrounded by this metaphorical type of textual organization is no longer the obstacle that it was to a realist literary enterprise bent on disclosing the meaning of reality, but becomes the text's best chance of gaining access to a stubborn and uncooperative reality which thwarts its every attempt to reduce it to a meaningful whole. It is its very opacity that enables language to accede to the nonsensical reality that precedes it. To quote Bernard:

> Le texte de Swift tisse les fils d'un écheveau métaphorique qui fait de l'écriture un maillage. Si le texte semble négliger son objet (l'exploration de la réalité), c'est pour y faire retour plus directement. Non plus transitive, tendue vers la restitution d'un référent hégémonique, l'écriture cultive ici une sorte d'opacité transparente qui redéfinit l'enjeu de la fiction. Elle ne vise plus à restituer un référent, à se plier à son image, mais, en ses plis et replis, se fait tissu organique, retrouvant une logique interne par le biais même de sa désorganisation.
>
> Swift's text interweaves the threads of a metaphorical skein that turns the writing into a network. If the text seems to neglect its object (the exploration of reality), that is to return to it more directly. No longer transitive, directed towards the restitution of a hegemonic referent, the writing here cultivates a kind of transparent opacity that redefines what is at stake in fiction. It no longer aims to restore a referent, to adapt itself to its image, but, through its folds and turns, becomes an organic tissue, rediscovering an internal logic by the very means of its disorganization. (94)

The novel's metaphorical logic 'lie paradoxalement la fidélité au sensible, au vivant, à l'intransitivité du dire' ('paradoxically ties fidelity to the sensible, to the living, to the intransitivity of speech', 96). Giving up on the attempt to represent reality through meaningful prose, the text effectively becomes continuous with its object, taking on its very form: 'en annulant la différence entre représentation et représenté . . . l'écriture double et révèle la densité de la réalité' ('by cancelling the difference between representation and represented . . . the writing mimes and reveals the density of reality', 97–98). Or, to put it another way:

> L'abolition des contours temporels et sémantiques, l'indirection de la narration témoignent de la versatilité d'une réalité 'unaccommodatable' ou que, du moins, seule la fluidité d'un dire métaphorique, perpétuellement mouvant, peut rendre sensible, sans espérer l'expliciter.
>
> The abolition of temporal and semantic contours, the indirection of the narration testify to the versatility of an 'unaccommodatable' reality or, at least, a reality that only the fluidity of a metaphorical speech, eternally on the move, can make meaningful, without hoping to make it explicit. (97)

According to Bernard, then – and this is the point at which her otherwise exemplary analysis goes astray – the text has successfully realized the project which Blanchot attributes to the second slope of literature. Through the use of poetical language, she contends, Swift has somehow managed to apprehend an elusive reality; indeed, his discourse 'incarne la complexité du monde' ('incarnates the complexity of the world', 99) which first-slope realism emphatically failed to convey. In the concluding paragraphs of her book, Bernard describes this supposed achievement in terms that implicitly recall the Orpheus myth. Having established that Swift conceives reality as 'foncièrement monstrueuse' ('thoroughly monstrous'), as something which 'ne saurait être regardée en face' ('could not be looked in the face'), she nevertheless maintains that the poetic logic which the text puts forward as an alternative to realism is fully 'comptable du réel' ('accountable to the real') and makes it possible to disregard the prohibition against looking directly at Eurydice *without thereby losing her* (109). Indeed, the use of this tactic allegedly allows one to 'soutenir son visage parfois grimaçant' ('maintain one's face while sometimes grimacing', 109) when faced with a monstrous reality.

As we have seen, however, Blanchot insists on the essential impossibility of any such endeavour. While one may cherish the illusion that one has successfully managed to look Eurydice in the face, in fact, Blanchot argues, she has always already returned among the shades. Put differently, the second slope of literature converts into its opposite as easily and inevitably as does the first. Rodolphe Gasché explains this insidious conversion as follows:

> on this second slope of literature on which meaning was to be left at the threshold, meaning reappears as the impossibility of leaving meaning behind. Its success at making things reveal their pre-linguistic reality by

> turning language itself into an opaque thing obtains only where this reality and its opaqueness signify the absence of meaning, hence where the project of this kind of literature fails and meaning returns as the meaningful absence of meaning. (58)

Thus, the second slope 'does not escape the light of day brought forth by the first' (Gasché 60), in the same way that the first slope is inevitably drawn to the radical obscurity pursued by the second. The unavoidable contamination of one slope by the other, which limits their ultimate accomplishment, is the uneasy condition in which literature exists:

> without the intrinsic impossibility that inhabits each slope, there would be no slope to begin with, and hence no literature. What Blanchot says about the impossibility of realizing in its purity each one of the two seemingly incompatible slopes, and in 'distinctly different works or goals', serves to emphasize further the constitutive power of the unresolvable contradictions. (Gasché 58)

Somewhat surprisingly, Bernard is not entirely unaware that the second slope lapses into its opposite. Indeed, at several points in her study she acknowledges that poeticizing the world ultimately becomes just another way of domesticating it, of making it fit into a human order of meaning which strips it of its unsettling force:

> Les infléchissements métaphoriques ainsi imprimés au lexique fondent le texte en une sorte de pan sémantique; l'exploration du matériau linguistique contribuant à produire le sens, à découvrir une cohérence née de l'écriture, qui donne forme aux choses et apprivoise leur violence.
>
> Cette structure métaphorique tente de bâtir un sens, de conférer au monde une cohérence autre, puisée à la source de l'imaginaire et de la vision qui poétisent le récit.
>
> The metaphorical inflections that are thus imprinted on the lexicon found the text on some sort of semantic plain; with the exploration of the linguistic material contributing to the production of meaning, to the discovery of a coherence born from writing, which gives shape to things and domesticates their violence.
>
> This metaphorical structure attempts to construct a meaning, to confer upon the world a different coherence, derived from the source of the imaginary and the vision which poeticize the narrative. (89)

However, even when Bernard does betray an awareness of the internal division of the second slope, she fails to consider this a problem. Indeed, in the course of her text, the aim of representation which she ascribes to Swift's work is redefined: almost imperceptibly, it shifts from gaining access to an unassimilable reality to appropriation and domestication. This surreptitious substitution leads her to state, by way of conclusion, that 'seule la force de dévoiement de la métaphore peut apprivoiser le monde, seul le vagabondage des mots peut apaiser la violence des choses' ('only the deviating force of metaphor can domesticate the world, only the vagrancy of words can appease the violence of things', 109). What she hereby fails to notice is that it was precisely a discontent with appropriation (which, at the start of her inquiry, was deemed to be the province of realism) that prompted the novel's quest for an alternative mode of representation which would do justice to – rather than negate – the strangeness of reality.[7]

The ease with which Bernard redefines the goal of *Waterland*'s engagement with reality results from the absence from her work of any reflection on the stakes involved, which in turn is a direct consequence of her decision not to address the urgent ethical questions raised by the novel. *Waterland* insists on the necessity of bearing authentic witness to an essentially traumatic reality, on the grounds that any attempt to deny or domesticate it leads to potentially cataclysmic consequences. The novel conducts a profound investigation of the various ways in which individuals and societies have traditionally engaged with trauma, exposing them as so many unproductive and ultimately pernicious variations on the persistent theme of negation and appropriation. However, rather than promoting despair or resignation, *Waterland* keeps a glimmer of hope alive: the promise which hovers over the novel is that a truly historical transmission of trauma, which literature can help bring about, may save us from apocalypse and offer a measure of redemption. Incidentally, the ethical impact of literature, construed in this way, also appears to be of the greatest concern to Blanchot. In the final footnote to *The Space of Literature*, Blanchot stresses the vital importance of 'the nontrue', the irreducible, traumatic non-sense at the heart of reality to which literature bears witness:

> the more the world is affirmed as the future and the broad daylight of truth, where everything will have value, bear meaning, where the whole will be achieved under the mastery of man and for his use, the more it seems that art must descend toward that point where nothing has meaning yet, the more it matters that art maintain the movement, the insecurity and the grief of that which escapes every grasp and all ends. The artist and the poet seem to have received this mission: to call us obstinately back to error, to turn us toward that space where everything we propose, everything we have acquired, everything we are, all that opens upon the earth and in the sky, returns to insignificance, and where what approaches is the nonserious and the nontrue, as if perhaps thence sprang the source of all authenticity. (247 n.8)

It falls on literature, then, to deliver us from fatal fantasies of full meaning by calling us back to the literal non-sense upon which all meaning is precariously founded. In so doing, literature becomes what Simon Critchley, in his reading of Blanchot, calls 'the *depoliticizing condition for politicization*, the precondition for a space of the political based on the vertiginous knowledge of finitude, a space that remains open and, dare one add, democratic' (65). In the remaining part of this chapter, we will examine the various false cures to the problem of trauma which *Waterland* condemns and discuss the merits of the alternative trajectory which the novel puts forward.

In fact, no sooner has Tom Crick articulated his theory of reality as nothing happening than he raises the question how people are to cope with reality so conceived:

> What do you do when reality is an empty vessel? You can make things happen – and conjure up, with all the risks, a little token urgency; you can drink and be merry and forget what your sober mind tells you. Or, like the Cricks who out of their watery toils could always dredge up a tale or two, you can tell stories. (61)

Both Tom's maternal ancestors and his paternal ancestors, though in different ways, engage in history-making in order to 'outwit reality' (17). The Atkinsons literally make history by making things happen through plans and schemes. Having worked their way up from shepherds to wealthy farmers, they conceive the idea of developing the as yet untamed Fens to further their business interests: 'If you have become prosperous by selling fine quality barley, if you can look down from your Norfolk uplands and see in these level Fens – this nothing-landscape – an Idea, a drawing-board for your plans, you can outwit reality' (17). Inspired by the 'Idea of Progress' (92), the Atkinsons set about draining the land and making the River Leem navigable, etching their vision deep into the fabric of the Fens nothing-landscape. Through the injection of ideas, they seek to transform the nothingness of the Fens into a meaningful setting for the unfolding of the emerging narrative of entrepreneurial capitalism. It is suggested that, in thus '[t]rying to assuage emptiness' (177), the Atkinsons are doing essentially the same thing as the alcoholic Jack Parr, whose drunkenness 'makes reality seem not so really real' (236).

The Cricks, for their part, attempt to outwit reality by telling stories. Just as the Atkinsons try to make the Fens fit into their economic schemes, so the Cricks inscribe the landscape with alternative, fictional realities, as a result of which it becomes 'peopled with ghosts and earnestly recounted legends', such as 'The Singing Swans of Wash Fen Mere; the Monk of Sudchurch; the Headless Ferryman of Staithe' (18). Tom's mother Helen shares her family-in-law's knack for story-telling, passing it on to her son, whose choice of profession was prompted by his mother's bedtime stories: 'My becoming a history teacher can be directly ascribed to the stories which my mother told me as a child, when, like most children, I was afraid of the dark' (61). Indeed, Tom has never recognized a categorical distinction between history and fiction: 'My earliest acquaintance with history was thus, in a form issuing from my mother's lips, inseparable from her other bedtime make-believe . . .' (62). Throughout his presentation, like a full-fledged narrativist philosopher of history, Tom draws attention to the constructed nature of historical discourse by disclosing its reliance on the fictional modes and strategies traditionally associated with literature. As a result, the distinction set up in the novel's first epigraph between the dictionary definitions of *historia* as 'a narrative of past events, history' and as 'any kind of narrative: account, tale, story' becomes increasingly precarious:

> So I began to demand of history an Explanation. Only to uncover in this dedicated search more mysteries, more fantasticalities, more wonders and grounds for astonishment than I started with; only to conclude forty years later – notwithstanding a devotion to the usefulness, to the educative power of my chosen discipline – that history is a yarn. (62)

When all is said and done, history, according to Tom, serves no other purpose than the tales his mother told him as a child, namely assuaging fear: 'And can I deny that what I wanted all along was not some golden nugget that history would at last yield up, but History itself: the Grand Narrative, the filler of vacuums, the dispeller of fears of the dark?' (62).

Grand narrative history, so it would seem, far from penetrating to the bedrock of reality, actually leads one away from it. This point is driven home by Price during an after-school meeting with Tom: 'explaining's a way of avoiding the facts while you pretend to get near to them' (167). According to 'The Price Explanation of Explanation' (167), explanation-hunting is 'a way of coming up with just another story, a way of giving reality the slip' (263). Driven by a 'longing for presence, for feature, for purpose, for content', grand narratives seek to repress the emptiness of reality: 'And there's no saying what heady potions we won't concoct, what meanings, myths, manias we won't imbibe in order to convince ourselves that reality is not an empty vessel' (41). In this respect, then, the story-telling mode of history-making resembles the Atkinson way of (dis)engaging with reality by making things happen.

This resemblance is further underscored by the way in which the inaugural scene of the Atkinsons' capitalist conquest of the Fens is mirrored by a scene which finds Tom taking stock of the past during a Sunday afternoon walk to Greenwich Park. Tom's eighteenth-century ancestor William Atkinson is pictured as standing on a Norfolk hilltop and 'direct[ing] his gaze towards the west, to where the Fens lurk in the misty distance' (67). Looking down on this 'backward and trackless wilderness' 'in an expansive and prophetic manner', he instils a vision of the future in his son's mind that will inspire several successive generations of Atkinsons and determine the destiny of the as yet undeveloped Fens region (67). This primal scene finds an echo in the late twentieth century, when Tom walks to the top of Greenwich Hill and 'surveys the outstretched view' (129), consciously imitating the pose of another illustrious eighteenth-century conqueror:

> Near longitude 0°, perched on a plinth, becloaked and tricorned, stands General Wolfe, in bronze, staring to the Thames. And beneath General Wolfe, imitating his vigilant pose, stands the history teacher, in coat and scarf, taking in for the umpteenth time the famous view. The Maritime Museum (relics of Cook and Nelson); the Naval College (painted ceiling depicting four English monarchs). History's toy-cupboard. The pastime of past time. (128–29)

The suggestion is that historiography is yet another way of imposing order on and thereby domesticating reality. History-writing strips the past of its unsettling force by mummifying and museumizing it. Indeed, museumization appears to be the inevitable outcome of the positivist-historical approach to reality which Tom embraces as a young man trying to keep the traumatic events at bay which have marred his childhood. By 'making a profession out of the past' (126) and becoming a history teacher, he attempts to throw up a barrier against the brute force of reality. As a result of Tom's fascination with history, his own house, stuffed with 'historical props' and referred to as his 'Regency retreat' (331), becomes a 'veritable museum' (267).

Whereas William projects his vision for the Fenland swamps from 'the dry and stable vantage point' (71) of the Norfolk hills, Tom looks out over London from near the Old Greenwich Observatory, where there are stored 'antique chronometers, astrolabes, sextants, telescopes – instruments for measuring the universe' (147). As Paul Smethurst points out,

> The site is significant as England's historical site for the scientific measurement of space and time. It was here that reference systems for dividing and bounding the world were developed, and here that the modern world was 'fixed' in a net of geographical coordinates, with Greenwich the zero space-time, from which the rest of the world was marked out. (166)[8]

From these solid, central locations, William and Tom lay claim to domination of the future and the past respectively. Just as William conjures a future for the Fens which his descendants will go on to realize, so Tom calls up a vision of the history of London through his imagination. Whether through visionary action or reflection, both history-makers strive to appropriate reality by fitting it into a conceptual framework which is radically alien to it. At the end of the day, the net result of this procedure is a persistent and systematic denial of reality.

Besides visionary-type action-men and reality-obscuring story-tellers, the novel also features two characters who appear to reject the two related modes of repression through history-making. They are Tom's grandfather Ernest Atkinson, who despises everything his forebears ever stood for, and Tom's wife Mary, who opposes the notion of story-telling as a way of coming to terms with past traumas. No sooner has Ernest Atkinson been introduced into the narrative than he is characterized as 'a renegade, a rebel' (156). Not only does he show 'scant interest in his future prospect as head of the Atkinson Brewery and the Atkinson Water Transport Company', but as an undergraduate at Cambridge he also flirts with socialist doctrines 'directly aimed at his father's Tory principles' (156). Ernest's reluctance to join the onward march of history sketched out by his great-grandfather is partly explained by the fact that, assuming control of the family business in 1904, he, unlike his forebears, 'could scarcely view the future with confidence': he is 'the first of the brewing Atkinsons to assume his legacy without the assurance of its inevitable expansion, without the incentive of Progress, without the knowledge that in his latter days he would be a richer and more influential man than in his youth' (157). Whereas his father Arthur Atkinson, MP, obstinately clings to the idea of progress, becoming 'a staunch advocate of forward imperial policies (for here, after all, expansion was still possible)' (157), Ernest finds it impossible to indulge in such ideological fantasies. It is suggested that his rebelliousness derives from the fact that he has seen through the veil of ideological mystification which had enchanted his ancestors: 'Ernest Atkinson saw as no Atkinson had clearly seen for four generations the essential desolation of the Fens' (158). His apparent frivolity is only a mask behind which hides 'a melancholy, a moody man' with an inclination 'to take the world in earnest' (158).

Aware of the nothingness at the heart of reality, Ernest takes it upon himself to warn the world that it is heading for disaster if it does not wake up from the illusions which it has created for itself. Standing as Liberal candidate during the 1910 general election, he

> did not shrink from accusing his own father (muttered protests), from berating him as one of those who had fed the people with dreams of inflated and no longer tenable grandeur, who had intoxicated them with visions of Empire (which ought to have been clouded for ever by the disgraces of the South African War), thus diverting attention from matters nearer home. (160–61)

Ernest puts himself forward as the advocate of 'realism' (161), who foresees in the years ahead 'catastrophic consequences unless the present mood of jingoism was curbed and the military poker-playing of the nations halted' (161). He speaks out against the war, which everyone feels is coming like 'a great adventure' (226), predicting it will be 'a terrible, a disastrous thing' (226), 'an inferno' (161). His warnings are not taken seriously, however, and, having lost the election, Ernest bids farewell to public life and retires to the family estate in Kessling. Even so, he remains active in the debunking business. In 1915, with the First World War in full swing, Ernest manages to 'make a mockery' of 'war-mongering proceedings' by taking his daughter Helen to attend a pompous military parade meant to attract new recruits (219). The soldiers, spellbound by Helen's beauty, fail to keep step or hold line, as a result of which the march-past 'turns into a shambles' (218). When the war is over, Ernest sees to it that its horrors are not forgotten. With the insurance money which came his way after the Atkinson Brewery had burnt down in 1911, he endows a convalescent home for shell-shocked war veterans, where his daughter finds employment as a nurse and which, in the years following the war, serves as 'a pretty big reminder' (221) of distinctly unpleasant events which people would much rather put behind them. The Kessling Home for Neurasthenics, by its mere existence, reminds one 'how evil lingers and how things of the past aren't things of the past' (227).

By the time of the hospital's foundation, however, Ernest appears to have devised his own strategy of reality-denial. Starting out as a fierce critic of ideological fantasies with no grounding in reality, he falls prey to such mystification himself later in life. After the aforementioned military parade which Helen had been instrumental in disrupting, Ernest becomes 'a worshipper of Beauty', clinging to his daughter as to 'some left-over fragment of paradise' (219). The narrator is quick to interpret this new development as a surrender to the previously detested family tradition: 'What is happening to my grandfather? Can it be that he too has succumbed to that old Atkinson malaise and caught Ideas? And not just any old idea, but Beauty – most Platonic of the lot. The Idea of Ideas' (219). To the idea of beauty is soon added the hope of messianic redemption: 'Ernest Atkinson beats a headlong retreat, backwards, inwards, to Paradise, and starts to believe that only from out of this beauty will come a Saviour of the World' (220). No longer content to imagine Helen 'effecting miracle cures' by 'the sheer magic of her beautiful presence', and to picture her patients, who entered the hospital as 'shattered creatures', leaving it as 'a redeemed race of men' (224), he conceives the idea that only the product of an incestuous union between himself and his daughter will be able to save the world from ruin. Despite serious misgivings about her father's plan, Helen consents to bear his child, which will be known to the world as the first-born of Henry Crick, one of the patients at the hospital whom she has nursed back to health. Having impregnated his daughter, Ernest writes a letter to his yet unborn son, to be handed over to him on his eighteenth birthday, revealing the truth of his parentage and enjoining him 'to save the world, which was a place in dire need of saving' (233). Committing suicide on the same day, Ernest does not live to see how his 'saviour-son' (233) 'proves to be a potato-head' (231): 'Not a saviour of the world. A potato-head. Not a hope for the future. A numbskull with the dull, vacant stare of a fish . . .' (242). In a grim parody of the role which was assigned to him as culmination of the Atkinson narrative of progress, Tom's mentally challenged older brother grows up to become a murderer, whose actions directly or indirectly mar the lives of many.

Ernest's final delusion is shared by Mary, who – according to the narrator – has travelled a similar path in her dealings with reality. Emerging from her father's farmhouse where she had shut herself up for three years after the abortion episode, she impresses Tom with 'her appearance of toughness, endurance, as if she has made the decision to live henceforth without any kind of prop or refuge' (120). During the years of her seclusion she may have sought solace in religion, but now she seems determined to make do 'with nothing' (126). Mary develops 'what this now ex-history teacher (who is no longer sure what's real and what isn't) would have called then a capacity for realism' (41), learning '[t]o withstand, behind all the stage-props of their marriage, the empty space of reality' (126). Her way of coping with reality is contrasted with the story-telling method championed by Tom and Helen. The difference between their respective approaches is particularly apparent in the scenes which find Helen and Mary tending a stricken Henry Crick. After the First World War, Henry is entrusted to the care of Helen, who believes in the healing power of narrative:

> she believes in stories. She believes that they're a way of bearing what won't go away, a way of making sense of madness. Inside the nurse there lurks the mother, and in three years at the Kessling Home for Neurasthenics Helen has come to regard these poor, deranged inmates as children. Like frightened children, what they most want is to be told stories. And out of this discovery she evolves a precept: No, don't forget. Don't erase it. You can't erase it. But

> make it into a story. Just a story. Yes, everything's crazy. What's real? All a story. Only a story . . . (225)

Admonishing against forgetting and erasure, Helen promotes story-telling as a way of 'bearing what won't go away', but by the end of this passage she seems to have forgotten her own caveat. Indeed, her assertion that stories make everything 'just a story' or '[o]nly a story' reintroduces by the back door the very erasure of reality which she has just denounced. Narrative repression is anathema to Mary, as is borne out by the advice she offers Henry while nursing him after a devastating flood hit the Fens region in 1947. Henry, dying from broncho-pneumonia, believes that the woman who is stooping over him is his wife who is trying to get him to tell a story, as in the olden days. Struggling to obey her supposed wish, he is stopped in his tracks by Mary: 'Don't speak . . . don't try to speak' (341). Speech, for Mary, constitutes a betrayal of reality. Indeed, being 'a realistic person', she herself 'won't ever tell about the time when –' (341).[9]

Like Ernest, however, Mary fails to stick to this supposedly realistic course. In 1980, at the age of fifty-two, she becomes an avid reader of books with titles like '*If Jesus Returned*' and '*God or the Bomb*' (128), and begins to attend church again, forcing Tom to take his traditional Sunday walks alone. When one Sunday she does come walking with him again, she curbs his initial enthusiasm by suddenly announcing: 'I'm going to have a baby. Because God said I will' (130). Like Tom's maternal grandfather, Mary has finally 'caught ideas': she has actually begun to believe in the 'miracle' (122) which, back in 1947, she had told Tom was their only chance of ever having a child. Where Dick had miserably failed to live up to his role as Saviour of the World, this child, 'sent by God', would succeed in 'sav[ing] us all' (329). What happens in reality, however, is that Mary abducts a baby from a supermarket, is arrested, charged with kidnapping, acquitted on grounds of extenuating circumstances (the 'voluntary' return of the child) and of diminished responsibility, and committed to a mental institution. Unable to remain true to her putative resolve to confront the absurdity of life head-on, Mary, like Ernest, reneges on her commitment and end ups embracing a fatal fantasy of plenitude and salvation.

Mary's abduction of the child is called a 'revolutionary' act by Tom, who thus establishes a link between his wife's delusion and his own reflections on revolution, which run as a red thread through the narrative: 'So one day, after teaching the French Revolution, I come home to find that my wife's committed a revolutionary – a miraculous – act . . .' (264). In chapter 14, entitled 'De la Révolution', Tom launches a scathing attack on revolutionary action. He argues that revolutions are generally not about 'categorical change, transformation – a leap into the future' (137), as it is commonly believed, but more often than not mark moments of catastrophic regression. Attempts to shake off 'the mountain of baggage called History, which we are obliged to lug with us – which slows our pace and makes us stagger off course' (136) do not necessarily bring us closer to salvation, but may lead us straight to hell:

> Let us throw down our baggage, let us cast aside all this cumbersome paraphernalia, and see. Every so often, there are these attempts to jettison the impedimenta of history, to do without that ever-frustrating weight. And because history accumulates, because it gets always heavier and the frustration greater, so the attempts to throw it off . . . become more violent and drastic. Which is why history undergoes periodic convulsions, and why, as history becomes inevitably more massive, more pressing and hard to support, man . . . finds himself involved in bigger and bigger catastrophes. (136–37)

Tom is primarily concerned with the French Revolution, the subject he is supposed to teach to his A-level class and about which, he suggests, we must ask ourselves some 'big questions' (141). After all, not only did this revolution in the name of liberty and equality end with an emperor, 'a reincarnation of the old Sun King', but in the process it managed to create a carnage:

> Why was it that this revolution which did indeed achieve lasting reforms could not do so without fear and terror, without the piling up, in the streets of Paris alone, of (at a modest estimate) six thousand corpses, not to mention the thousands of corpses in greater France or the unnumbered corpses of Italians, Austrians, Prussians, Russians, Spaniards, Portuguese, Englishmen – which were to be strewn over the battlegrounds of Europe? Why is it that every so often history demands a bloodbath, a holocaust, an Armageddon? (141)

For a fully developed answer to these questions, we have to wait till chapters 25 and 27, 'Forget the Bastille' and 'About Natural History' respectively. There, it is argued that revolutionaries – and proponents of any kind of redemptive ideology – fail to take account of 'human nature', conceived in terms of love of life, which is why they turn into active agents of death:

> Children, there's something which revolutionaries and prophets of new worlds and even humble champions of Progress (think of those Atkinsons and their poor living fossil of a Sarah) can't abide. Natural history, human nature. Those weird and wonderful commodities, those unsolved mysteries of mysteries. (205)

The narrator goes on to contend that

> this unfathomable stuff we're made from, this stuff that we're always coming back to – our love of life, children, our love of life – is more anarchic, more seditious than any Tennis-Court Oath ever was. That's why these revolutions always have a whiff of the death-wish about them. That's why there's always a Terror waiting round the corner. (205–6)

In other words, revolutionaries and other types of world-builders are doomed to fail, and to fail dismally, because of their systematic repression of precisely that element which might be the nucleus of a true and truly successful revolution: the life-affirming force of human nature.

An essential ingredient of this human nature is the quality of curiosity, which 'begets love. It weds us to the world. It's part of our perverse, madcap love for this impossible planet we inhabit' (206). '[O]ur natural and fundamental condition', curiosity is called 'the true and rightful subverter' by the narrator (194). Yet it is stifled by revolutions which 'divert and impede the course of our inborn curiosity', with all the attendant consequences:

> Have you ever considered that why so many historical movements, not only revolutionary ones, fail, fail at heart, is because they fail to take account of the complex and unpredictable forms of our curiosity? Which doesn't want to push ahead, which always wants to say, Hey, that's interesting, let's stop awhile, let's take a look-see, let's retrace – let's take a different turn? What's the hurry? What's the rush? Let's explore. (194)

Curiosity being a source of life, '[p]eople die when curiosity goes', which is why '[n]othing is more repressive than the repression of curiosity' (206).

In the field of historiography, the repression of curiosity takes the form of grand narrative history. As a history teacher, Tom has always been concerned to impress upon his students the necessity of the pursuit of history. He starts out by holding history up as a valuable body of knowledge which may guard against the repetition of past mistakes. Challenged by his students to address the question 'Why history?' (106), he ventures the following answer: 'To shut stable doors, so that next time, at least, the horse – . . . To learn (the history master's hoary stand-by) from our mistakes so it will be better, in future . . .' (107). However, Tom's belief in the preventative power of historical knowledge is badly shaken by the succession of catastrophes which have marked the twentieth century. As Tom points out during one of his exchanges with Lewis, if 'the past actually had something to teach us', 'history would be a record of inexorable progress' and '[t]he future would be an ever more glowing prospect' (153). This clearly not being the case – what with history demanding 'a bloodbath, a holocaust, an Armageddon' every so often – Tom is left to wonder: 'why is it that every time the time before has taught us nothing?' (141). His initial trust in the prophylactic purpose of history gives way to an awareness that the only kind of knowledge which history provides is knowledge of the limits of our power to explain reality:

> history is that impossible thing: the attempt to give an account, with incomplete knowledge, of actions themselves undertaken with incomplete knowledge. So that it teaches us no short-cuts to Salvation, no recipe for a New World, only the dogged and patient art of making do. I taught you that by forever attempting to explain we may come, not to an Explanation, but to a knowledge of the limits of our power to explain. Yes, yes, the past gets in the way; it trips us up, bogs us down; it complicates, makes difficult. But to ignore this is folly, because, above all, what history teaches us is to avoid illusion and make-believe, to lay aside dreams, moonshine, cure-alls, wonder-workings, pie-in-the-sky – to be realistic. (108)

Tom ends up accusing grand narrative history – which he has practised for the best part of his life – of a staggering lack of realism. In its conviction that reality can be definitively explained, grand narrative history denies the inevitable incompleteness of our knowledge of the past, thereby reducing itself to the deplorable status of illusion and make-believe. Indeed, its promise of absolute positivity can only be sustained by the exclusion of an intractable traumatic reality. A fantasmatic conception of a fully sutured reality is called in to cover over the ineradicable gap between representation and an always escaping, impossible reality. Unprepared to acknowledge the existence of a reality beyond meaning and cognition, ideology promotes the illusion that curiosity can be – and has been – definitively satisfied, that the world can be fully known and comprehended. A cornerstone of ideological thinking, the misguided notion that representation can somehow exhaust reality has potentially murderous consequences: 'What every world-builder, what every revolutionary wants a monopoly in: Reality. Reality made plain. Reality with no nonsense. Reality cut down to size. Reality minus a few heads' (205–6).

The duty of history as Tom eventually comes to see it is to recognize the limits of our power to explain, to avoid the pitfall of reality-denial and to inscribe, without neutralizing it, the ultimate impossibility of reality as it is revealed in our traumatic encounters with it. This conception of history gives free rein to curiosity: after all, it is curiosity which, never satisfied with any explanation, no matter how conclusive it may seem, spurs us on to penetrate the darkest recesses of reality, to try to encircle its traumatic kernel, without ever giving in to the tempting but reality-negating easy answers of ideology. The pursuit of the establishment of a social and political framework in which curiosity can thrive is called 'civilization' by the narrator, a notion which he obviously sets great store by: 'this thing called civilization, this thing we've been working at for three thousand years, so that now and then we get bored with it and even poke fun at it, . . . is precious. An artifice – so easily knocked down – but precious' (239–40). The forces of civilization constitute an antidote to the threat of apocalypse exemplified by Robespierre's Terror and the First and Second World Wars, claiming successively heavier death tolls:

> This artificial stuff, this man-made stuff. In 1793 the Apocalypse came to Paris (just a few thousand heads); in 1917 it came to the swamps of Flanders. But in August, 1943 (yes, history soberly records that, despite the scale of that earlier bloodbath, the death toll in the First War was smaller than in the Second, and included few civilians), it came in the form of detonating goose eggs to Hamburg, Nuremberg and Berlin . . . (299)

Waterland's defence of civilization thus understood goes hand-in-hand with the active promotion of a particular conception of progress, which appears to be inspired by the Fens landscape in which a large part of the narrative is set. Tom elaborates a realistic model of progress in terms of land reclamation, which is clearly set against foundationalist and positivist models. Whereas the latter risk letting the world 'slip away', the former is explicitly meant to prevent it from doing so:

> There's this thing called progress. But it doesn't progress, it doesn't go anywhere. Because as progress progresses the world can slip away. It's progress if you can stop the world slipping away. My humble model for progress is the reclamation of land. Which is repeatedly, never-endingly retrieving what is lost. A dogged, vigilant business. A dull yet valuable business. A hard, inglorious business. But you shouldn't go mistaking the reclamation of land for the building of empires. (336)

As a structural activity essential to man's continuing presence in the waterland of the novel's title, the process of land reclamation is never completed. In fact, since the Fens are 'not quite solid' (8) even today, it is misleading to use the term 'reclaimed land' in this connection: 'Strictly speaking, they are never reclaimed, only being reclaimed' (10). Transposing this observation to the realm of history, we may assume that there is no pre-established telos for history which could be recognizable now, programmatically striven for and ultimately achieved in some particular organization of social life. The civilized world to which the novel aspires is an aporetic world whose idea lies in infinite conflict with its every singular actualization and in conflict with its always possible annulment. Civilization can never be definitively instantiated in the institutions of any society, which is why we should resist the ever-present temptation to essentialize its identity. Progress as conceived by the narrator militates against the organization of the future according to an immutable plan, prescription or programme which leads us to ignore the reality before us. Rather than as a movement towards a definite goal on the basis of predetermined principles, it should be understood as a continual interruption of the ordinary course of things which opens it up to an irreducible otherness.[10]

Though in the above quotation the narrator takes pains to set his notion of progress in the service of an inviolable human nature apart from the eminently ideological project of empire-building, this move may raise a few eyebrows among a contemporary reading public familiar with the infamous track record of historical humanism. Is not humanism itself, one might ask, a quintessential imperialist ideology which has only too often led people to 'let the world slip away' and to commit the vilest of atrocities? Indeed, as Tony Davies points out,

> All humanisms, until now, have been imperial. They speak of the human in the accents and the interests of a class, a sex, a 'race'. Their embrace suffocates those whom it does not ignore. . . . At various times, not excluding the present, the circuit of the human has excluded women, those who do not speak Greek or Latin or English, those whose complexions are not pink, children, Jews. It is almost impossible to think of a crime that has not been committed in the name of humanity. (131)

While recognizing that the master narrative of transcendental Man has been discredited by the long list of injustices which it has spawned, Davies nevertheless insists on the continued relevance of and need for some form of humanism in the world today. Humanism is not irredeemably tainted by its history of oppression, but needs to be reconceptualized for it to become a genuine asset to emancipatory struggles in this day and age. The new humanism which Davies envisages would have to avoid the essentialism and imperialism inherent in its predecessors. Inspired by Levinas's notion of an '*humanisme de l'autre homme*', Davies proposes a conception of humanism which sees humanity as 'neither an essence nor an end, but a continuous and precarious process of becoming human, a process that entails the inescapable recognition that our humanity is on loan from others, to precisely the extent that we acknowledge it in them' (132). A self-centred conception of the human is replaced by an other-centred one, which means that humanity is no longer to be regarded as an intrinsic property of the self but is made dependent on one's relation to an alterity that resists comprehension: 'the human can no longer be taken for granted, but must be rediscovered anew in each encounter with a ceaselessly changing reality'

(135). Humanism thus comes to be associated with a certain disposition towards alterity within the subject, with a readiness to bear witness to trauma, which is what *Waterland* is gesturing towards with its insistence on the cultivation of our innate curiosity. In other words, *Waterland* does not simply rehabilitate and reinstate the values which have contributed to producing the historical crisis whose diagnosis the novel makes, but offers a rethinking or reinvention of those values which opens up the possibility of true renewal.[11]

The course for ethical action which *Waterland* sets out strongly recalls the argument laid out by Albert Camus in *L'homme révolté* (*The Rebel*), the study of rebellion and revolution whose publication in 1951 generated a bitter conflict between Camus and Jean-Paul Sartre over the merits of Soviet-style communism. Camus's argument revolves around the tension that obtains between rebellion and revolution, two related notions to which, however, the author attaches very different valuations. Revolution is presented as a regrettable perversion of an authentic rebellious impulse which is praised as 'a force of life' (252) and 'a preliminary to all civilization' (241). When legitimate rebellion 'forgets its purpose', however, it 'plunges into a mire of tyranny or servitude' (28). Oblivious of its noble origins, innovative revolt degenerates into the terror of revolution: 'There is, it would seem, an ineradicable opposition between the movement of rebellion and the attainments of revolution' (255). Camus's reflection on this subject was occasioned by his indignation at the existence of concentration camps in Stalin's Soviet Union, which comes in for some damning criticism as instantiation of the 'revolution of the twentieth century' (255, *passim*). Camus accuses Stalinism, which conceives history as a process of dialectical totalization, of being as harmful and as deluded as the totalitarian impulse of the ideology that seems to be its opposite, that of idealist anti-historicism. In both cases, the crux of the problem turns out to lie in a denial of reality:

> If, in fact, to ignore history comes to the same as denying reality, it is still alienating oneself from reality to consider history as a completely self-sufficient absolute. The revolution of the twentieth century believes that it can avoid nihilism and remain faithful to true rebellion, by replacing God by history. In reality, it fortifies the former and betrays the latter. . . . Purely historic thought is therefore nihilistic: it accepts wholeheartedly the evil of history and in this way is opposed to rebellion. (255)

Unlike those who invoke a divinized history to justify the atrocities committed by the Stalinist regime, the true rebel refuses to avert his gaze from the reality of human suffering, since he 'cannot turn away from the world and from history without denying the very principle of his rebellion'

(254). Camus attributes to rebellion a profound sense of realism, which is sadly lacking in revolution: 'Despite its pretensions, it [the revolution of the twentieth century] begins in the absolute and attempts to mould reality. Rebellion, inversely, relies on reality to assist it in its perpetual struggle for truth' (265). Hence, 'Far from being a form of romanticism, rebellion, on the contrary, takes the part of true realism' (265). Here as in *Waterland*, a truly progressive world-view presupposes a determination to face up to reality.

Like Tom Crick, Camus identifies the fatal flaw of revolutionary thinking as a tragic misconception of human nature: 'The errors of contemporary revolution are first of all explained by the ignorance or systematic misconception of the limit which seems inseparable from human nature and which rebellion accurately reveals' (261). Whereas revolution even goes so far as to attempt to prove 'that there is no such thing as human nature' (219), rebellion can be defined precisely as 'the affirmation of a nature common to all men' (219). At the end of his itinerary, Camus calls for a 'renaissance' (272) – or 'a truly realistic revolution' (245) – to be prepared 'beyond the limits of nihilism' (272) which would take due account of human nature. Its law would be the rebellious elaboration in the face of history of a 'rule', 'neither formal nor subject to history', which is defined in terms of respect for the value and the dignity common to all men: 'instead of killing and dying in order to produce the being that we are not, we have to live and let live in order to create what we are' (221).

What makes Camus's anticipation of *Waterland* all the more striking is the fact that the notion of progress which his study implies is very similar to the novel's model of land reclamation. The 'rule of conduct' which rebellion defines, contrary to nihilism, opens the way to

> a morality which, far from obeying abstract principles, only discovers them in the heat of battle and in the incessant movement of debate. Nothing justifies the assertion that these principles have existed eternally, nothing serves to declare that they will one day exist. But they do exist, in the very period in which we exist. With us they deny, throughout all history, servitude, falsehood and terror. (250)

Renouncing the resort to a transcendental alibi for his actions, the rebel 'can never find peace': 'The value which supports him is never given to him once and for all – he must fight to uphold it, unceasingly' (252). For the utopian prospect of a just society at the end of history which permits murderous excesses to be committed in the present, Camus substitutes an awareness that justice is an elusive quality which can never be achieved once and for all, and which must therefore be continually reclaimed. Justice demanding constant pursuit, a society can be called just only to the extent that it is prepared to join this never-ending quest and hence to maintain its own interruption as that which sustains it.

In *Testimony: Crises of Witnessing in Literature, Psychoanalysis, and History*, the book she co-authored with Dori Laub, Shoshana Felman associates the ethical programme put forward in *The Rebel* with an important evolution in Camus's thinking about trauma apparent in his literary work published on either side of his seminal essay. A crucial turning point in his career as a theorist and writer, *The Rebel* is said to mark a major change in Camus's conception of the relationship of narrative to history, which is Felman's primary concern in her readings of two of his novels, situated at the beginning and at the end of his writing career: *La peste* (*The Plague*) (1947) and *La chute* (*The Fall*) (1956). The conclusion which she draws from these readings is that 'the author of *The Fall* precisely *deconstructs* the very ideology of salvation and the very witnessing authority which, governing *The Plague*, gave it its momentum as an exemplary *therapeutic* testimony' (176). Felman centres her interpretation on the scenes of witnessing embodied by the two novels, which turn out to be radically different:

> In *The Plague*, the scene of witnessing is thus the scene of the historical recording – and of the historical documenting – of an event. In *The Fall*, the scene of witnessing is, paradoxically enough, the scene of the non-recording and of the non-documenting of an event . . . In *The Plague*, the event is witnessed insofar as it is fully and directly experienced. In *The Fall*, the event is witnessed insofar as it is *not experienced*, insofar as it is literally *missed*. (168)

On Felman's reading, *The Plague* suggests a simple but false cure for the problem of trauma. Witnessed directly, the event can be incorporated into a meaningful story in a relatively straightforward manner. Once this narrative integration has been achieved, it becomes possible to envisage 'a new beginning that will altogether do away with the contamination of disease, a new beginning that, indeed, would totally erase, forget, deny the Plague' (177). Having been reduced to 'just a story', 'only a story' – to use the words of Helen Crick – the traumatic event can be safely dismissed as a thing of the past which does not in the least affect the attempt to construct the present or the future. Felman goes on to associate Sartre's position with this misguided perspective. As an apologist for Stalinism, Sartre 'neglects to witness and to take into account the labor camps in Soviet Russia, and fails to recognize through them the non-cessation of the Plague' (178).

Benefiting from the insights developed in *The Rebel*, *The Fall* denounces the delusion of salvation of the ending of *The Plague*. According to Felman, the later novel makes a mockery of the notion of redemption to be had through erasure and denial of an essentially traumatic reality. What has been witnessed in *The Fall* 'cannot be made whole and integrated into an authoritative telling': 'Unlike *The Plague*, whose testimony celebrated and recorded the significance of the dead, *The Fall* bears witness to the failure of the Other's death to claim significance' (171). Affording direct access to events, the testimony of *The Plague* fails precisely to account for 'the specificity of a disaster that consisted in a radical failure of witnessing, an event to which the witness had no access, since its very catastrophic and unprecedented nature as event was to *make the witness absent*: absent to the very presence of the event; present in, but not to, what was taking place' (194). In bearing witness to the impossibility of bearing witness to the Holocaust, *The Fall* not only radically revises the traditional understanding of witnessing as a transparent mediation between seeing and telling, but also displaces the very concept of what history is in relation to narration: 'Narrative has thus become the very writing of the impossibility of writing history' (200–1). According to Felman, the significance of the transformation of literature's testimonial task that she sees taking place in Camus's work can hardly be overestimated:

> Camus, I would maintain, exemplifies the way in which traditional relationships of narrative to history *have changed* through the historical necessity of involving literature in action, of creating a new form of narrative as testimony not merely to record, but to rethink and, in the act of its rethinking, in effect *transform history* by bearing literary witness to the Holocaust. (95)

Literature's determination to bear witness to history as trauma is construed by Felman as a commitment to a future which would steer clear of the havoc wreaked by ideological mystification. This conception of the future is clearly to be distinguished from the sort of future projected by Sartre, which cannot avoid repeating the horrors of the past. Indeed, Sartre stands indicted as 'a man who, in the name not of a real future but of the prophetic gesture – and projection – of an ideology, fails to *recognize the present* and thus *denies*, specifically, *the implications of the past* and the ineradicability of these implications from any possible future construction' (178). By constantly calling us back to the essential 'incurability' (177) of the past, literature gives the lie to the harmful 'dreams, moonshine, cure-alls, wonder-workings, pie-in-the-sky' embraced by the likes of Sartre, and intimates the possibility of endless, genuinely future-oriented progress.

Waterland too sketches out a tentative alternative to being deluded by revolutionary fictions and absolutist dreams. Painfully aware of the fact –

amply borne out by the horribly failed experiments of the twentieth century – that there are 'no short-cuts to Salvation', the novel yet refuses to retreat into passive stoicism and despair. Rather, it promotes a life of radical curiosity in relentless pursuit of an elusive, traumatic reality. Our questioning zeal, which continually pushes beyond the boundaries of the status quo, is hailed as our greatest asset in the search for an ethical way of being in the world. Always wary of definitive explanations and final solutions, it impels us to avoid complacency and sensitizes us to an irreducible alterity in perpetual danger of being repressed from our constructions of reality. Disillusioned with the reality-denial of grand narrative history, *Waterland* resorts to an essentially literary way of bearing witness to a traumatic history in the hope of preventing it from returning with a vengeance.

5 Cathartic Fables, Fabled Catharses

Photography, Fiction and Ethics in Out of this World

The crisis consists precisely in the fact that the old is dying and the new cannot be born; in this interregnum a great variety of morbid symptoms appear.
Antonio Gramsci, *Prison Notebooks*

No matter when it is written, every story from now on will be from before Auschwitz.
Maurice Blanchot, 'After the Fact'

Graham Swift's writing space may, with some justification, be described as the liminal zone between a now-defunct modernity and a tentative and tantalizing postmodernity, to be created out of the debris of the past. In an interview conducted shortly after the publication of *Out of this World*, Swift admits that his main interest is in the exploration of the 'no man's land' between 'some past, traditional world' which has disintegrated and an elusive sense of 'a viable, vital future' which would avoid the pitfalls of the past:

> So I'm interested in people who are caught between a traditional world and a sense of a viable, vital future. It's that sort of no man's land that interests me, and I'm not so sure that that isn't the position of a lot of people nowadays. I mean, we're seeing so many of our visions of the future prove delusory, whilst we cannot really go back to the old, traditional world, or when we do, we do it in a rather crass sense, you know, evoking some sentimental vision of England, Britain, in the past, which no longer pertains, even if it did a hundred years ago. And there are obvious political examples of that, like the Falklands episode, which was so absurdly grotesque, you know, it's very disturbing. (quoted in Profumo, ICA *Guardian* Conversation)

This comment acutely captures the precarious situation of many of the characters in *Out of this World*, who find themselves wandering between two worlds, one dead but eminently resurrectable, and another full of promise but still struggling to be born. The novel reflects at great length on the part (to be) played by photographic and textual representation in mediating this critical transition. The aim of this chapter is to analyse this mediating process and to assess its ethical import.

At first glance, the function ascribed to both photography and fiction is an unequivocally liberatory one. *Out of this World* engages with a range of major events in twentieth-century history, including the two world wars and the Nuremberg trials, the Vietnam War, the landing on the moon, the colonels' coup in Greece, the IRA bombing campaign and the Falklands/Maldivas conflict. Many of these events have been witnessed at close hand by Harry Beech, one of the novel's main figures, who has pursued a successful career as a photojournalist capturing harrowing images from the world's trouble spots. During his professional days, Harry was driven by a desire to open people's eyes to the woes of the contemporary world: 'Seeing is believing and certain things must be seen to have been done. Without the camera the world might start to disbelieve' (107). He used to say that photography should be about 'what you cannot see', not just because 'it is far away and only the eye of the camera will take you there', but also because 'it happens so suddenly or so cruelly there is no time or even desire to see it, and only the camera can show you what it is like while it is still happening' (55). By 'hold[ing] open the shutter when the world wants to close its eyes' (92), Harry had hoped to produce images that could speak directly to people's conscience. He held the view that photographic evidence, being 'truth positive, fact incarnate and incontrovertible' (205), has the potential to strip away layers of ideological sediment which have historically prevented people from assuming their ethical responsibilities towards their fellow men. According to Harry, 'The problem is what you don't see. The problem is your field of vision' (119); hence his fantasy of taking '[a] picture of the whole world' (119): 'The ultimate photo. All of it, the whole of it, everything' (38). In extending the limits of sympathy far beyond the bounds imposed by one's immediate field of vision, photography seems to provide a solution to the problem posed by the novel's motto: 'What the eye sees not, the heart rues not.'

Apparently, the same purpose is served by textual representation, to the extent that it aspires to a condition of overwhelming realism. *Out of this World* proceeds by constant reference to photographic images, whether real or imagined,[1] whose primary function seems to be to confer upon the text the mimetic authority traditionally attributed to photography. If, as Nancy Armstrong argues in *Fiction in the Age of Photography: The Legacy of British Realism*, since the mid-nineteenth century fiction has derived its realist credentials from fidelity to a 'shadow archive' (27) of photographic images which has come to define our notion of the real, then *Out of this World* presents itself as the prototypical realist novel.[2] In addition to relying on a straightforward realist aesthetic, *Out of this World* hinges on a traditional plot structure and uses a conventional cast of characters. Through the first-person narratives of Harry and his daughter Sophie, it tells a fairly familiar story of estrangement and reconciliation, of divergent paths that meet again. Alienated from one another ever since Harry's father Robert was killed in a terrorist attack in 1972, Harry and Sophie attempt to come to terms with the past through their interlocking monologues, with the assistance of a dream-woman and an analyst respectively. The narrative inexorably moves towards their final reunion, which is not actually recounted in the text but which seems bound to take place within the fabulous logic of sorrow to salvation or – to use the novel's preferred terminology – mud to air. Thus, the text would seem to suggest that redemption can be had and that discord can be overcome through a concerted investment in the healing powers of love and narrative communication.

The sense of moral optimism which the novel projects is tempered, however, by the doubts expressed by several characters about the ethical efficacy of both photography and fiction. Disillusioned with his former profession, Harry reflects that, rather than exposing ideological mystification, photography actually promotes it:

> I used to believe once that ours was the age in which we would say farewell to myths and legends, when they would fall off us like useless plumage and we would see ourselves clearly only as what we are. I thought the camera was the key to this process. But I think the world cannot bear to be only what it is. The world always wants another world, a shadow, an echo, a model of itself. (187)

The 'new myth' which the world so craves is that of 'its own authentic-synthetic photographic memory' (189). In true Baudrillardian fashion, Harry wonders: 'When did it happen? That imperceptible inversion. As if the camera no longer recorded but conferred reality' (189). Rather than putting us in direct contact with the world, the sheer mass of visual images by which we are bombarded on a daily basis effectively makes the real disappear into hyperreality. Despite its pretensions to mimetic verisimilitude and truthfulness, photography in the age of simulation ends up producing a sense of reality-loss. Thus, it can be seen to fulfil the same reality-obscuring function as the myths and legends which it was expected to dispel.[3]

In particular, photography appears to collude with the myth of the sovereign subject, one of the basic tenets of modernity. As Susan Sontag points out, photography celebrates the imperial self: 'To photograph is to appropriate the thing photographed. It means putting oneself into a certain relation to the world that feels like knowledge – and, therefore, like power' (4). Sontag detects 'something predatory' in the act of taking a picture:

> To photograph people is to violate them, by seeing them as they never see themselves, by having knowledge of them they can never have; it turns people into objects that can be symbolically possessed. Just as the camera is a sublimation of the gun, to photograph someone is a sublimated murder . . . (14–15)

The analogy of the camera and the gun is frequently invoked in *Out of this World* by both of the main narrators. Sophie observes that 'You can shoot with both. You can load and aim with both. With both you can find your target and the rest of the world goes black' (77). The cameramen and photographers at her grandfather's funeral are compared to snipers (84) and seen to be 'waiting in full ambush . . . Primed and loaded' (85). When Harry and Sophie walk through the lych-gate, 'they all fired away' (85). Harry, for his part, recalls that, as a serviceman during the Second World War, he 'was taught the parts and use of a camera in much the same manner as rifle drill' (49). He too is struck by the resemblance between camera and gun when he is caught off his guard by a swarm of photographers covering the death of his father: 'The flash-bulbs, like pistol shots' (93).

If it is indeed the case that 'the world cannot bear to be only what it is', or, in other words, that the confrontation with a demystified reality is a frightening and horrific (non-)experience, photography makes it possible to reduce the unsettling impact of this traumatic encounter. Harry recounts how the camera seems to confer 'a heady sense of immunity' on news photographers finding themselves in the most dangerous situations: 'The camera seems to make them invisible, invulnerable, incorporeal. They are like those immortal gods and goddesses who flitted unharmed round the plain at Troy' (121). A photo is 'a reprieve, an act of suspension, a charm' which allows one to remain unaffected in the face of potentially overwhelming events: 'If you see something terrible or wonderful, that you can't take in or focus your feelings for – a battlefield, the Taj Mahal, the woman with whom you think you are falling in love – take a picture of it, hold the camera to it. Look again when it's safe' (122). The alliance between photography and tourism, which the novel also touches upon, can be explained by reference to the same detraumatizing logic. As Sontag writes, 'The very activity of taking pictures is soothing, and assuages general feelings of disorientation that are likely to be exacerbated by travel. Most tourists feel compelled to put the camera between themselves and whatever is remarkable that they encounter' (9–10). A similar analysis is put forward by Sophie: 'I used to think, Why is it so desperate, so sad, so urgent – everyone taking the same pictures? And I'd come to this conclusion: They are trying to possess something that doesn't belong to them' (130). Using a camera is a way of maintaining one's self-assertiveness when confronted with situations that might pose a threat to one's self-conception. By reducing the outside world to one's own terms, one effectively absolves oneself of the responsibility to negotiate the demands of alterity. Rather than denouncing indifference and effecting a genuine moral transformation, then, photography appears only to confirm people in their habitual patterns of thought and behaviour.

Throughout his career as a photojournalist, Harry struggled with the profound ambivalence of photographic representation. For all his missionary zeal, he was well aware that his ambition to awaken people's conscience by shoving the naked truth down their throats was counteracted by an aestheticizing tendency within photography itself which could never be entirely suppressed. However, this realization did not stop him from trying to achieve just that:

> When I took that photograph I thought to myself, if not in so many words: Let this have no aesthetic content, let this be only like it is, in the middle of things. Since I knew already that photos taken in even the most chaotic circumstances can acquire, lifted from the mad flow of events, a perverse formality and poise. (106)

The kind of 'straight photography' which Harry favours strives to '[a]void beauty, composition, statements, symbols, eloquence, rhetoric, decorum, taste' (92), but cannot help being always already contaminated by these elements. As aesthetic artefacts, pictures meant to shock and to disturb can produce the very opposite effect of the one intended.

This state of affairs is aggravated, according to Harry, by the fact that nowadays photographs are often required to tell stories to satisfy the demands of a smug and complacent public which has no taste for the kind of 'unaccommodatable fact' that Harry seeks to transmit:

> People want stories. They don't want facts. Even journalists say 'story' when they mean 'event'. Of the news photo they say: Every picture tells a story – worth two columns of words. But supposing it doesn't tell a story? Supposing it shows only unaccommodatable fact? Supposing it shows the point at which the story breaks down. The point at which narrative goes dumb. (92)

The rivalling conceptions of the relationship between photography and narrative which Harry plays off against each other in this passage can be usefully reformulated in terms of the tension between the two dimensions of photography which Roland Barthes, in *Camera Lucida*, calls *punctum* and *studium*. If the *studium* represents the world of codes, of culture, of conventionalized context, the *punctum* refers to a moment of breakdown in the photograph's cultural coding: 'The second element [the *punctum*] will break (or punctuate) the *studium*. This time it is not I who seek it out (as I invest the field of the *studium* with my sovereign consciousness), it is this element which rises from the scene, shoots out of it like an arrow, and pierces me' (26). By privileging the readability of the *studium* at the expense of the traumatic force of the *punctum* – for example, by considering the photograph as the vehicle of a meaningful story – one 'tame[s]' the photograph, 'temper[ing] the madness which keeps threatening to explode in the face of whoever looks at it' (117). Such, according to Barthes and Harry, is the way in which society tends to deal with photographs. Their fascination, however, is with the *punctum*, the photograph's self-shattering power, and the confrontation with 'the wakening of intractable reality' which it invites (Barthes 119).[4]

The trouble with narrativization, according to Harry, is that the domestication of unaccommodatable fact which it entails amounts to an abdication of ethical responsibility, which may lead in dubious directions. This is apparent from his remarks on the Nuremberg war trials, which, as a fledgling news photographer, he had been sent out to cover. The directives which he had received for this, his first foreign assignment, were clear:

> I was looking, as my employers were looking, as the whole world was looking, for monsters. Goering, Hess, Keitel, von Ribbentrop . . . Capture in their faces the obscenity of their crimes, capture in their eyes the death of millions, capture in the furrows of their brows the enormity of their guilt. Jodl, Sauckel, Kaltenbrunner . . . (101)

The story which people wanted to hear and see was one of crime and punishment, in which a bunch of devilish arch-villains, whose very physical appearance betrays the magnitude of their crimes and the full extent of their guilt, are made to pay for the atrocities which they committed. By finishing off these monsters, the world can finally return to business as usual, secure in the knowledge that the horrors of the Second World War have been properly dealt with and laid to rest. However, Harry is forced to conclude that this reassuring narrative is contradicted by the facts: 'But I didn't find monsters. I found this collection of dull, nondescript, headphoned men, thin and pale from months in prison, with the faces of people in waiting rooms or people co-opted into some tedious, routine task' (101). Finding his mission to capture the monstrous face of Nazism thwarted, he realizes that what he should put before the world is precisely the fact of this 'terrible ordinariness':

> I thought: So what is there to capture? And then I realized. It is this ordinariness I must capture. This terrible ordinariness. The fact of this ordinariness. I must show that monsters do not belong to comfortable tales. That the worst things are perpetrated by people no one would pick out from a crowd. (102)[5]

The fact that monsters are not necessary for extreme evil, that there can be such a thing as 'routine atrocity' and 'casual' killing carried out by normal individuals, is something which people 'cannot comprehend' and which is therefore 'pushed to the remote borders of the mind' (102). Rather than taking on board this unaccommodatable fact, they prefer to cling to a self-absolving monster story which precludes any need for moral soul-searching:

> And they watch, almost with glad relief, when the unthinkable facts of a decade are unloaded on to the figures of twenty-one men who are placed, as it were, on a stage with the entire world as audience, and the whole thing takes on the solemnized aspect of ritual. Nothing is more edifying than a courtroom drama. Nothing is more conscience-cleansing than an exhibition of culprits. Nothing is more cathartic than the conversion of fact into fable. (102–3)

The fable which is meant to close the book on the Second World War and to foster an unburdened present conveniently avoids the thorny issue of ordinary people's implication in the extra-ordinary event of the Holocaust. Harry, however, relentlessly insists on the commonalities between the accused and other people. He describes the faces of the crowd of people – mostly 'members of the Allied occupying forces and administration' (103) – gathered outside the prison where the executions had been carried out as wearing a look of 'murderous exultation', and comments that '[t]hese too were the faces of ordinary people' (104). About the executioner who is said to have deliberately bungled the hangings of the condemned so that at least some of them 'died slowly and horribly', Harry provocatively asks: 'Was this a crime against humanity?' (104). Thus, a connection is suggested between the executioner's ruthlessness and the offences committed by his victims. The implication appears to be that, for as long as the world refuses to face up to the self-critical requirements of historical understanding, the murderous cycle will continue uninterrupted.[6]

Harry's musings on the Nuremberg trials are, of course, indebted to Hannah Arendt's well-known analysis of the 'banality of evil',[7] which was occasioned by the 1961 trial of Adolf Eichmann. According to Seyla Benhabib, Arendt was 'among the first to encourage facing the facts of the

Nazi regime and the Holocaust in all their naked horror' (71). Attending the Eichmann trial as a reporter for the *New Yorker*, Arendt was struck by the fact that the defendant lacked any of the demonic qualities attributed to him by the prosecution. Irritated by what she viewed as the chief prosecutor's courtroom dramatics, she insisted on the need to resist the temptation to make a shocking, outrageous reality comprehensible in terms of reductive commonplaces. Against the traditional concept of evil seen in metaphysical terms as ultimate depravity, corruption or sinfulness, she argues that the phenomenon which 'stared one in the face' at the trial was precisely 'the fearsome, word-and-thought-defying *banality of evil*' (287). While 'it would have been very comforting indeed to believe that Eichmann was a monster', Arendt maintains that '[t]he trouble with Eichmann was precisely that so many were like him, and that the many were neither perverted nor sadistic, that they were, and still are, terribly and terrifyingly normal' (276).

For Arendt, the crucial lesson of the Eichmann trial was that such everyday vices as 'thoughtlessness' and 'remoteness from reality' can 'wreak more havoc than all the evil instincts taken together which, perhaps, are inherent in man' (288). Though this should not be taken to mean that all of us share culpability for the Holocaust,[8] it does suggest that a painstaking process of self-reflection and self-questioning may be in order to avoid a recurrence of past horrors. As Dominick LaCapra writes, 'all of us in the postwar world are, in one way or another, implicated in – indeed fractured and dispossessed by – the events of the Holocaust and under the obligation to come to terms with them in a manner that does not simply deny or repress their radically disorienting import' (*Representing* 97). After all, 'denial of transference and the need to work critically through it encourages blind repetition and return of the repressed' (*Representing* 87). Only by engaging in the arduous process of working through trauma can one legitimately hope to create a future which will be truly different, not a stale repetition of the past but something radically new and as yet unimaginable.

The primary instance of a return of the repressed in *Out of this World* is undoubtedly the Falklands War, whose threatening shadow looms large over the narrative. Not only is the time of the narration made to coincide with the beginning of this conflict – the novel being explicitly headed with the date 'April 1982' – but the characters' repeated allusions to it also ensure that it is never far from mind.[9] The Falklands episode can be seen as a symptom of Britain's failure to come to terms with the trauma of its loss of status in the world. In the post-war period, Britain's status shifted from a global empire to a middle-sized country with chronic economic difficulties. Its political and economic downfall was sealed by the Suez crisis of 1956, which conclusively signalled the end of British imperial power. Britain's decline sparked a national identity crisis and gave rise to a profound sense of insecurity, which the Falklands War was expected to assuage if not surmount. Indeed, the conflict with Argentina was seen by many as 'a priceless opportunity' to 'lay the ghost of Suez – that haunting moment when Britain's Great Power pretensions were finally unmasked' (Greengrass ix). The war, which – in Margaret Thatcher's words – was to 'put the Great back into Great Britain', became 'a national exercise in myth making', acquiring the stature of 'a kind of Suez in reverse' (Greengrass ix–x). The conflict was enveloped in a fervent New Age rhetoric expressing 'a moral idea of England that is confident and steeped with evangelical fervour' (Aulich 2). As a result, 'a potent narrative developed which was cogent, pervasive and persuasive, despite the fact that it was built on the spurious foundations of partial understandings of national history and contemporary conditions' (Aulich 2). Reliant on hazy, rose-tinted memories of Empire and two world wars and oblivious to Britain's current predicament, this narrative of national pride and moral superiority – 'a lethal fix of jingoism and xenophobia' (Greengrass x) – has been characterized as 'Blimpish nostalgia' (Aulich 5).

In *Out of this World*, the Falklands War is invoked as a warning against the revivication of decrepit and obsolete ideologies. As Swift has repeatedly stated in interviews, he sees the Falklands as 'an example of an event which in some grotesque, farcical way illustrated the fact that there is a myth, and it can suddenly be revived, and there is a great urge to make it real. I think it's utterly misguided, but it's there' (quoted in Profumo, 'Attraction').[10] The nostalgic resurrection of outworn mythologies precludes the construction of a truly new, post-modern, post-imperial future. The embrace of salvific narratives provides no real solution to the contemporary crisis of meaning but fatally obscures the problem. The pursuit of redemptive meaning offers no genuine catharsis but a false semblance of it, enabling a comfortable return to the old ways which ensures that the future will be no less catastrophic than the past. Indeed, the novel paints a rather sombre picture of human history, presenting it as a long succession of variations on the age-old theme of violence and bloodshed. The Falklands War, for example, is regarded by Harry not just as an imitation of Victorian imperial campaigns but as a faithful re-enactment of the Trojan War. Thus, the official send-off ceremony for the *HMS Canberra* at Portsmouth leads him to reflect:

> It wasn't even a re-run, with twentieth-century props, of grand Victorian send-offs for illustrious imperial expeditions. It was the Trojan War all over again. Someone had raped our precious Falkland Isles, so the ships must sail. And somewhere, in a sacred grove, behind the harbour, before the bands

> could strike up and the ships slip their cables, someone had discreetly cut the throat of a modern-day Iphigeneia. (186)

The world appears to be caught up in a grim cycle of war and misery, with the destructive patterns of the past being perpetually re-enacted. As Hermione Lee points out in her review of *Out of this World* for the *Observer*, 'There's no decline or progress, just monstrous repetition.'

In light of all this, the novel's dependence on a classic narrative formula may seem strangely paradoxical. If the text is concerned with the possibility of coming to terms with the past and inventing a radically different future, its continued adherence to the logic of denial or repression does not make any sense. After all, one does not liberate the future from the prison of the past by perpetuating the very mechanisms which have consigned it to the dungeon in the first place. A great deal of critical dissatisfaction with the novel's fictional strategies can be traced back to this apparent paradox.[11] In effect, several commentators object to the discrepancy between the chaotic and overwhelming nature of the fictional universe and the rigid conventionality of the form meant to contain it. According to Jonathan Coe in the *Guardian*, for example, the novel 'lacks . . . a radical approach to structure which would in some way reflect the sheer mess of the events with which it attempts to deal'. Coe's observation that *Out of this World* represents 'an essential [sic] tidy sort of novel' which 'never quite reaches' the point 'where the story "breaks down"' is taken up and further developed by Michel Morel, who calls attention to the 'facture classique' ('classical make-up', 'Le romancier' 24) of a text which leaves the reader 'maître d'une image lisse et globalisante qui naturalise l'univers de fiction en tant que tel' ('master of a smooth and globalizing image which naturalizes the fictional universe as such', 'Le romancier' 26). Morel alleges that, for all its criticism of the sinister pseudo-catharsis offered by photography, the novel actively encourages complacency and conscience-cleansing on the part of the reader: 'Ce qui frappe ici, c'est que le texte paraît autoriser chez le lecteur des démarches de perception et de pensée qui sont dénoncées en matière de document photographique' ('What is striking here is that the text appears to authorize modes of perception and of thought for the reader that are denounced with regard to photographic documents', 'Le romancier' 26). According to Morel, the mock-cathartic recuperation of textual representation sadly goes uncensured in *Out of this World*: 'Comme la contemplation photographique, la lecture se fait cathartique, et ceci de façon à peine distanciée. La crise du sens paraît surmontée' ('Like photographic contemplation, reading becomes cathartic, and this almost unreservedly. The crisis of meaning appears to have been overcome', 'Le romancier' 26). In other words, the reader comes away from *Out of this World* assured of the fulness of his or her own identity, the self-evidence of his or her preconceptions and the correctness of the frames in which he or she habitually seeks to enclose the world.

Although Morel's reading fails to take into account an important dimension of the novel which sheds a very different light on this matter, namely its all-pervading irony, it does put its finger on an issue which other critics have ignored at their peril: the tension between the text's allegiance to a critical ethics and its simultaneous adoption of a realist framework. Mecklenburg and Bernard – to give but two examples – have sought to avoid this tangle in diametrically opposed ways: the former by reinterpreting the novel's ethical stance in traditional humanist terms compatible with a realist aesthetic, the latter by reinterpreting the textual make-up in terms of a defiantly experimental aesthetic consistent with a non-foundational ethics. These two contrasting readings both misconstrue the way in which the text operates.

In *Graham Swift: La parole chronique*, Bernard offers a reading of *Out of this World* which all but disavows the 'facture classique' of the novel. Bernard makes a case for *Out of this World* to be considered as a thoroughly experimental text, irreparably fragmented by the violence of the referent it seeks to capture, yet tentatively held together by an intricate network of repetitions and metaphors. This essentially poetical logic has allegedly displaced traditional realist conventions of textual organization, which have been found unequal to the task of representing an excessive reality with any kind of credibility. In stark contrast to Morel, who argues that the fiction continually assures the reader as to the meaningfulness of the story and thus invites a naively cathartic reading, Bernard maintains that the fractured text effectively cuts off any easy access to redemptive meaning: 'Jamais le texte ne parviendra à la catharsis de la désignation' ('Never will the text arrive at the catharsis of designation', 47).

Bernard's argument works extremely well for *Waterland*, the novel which constitutes her primary object of study, but less so for *Out of this World*. In fact, the latter novel is forcefully assimilated to an analysis uniquely tailored to the specific textual constellation of the former. That *Out of this World* plays only a tangential role in Bernard's study is apparent not only from the relative infrequency with which it is invoked to sustain the main argument, but also from Bernard's repeated admission that a textual strategy allegedly employed in both novels is actually more readily discernible in *Waterland*. Such is the case, for example, when she discusses the temporal and narrative structure of *Out of this World*. Eager to show how the novel is thrown into disarray at these levels, Bernard finds herself forced to admit that, all things considered, the sense of fragmentation is not quite so marked here as it is in *Waterland*: 'L'architecture temporelle et narrative de *Waterland* est complexe et ondoyante; celle de *Out of this World* opte pour plus de systématisme et fait de l'entrelacement une loi opératoire' ('The temporal and narrative architecture of *Waterland* is complex and unsteady; that of *Out of this World* opts for more systematicity and makes an operative law of interlacement', 70).

In order to compensate for its – admittedly minimal – disjointedness, *Out of this World* is said to weave a web of verbal linkages between the various strands of the narrative:

> Bien que fragmenté par la polyphonie de la narration, il [le texte] recouvre une unité par le biais de cette structure répétitive. Elle apparaîtra plus nettement encore lorsque nous aborderons la structure métaphorique des deux romans.
>
> Though fragmented by the polyphony of the narration, it [the text] restores unity by way of this repetitive structure. It will appear even more clearly when we go into the metaphorical structure of the two novels. (72)

Though several of these repetitions are duly listed, the promised analysis of the more significant metaphorical structure supposedly underpinning *Out of this World* fails to materialize. Bernard's claim that '*Waterland* plus encore que *Out of this World* est en effet soustendu par une armature répétitive et métaphorique qui confère sa réelle unité au texte' ('*Waterland*, even more than *Out of this World*, is in fact propped up by a repetitive and metaphorical armature that confers its real unity on the text', 86) therefore seems unwarranted insofar as it suggests that *Out of this World* too relies on a unifying metaphorical logic. Given its compliance with realist orthodoxy, the more recent novel has no need for a poetical logic to restore a sense of order to an utterly fragmented and radically disjointed textual universe – which is why it is not to be found there.[12]

Operating at the other end of the literary-critical spectrum is Mecklenburg, who readily accepts the realist premises of the narrative and assimilates the novel's ethical orientation to a set of humanist values. According to Mecklenburg, *Out of this World* is vintage Swift material. More than any of the author's other novels, with the sole exception of *Last Orders*, *Out of this World* allegedly constitutes a perfect instantiation of Swift's literary ideals and ambitions, which Mecklenburg believes to revolve around the propagation of a humanist type of morality. Thus, *Out of this World* is seen as a singularly effective vehicle for the transmission of values such as love, hope and communication, Swift's purported panacea for all the woes of the contemporary world. Whereas the main characters of his previous novels never quite manage to achieve the envisaged moral transformation, *Out of this World*'s protagonists exemplarily go all the way:

> Alle Individuen sind in der Lage, sich von der Last ihrer persönlichen Familiengeschichte zu befreien und ihren Platz in der Gegenwart der überzeitlichen Weltgeschichte anzunehmen. Die von Graham Swift gleichsam literarisch dargebotenen moralischen 'Heilmittel' der Kommunikation, der Hoffnung und Liebe sind allerdings ganz unverändert dieselben wie bisher, doch ist der Grundton dieses vierten Romans deutlich optimistischer als der seiner bisherigen Werke: Das Leben im Moment steht grundsätzlich allen seinen Charakteren offen, unabhängig von dem Schweregrad ihrer Verletzungen.
>
> All individuals are able to free themselves from the burden of their personal family history and to take up their place in the present of everlasting world history. The moral 'remedies' of communication, hope and love which Graham Swift provides through literature, as it were, are exactly the same as before, but the prevailing tone of this fourth novel is clearly more optimistic than that of his previous works: life in the present moment is in principle within the reach of all of his characters, regardless of the gravity of their wounds. (162)

Mecklenburg's supremely optimistic reading of *Out of this World* maintains itself by manifestly ignoring the profound concerns which the text raises about the ethics of representation. Whole-heartedly embracing the redemptive promises of the narrative, it takes no account whatsoever of the text's misgivings about the pursuit of liberating cathartic relief.

Moreover – and this criticism also pertains to Morel's more incisive interpretation – Mecklenburg's reading fails to appreciate the fact that the text's engagement with realism is marked by a sense of irony which subtly but significantly undermines the narrative's redemptive pretensions. *Out of this World* performs an insidious critique of the traditional model of textual organization to which it is so obviously indebted, denouncing it as a ploy to hold a traumatic reality at bay and to reassert the spontaneous dogmatism of the self in the face of a discomforting and dislocating alterity. The cathartic logic which the narrative enacts and promotes is exposed as a cop-out solution to the problem of coming to terms with a disenchanted world which holds out little hope for the future. The way in which the novel goes about its debunking business is by ironically mimicking the conventional model for dealing with trauma, and by having its characters loudly dispute the theoretical premises of this approach and subsequently express their bemusement at being caught up in its clutches.

Although ostensibly a novel about the triumph of story-telling, *Out of this World* shows clear signs of unease with the programme in whose service it is deployed. *Pace* Morel, Harry's trenchant critique of the conversion of fact into fable has repercussions beyond the field of photography which may have originally prompted it; indeed, it acts as a warning for the reader not to be seduced by this procedure wherever it manifests itself – including in the fictional narrative which he or she is reading. Harry's remarks all but impede easy consumption of the fabulous story at hand and incite the reader to a resistant reading. Taking the narrative at face value is rendered even more difficult by the fact that the protagonists themselves turn out to look upon the redemptive course on which they are set with great scepticism and disbelief.[13] Harry and Sophie find their journey towards healing and reconciliation to be so facile, expedient and steeped in cliché that they can hardly believe what is happening to them.

Harry in particular makes no attempt to hide his incredulity at the easy ride he is getting. Being saved from numbness and despair by a pretty young wife in an idyllic picture-book cottage seems just too good to be true:

> Miracles shouldn't happen. Picture-books aren't real. The fairy-tales all got discredited long ago, didn't they? There shouldn't be thatched cottages still, tucked away among green hills. You shouldn't be able to advertise in the local papers for an assistant and fall in love with the very first candidate who comes along. (79)

Much to his amazement, Harry finds himself pressed into playing the part of a character in the very kind of fairy-tale or fable which he knows to be an illusory way of escape from trauma. Settling into his role, he describes the healing process which he is made to undergo at Jenny's hands in terms suggestive of a cover-up operation: 'She makes me feel that the world is never so black with memories, so grey with age, that it cannot be re-coloured with the magic paint-box of the heart' (141). Far from being confronted head-on, Harry's haunting past is conveniently overpainted and thus obliterated through the intervention of fairy-tale magic.[14] Sophie is no less astonished than Harry at the ease and smoothness with which all tensions and turmoils are being resolved. The prospect of being reunited and reconciled with her father at the latter's wedding fills her with a sense of unreality: 'Shit, I know this is pure theatre, I know this is like a bad movie, like the way it isn't. But what's the point of life, and what's the point of goddam movies, if now and then you can't discover that the way you thought it isn't, the way you thought it only ever is in movies, really is the way it is?' (145).[15]

However, *Out of this World* drops the pretence of being a bad movie in the end. Though the narrative is inexorably drawn to the fulfilment of its promise of healing, reparation and revival, the reader's desire for closure is ultimately thwarted. Indeed, the narrative ends 'up in the air', literally as well as figuratively. Harry and Sophie both find themselves aboard an aeroplane in the last section of the novel which they narrate. When Sophie's voice goes silent, we know her to be en route to England with her two sons, and Harry, in the final section of the text, fondly reminisces about a flight which he once took with his father. A veteran of the First World War, Robert made a point of attending the celebrations marking the tenth anniversary of the 1918 Armistice in France. These proceedings were lost on his son, however, who was entranced by the wonders of air travel which he had just tasted for the first time. The Armistice 'meant nothing' to Harry, his thoughts being on 'that astonishing aerial journey and the equally astonishing one we would have to make back' (206–7). On seeing Europe from the air, Harry was struck by the absence of visible boundaries between nations, which made 'the demarcations of maps and atlases' seem 'a sham' (206). The novel ends with a lyrical evocation of an 'age of air', that is, an era of international co-operation, solidarity and understanding, which has supposedly superseded the 'age of mud', the era of strife and misery epitomized by the muddy and bloody trenches of France: 'I can see now that throughout that homeward journey his [Robert's] feet must have been, so to speak, still on the ground, still caught in the mud. And I was being lifted up and away, out of his world, out of the age of mud, out of that brown, obscure age, into the age of air' (208).

There are at least two layers of irony at work here. On the one hand, the fact that Sophie and Harry are left hanging in mid-air is arresting in that it frustrates traditional readers' expectations. Eventually, the promise of redemption and reconciliation which has kept the reader hooked for so long is postponed indefinitely to a moment beyond the time-frame of the narrative. The novel's inconclusive ending can be seen to throw into doubt the validity of the redemptive logic by which the narrative set such store. Indeed, the suggestion is that the moment of apotheosis which the story seemed to be working towards cannot simply be taken for granted. Nothing guarantees, for example, that Sophie's plane will not crash before it reaches its appointed destination – as did another plane soaring to mythical heights earlier in the narrative: that of Harry's first wife Anna, which unceremoniously slammed into Mount Olympus.[16] That *Out of this World* does not uncritically go along with the consummation of mythical redemption is also apparent from the fact that the euphoric vision of a continent without boundaries with which the novel ends is subtly undermined by another ironic echo from the past. The age of air, whose arrival is so triumphantly announced by Harry, produced another devastating world war, whose haunting presence is felt throughout the novel. Fought largely from the air, the Second World War – in which Harry served as an aerial photographer documenting the destruction after Allied bombing raids – did indeed dissolve boundaries, but through hostility rather than co-operation.[17]

We can concur, then, with Patrick Parrinder, who, in his astute review of *Out of this World* for the *London Review of Books*, states: 'We are not going to get out of this world, with its accumulations of images and memories and deposits of mud, as easily as all that; the power and fascination of each of Swift's novels, including this one, rest on some such dogged affirmation.' The bottom-line of *Out of this World*'s reflection on photography and fiction as ways of engaging with the exigencies of our contemporary situation is indeed a dogged affirmation of the need critically to work through the traumas of the past and to avoid becoming mired in self-defeating strategies of denial. Complacent attempts to compensate for trauma through a hasty investment in essentially narcissistic ideologies are shown to entail an evasion of ethical responsibility and to sacrifice the possibility of the future on the egotistical altar of short-term expediency. While the novel does not presume to offer any clear-cut formulas or ready-made solutions for navigating our post-traumatic condition, it spares no efforts in identifying pressures, possibilities and pitfalls that will have to be confronted if the future is to be anything other than a depressing and debilitating reprise of the past.

6 When Mourning Comes

Ever After, *or The World Well Won*

Who lets a Big Question upset his small, safe world?
Graham Swift, *Ever After*

Of all Graham Swift's novels, *Ever After* seems to be the most reluctant to expose itself to a critical reading informed by contemporary theory. As an English literature professor at what appears to be Cambridge University, Bill Unwin, the novel's narrator-protagonist, makes no secret of his intense dislike for the theoretical turn which his discipline has taken in recent decades. From the very start of the narrative, he takes pains to set himself apart from 'those sexy young studs of academe who attempt to go against the grain' (1). His loudly-voiced dissatisfaction with the current state of literary studies derives from the familiar misconception that theory, in proclaiming the death of God, Truth, Meaning, the Subject, the Author and so on and so forth, has reduced the study of literature to the dissection of a corpse. Nowadays, 'in a place like this', so Bill believes, literature is being 'forever chopped up and flung into preservatives as if it were a subject for an autopsy' (5). The profession's way of 'tak[ing] apart' its object is said to amount to a 'brutal' act of aggression (211). Exploiting the *faux*-reifying effect of the figure of death, theory's favourite trope for the dissolution of all sorts of concepts, Bill indicts the academic literary establishment of cold-blooded murder and casts literature itself in the role of the victim.

The interpretation of Bill's narrative offered in this chapter will do exactly what he most abhors, that is, read the text 'against the grain'; not on his own traditionalist terms, but according to the very poststructuralist principles which he so vehemently rejects. This approach is, after all, antithetical to Bill's personal conception of literature, which regards literature as 'the speech, the voice of the heart' (5) and values it primarily on account of its beauty.[1] 'Say things like that round here and see what happens' (5), Bill writes at one point, showing his awareness that the expressivist theory of literature to which he has just reaffirmed his allegiance puts him in a beleaguered position on account of the theoretical leanings of his colleagues. It is with the same defiant attitude – though from the opposite direction – that this chapter will approach a textual universe governed by Bill's distinctly unfashionable assumptions about literature.

The text shows clear signs of resistance to the project of narcissistic self-enclosure in whose service it has been enlisted by the narrator, whether consciously or not.[2] Having lost his wife, his mother and his stepfather in eighteen months, Bill is recovering from a failed suicide attempt when we first meet him. From what he tells us, we can infer that Bill's main problem is, and has always been, a radical refusal or inability to acknowledge the fact of loss. Framed in psychopathological terms, his condition is one of melancholia, an affliction which can be succinctly described as unhealthy mourning and which, as Freud points out, is intimately bound up with narcissism (250). Mourning, according to Freud, consists in a withdrawal of affection from the lost object and a subsequent reattachment of affection to some substitute for that object. The melancholic, however, responds to loss not by accepting this principle of substitution, but by taking recourse to narcissistic fantasies of plenitude and self-completion which effectively deny the fact of loss and preclude any possibility of personal renewal. Such is Bill's predicament: his inability as a child to come to terms with the shattering experience of his father's suicide has led him throughout his life to embrace a succession of redemptive discourses – Literature, Romantic Love and History – which have allowed him to ignore loss as a constitutive dimension of the human condition. Eventually, though, Bill comes to realize the impossibility of capturing 'the real thing', the self-completing object which he has continually attempted to seize hold of in this way. Time and again, his appropriative strategies turn out to leave him with no more than a substitute for the real stuff, which itself remains forever out of reach. The ultimate demise of the notions of self-sufficiency, sovereignty and wholeness in which Bill has so heavily invested is signalled by his botched suicide bid. Ironically, then, the cunning literalization of a rhetorical figure by means of which Bill had sought to discredit dominant trends in literary scholarship is reversed in this reading, as Bill's literal (near-)suicide comes to function as a figure for – precisely – the death of the subject.

Ominous though the phrase may sound, this disenchantment of the self is not something to be deplored. Far from it, in fact: the destabilization of the identity principle can be seen to liberate the narrator from his sinister solipsistic fantasies and to return him to the world he had forsaken. Whereas his 'former self' (3) displayed a disturbing degree of unconcern for others, in his 'quasi-afterlife' (239) Bill may yet learn to see through his self-intoxication and to enter into non-totalizing relations with other people. Though such an evolution is intimated rather than fully stated in the novel, Bill does record his experience of having '*moved on*, in some critical but indefinable way, from what I was before' (3). His recent brush with death having 'changed' him, he feels 'as though I have become someone else' (3). His new self shows tentative signs of a readiness to abandon the principle of self-sameness, to accept the inevitability of substitution, and thus to engage in a process of genuine mourning which may produce ethically desirable results.

This interpretation, which considers the novel to be cautiously promoting an ethical self-disquiet, differs in fundamental ways from another type of reading also concerned with issues of ethics, which is exemplified by Susanne Mecklenburg. Mecklenburg claims that all of Swift's novels promote a traditional humanist morality, albeit with varying degrees of success. From the first to the latest, she argues, they work towards a fictional realization of 'die Möglichkeit eines erfüllten Lebens im Moment' ('the possibility of a fulfilled life in the present moment', 164). Though the contours of this fulfilled life allegedly become increasingly apparent with each subsequent novel, *Ever After* is singled out as constituting an exception to this supposed general rule:

> Während besonders die männlichen Figuren in den frühen Werken nur sehr langsam und oft zu spät ihre entsprechenden 'Lektionen' lernten, gab es doch in jedem Buch dieses Autors von Beginn an zumindest einen dezidierten Hoffnungsträger, der eine vorwärtsgewandte ethische Grundhaltung verkörperte. Jene Tendenz verdeutlicht sich in einer langsam ansteigenden chronologischen Entwicklung, in dem [sic] der Autor immer mehr Figuren sein Moralkonzept auch leben ließ. Nur in Swifts vorletztem Werk mit dem programmatischen Titel *Ever After* konnte der Protagonist sich nicht aus seinem überwältigenden Verlustgefühl lösen: 'Unwin' scheiterte auf allen Ebenen, was mit der unverändert damit verbundenen moralisierenden Betonung eines notwendigen Daseins im Hier und Jetzt zu Unklarheiten über die Zielsetzung des Romans führte.
>
> Though especially the male characters in the early works learnt their appropriate 'lessons' only very slowly and often too late, in every book by this author from the start there was at least one determined bearer of hope who embodied a forward-looking ethical stance. That tendency becomes clearer in a slowly progressing chronological evolution, in which the author made an ever greater number of characters live his moral concept. Only in Swift's penultimate work with the programmatic title *Ever After* was the protagonist unable to free himself from his overwhelming sense of loss: 'Unwin' failed in every respect, something which, considering the moralizing

> emphasis on a necessary existence in the Here and Now which is always connected with this, led to obscurities regarding the purpose of the novel. (181)

Mecklenburg remains in the dark as to the exact 'purpose' of *Ever After*, a novel whose principled refusal simply to overcome loss utterly confounds her.[3] In her view, Bill is a complete and absolute failure: having once had a fulfilled life at the side of his late wife, but paralysed with grief ever since her death, he cannot seem to muster the strength to put his losses behind him, and as a result squanders another opportunity for perfect bliss which he is offered by Katherine Potter, the long-suffering wife of a colleague of his who is clearly attracted to him. Mecklenburg ends her analysis of *Ever After* by calling the novel a 'konsequente Negativfolie seines [Swifts] ethischen Konzeptes' ('consistent negative foil for his [Swift's] ethical concept'), a conclusion which she admits to be less than satisfying (171). In fact, the reason why Mecklenburg fails to detect any positive ethical relevance in the novel is that she is looking in the wrong places. Ethics, in *Ever After*, is not a matter of self-realization and the repression of loss, but rather of dissolution of the presumptuous, narcissistic self and the acknowledgement of loss.

The very first loss which Bill is confronted with, and which is to have a lasting influence on his life, is that of his father, a military officer who kills himself when his son is only nine. Colonel Unwin's suicide puts an abrupt end to his family's stay in Paris, the city to which he had been sent in November 1945 on a military or diplomatic mission whose exact nature remains unclear. It is during this period that Bill begins to perceive a collusion between 'Reality and Romance' (13), a notion of which he will not be disabused until several decades later:

> I had never seen Paris before, and yet even at nine years old I had this recurring sensation of encountering a vision made fact. If the *trompe-l'oeil* Paris of *La Bohème* was an illusion, then on my journeys on foot between our apartment and the *école*, . . . I daily disproved the illusion: Paris was the living, breathing rendition of itself. (18–19)

As a child in Paris, Bill is unaware of any gap between representation and the reality it purports to embody. He believes the world in which he moves to be saturated with meaning, an experience best captured by his sense of things being 'divine'.[4] This outlook on life is planted and nurtured in him by his charismatic mother: 'And, yes, that word [*divine*] had only to spring from her lips and I believed it to be so' (17). At this stage, Bill is completely spellbound by his mother and could hardly care less about his distant father, who is absent most of the time anyway: 'if I had an allegiance, it was to her, not to him' (23). Moreover, Bill's relationship with his mother has an important physical dimension, in the form of recurrent hugs and squeezes: 'I could have lived for, lived in that squeeze' (16). This symbiosis is typical of the pre-Oedipal state of primary narcissism, in which the infant experiences a total fusion with the mother.

In the normal course of events, the dyadic unity between mother and child is split up by the father, whose intervention prompts the child to enter into the symbolic order. As Peter Sacks points out, the Oedipal resolution shares some crucial features with the work of mourning: both procedures require 'a detachment of affection from a prior object' and posit 'the acceptance not just of a substitute, but of the very means and practice of substitution' as 'the price of survival' (8). Just as the outcome of the Oedipal crisis is the child's accession to the order of the sign, so the successful mourner eventually (re)submits to the constraints of language, turning from the object of his love to a sign of it. In Bill's case, however, such an evolution is prevented by his father's dramatic suicide. Though there is another character present in the text who is more than eager to step into his role, he is not given a chance by Bill. It is his stepfather Sam Ellison, an American plastics manufacturer who has come to the Old World to spread the gospel of substitution, his goal being 'nothing less than the polymerization of the world' (7), or so Bill tells us. 'You gotta accept it, pal', he is quoted as saying, 'the real stuff is running out, it's used up, it's blown away, or it costs too much. You gotta have *substitoots*' (7).[5] Bill, however, rejects Sam's authority and refuses to be instructed by him. He obstinately clings to his conviction that the fulness of reality can be seized hold of and that plastic, as 'the epitome of the false' (7), deserves to be treated with contempt. Holding Sam responsible for his father's death, Bill thwarts his every attempt to take over the paternal role: 'He failed, of course. . . . The more he strove, not being my father, to become my father, the more I resurrected, like a shield, my real –' (150). The dash at the end of this quotation highlights the supreme irony that Colonel Unwin, the man whom Bill believed to be his real father, was already a substitute, Bill being the product of an illicit affair between his mother and an anonymous engine driver.

The narrator's failed Oedipal development can be recoded as the mother of his later melancholias, which see him trying to recover the prelapsarian state of Parisian plenitude by various means. It should be noted, however, that the meaningfulness or divinity which as a child Bill was taught to recognize in all things is exposed as an illusion by Bill in the narrative present. The conflict between these two opposed perceptions is played out in the novel's second chapter, which tells the story of Bill's Paris days by alternating internal and external focalization, with the latter serving as a constant corrective to the former: 'now I know, in any case, that certain things were not as they once seemed' (13). Thus, his mother's way of divinizing the world and emphasizing the bond between them is revealed as a crude strategy of self-aggrandizement and egotistical projection: '"But isn't it just *heavenly*, darling?" I could have lived for, lived in that squeeze. Until I grew up and realized it was almost entirely selfish. She might as well have been hugging herself, or a handy cushion or spaniel' (16). What Bill realizes from his vantage point in the narrative present is that the pre-Oedipal unity with the mother and the sense of wholeness and identity associated with it – which, in Lacan, are explicitly situated in the Imaginary – are not an objective reality but a mere fiction. The question, therefore, is not one of attempting to regain a supposedly lost golden[6] or paradisiac age, but of acknowledging and affirming its radical absence.[7]

The benefit of hindsight being unavailable to him as a child in the thick of the action, however, Bill sets out to recover the sense of fulness lost with his father's suicide. His objective is to restore the alleged former integrity of a world which has 'fallen apart' (114) as a result of the drastic course of action taken by his father. He seeks to do so, first, by turning his attention to 'Literature' (5), and to one literary text in particular. Literature, variously described as a 'redeeming balm', a 'lifelong refuge' (71), 'verbal eternity', the 'divine spark' (233), is something which Bill firmly 'believe[s] in' (5). His use of religious terminology in this connection is hardly accidental. After all, Bill has unusually high expectations of literature, attributing it the redemptive power traditionally associated with religion. His expressivist/aestheticist conception of literature leads him to assert that there is something about literature which makes us 'better off than we were before' (71). To substantiate his position, he quotes a poem by Sir Walter Ralegh:

> *Even such is time, which takes in trust,*
> *Our youth, our joys, and all we have,*
> *And pays us but with age and dust;*
> *Who in the dark and silent grave,*
> *When we have wandered all our ways,*
> *Shuts up the story of our days.*

> So? We all know this. We have heard this before, and we would rather not dwell, thank you, on the subject. But the words hold us with their poise, their gravity – their beauty. They catch us up and speak to us in their eloquence and equilibrium, and just for a little moment (are you listening, my fine Fellows, my prize pedants?), the obvious is luminous, darkness is matched with light and life is reconciled with death.
>
> I rest my case. (71)

Bill's love of literature, then, is predicated on the sense of stability – poise and equilibrium – which it seems to provide. In a world which has collapsed following the death of his father, literature is seen by Bill as an instrument which may help him to recover his sense of balance. Indeed, the suggestion is that death and darkness can be redeemed through the operations of literature.

Bill's omission of the final couplet from Ralegh's poem – whose sixth line does not end with a full stop but with a comma – is highly significant in this regard. It runs as follows: 'And from which earth, and grave, and dust, / The Lord shall raise me up, I trust' (quoted in Jacobmeyer). In Bill's interpretation of the poem, however, there is no need for the Saviour to put in a redemptive appearance, divine agency having been displaced onto literature itself. Hence God, having become redundant, is unceremoniously sent packing. Literature's usurpation of the position of religion is further underscored by the structural parallel between Bill's life-story and that of Matthew Pearce, his great-great-grandfather whom, later on in life, he sets about resurrecting through writing. Both men turn out to have reacted in very similar ways to the loss of close relatives in their childhood and adulthood. Though managing to overcome the loss of a parent at a relatively young age (Bill's father and Matthew's mother), they prove incapable of performing the same feat when confronted with the loss of another family member during their adult life (Bill's wife Ruth and Matthew's son Felix). However, the specific survival strategy adopted after the first loss is markedly different in the two cases. While Bill seeks refuge in literature in the wake of his father's suicide, Matthew turns to religion for consolation after his mother's demise. Just as literature is considered a source of stability by Bill, religion is held to provide 'a *basis*, a sure foundation' (92) for the world by Matthew, who moreover comes to see the Bible as 'the only true reply to death' (95).

Although enamoured with literature in general, Bill is particularly fascinated by *Hamlet*, the play to which he is introduced by his English master Tubby Baxter on returning from Paris to England. His infatuation with *Hamlet* stems from the 'particularly acute rapport' (5) which he presumes to exist between the tragic prince of Denmark and himself. Both Hamlet's mother and Bill's have remarried with unseemly haste after the violent death of their respective husbands. These parallels are seized upon by Bill to imagine himself 'surreptitiously, presumptuously, appropriately, perversely' (4) as a latter-day Hamlet. Shakespeare's play thus furnishes Bill with an identity-model which allows him to make sense of his own life, a life which has been rendered meaningless and purposeless by his father's death. Throughout the narrative, Bill persistently filters his own experience through the Shakespearean intertext, which, as Hannah Jacobmeyer points out, performs a 'stabilizing and ordering function' in shoring up the narrator's shaky sense of identity and counteracting the reader's initial disorientation.

A clue for understanding Hamlet's appeal as an identity-model for Bill lies in what has been perceived, by a critical tradition stretching at least as far back as H. D. F. Kitto, as the promise of redemption hovering over the play. Bill's 'fixation' (5) with Hamlet may well be due to the fact that Shakespeare's hero, for all his despair, can be seen to find redemption in the end by submitting to divine providence and righting the wrong that has been committed against his father. This pattern is prefigured in the early exchange between Marcellus and Horatio:

> MAR. Something is rotten in the state of Denmark.
> HOR. Heaven will direct it. (1.4.90–91)[8]

The appearance of the ghost is recognized by Hamlet as a divine response to human disruption of the natural order of the realm. It precipitates a sequence of human responses which end when Hamlet becomes the main agent through which Heaven 'directs', or sets right, the rottenness of Claudius's Denmark. Discovering a design in the universe he had previously failed to find, Hamlet winds up surrendering to providence. Instead of inveighing against 'all the uses of this world' (1.2.134), regarding the 'goodly frame' (2.2.298) of the earth as 'a sterile promontory' (2.2.299) and lamenting that he was born to set right what is 'out of joint' (1.5.196), he now asserts his faith in 'a divinity that shapes our ends / Rough-hew them how we will –' (5.2.10–11). Having resigned himself to being an instrument of divine will, Hamlet kills Claudius, thereby presumably restoring the violated order. Losing his own life in the process of administering revenge on his uncle, he is applauded for his vengeful act by Horatio, who prays for his friend to be blessed with heavenly benediction: 'And flights of angels sing thee to thy rest' (5.2.365). On this reading, then, taking revenge on Claudius is a way of restoring meaning to a world which has been rendered meaningless by the death of Hamlet's father.

Inspired by Hamlet's example, Bill sets out on a 'theoretical vendetta' against his own stepfather: 'For Claudius, read Sam Ellison' (6).[9] Unlike Hamlet, however, Bill does not find himself summoned by the ghost of his father to avenge him; rather, he has to summon this ghost (as) himself:

> There were Sam and my mother testing the springs of a new double bed, and there was I, an adjunct, an accessory, a supernumerary. This had been my father's position. I stood in his vacant place. And out of this ghostly identifi-

> cation I began to summon a father I had never really known: noble, virtuous, wronged.
>
> I'd like to think I wasn't as slow as I was in opening my account of vengeance; that at least by that day the India photos were removed, I had taken my first vow of retribution; and that if I took such a vow, it was as authentic and spontaneous as the pang that prompted it. But I'm not so sure. I'm not sure if our passions seek out models of behaviour or if models of behaviour are the springs of our passions. It was a while before the first blow was struck. (63–64)

The fact that the ghost in Bill's narrative turns out not to be an objective reality but an imaginative (self-)projection on the part of the narrator alerts the reader to the precariousness of the Hamlet connection, which becomes ever more apparent as the story progresses. Still in this passage, it is weakened further by Bill's calling into question of the originary status of the vengeful emotion that drove him to conduct a retributive campaign against Sam. Indeed, he raises the possibility that his passion for revenge was not 'authentic and spontaneous' in the sense of being a transparent or direct translation of 'the pang that prompted it' (grief over the death of his father[10]), but required the intervention of an external 'model of behaviour' (the example of Hamlet) to come into its own.[11]

This hypothesis, launched by Bill from his 'posthumous' position in the narrative present, subverts the notion of the fully autonomous, self-present subject by which he has always set great store and which underlies his expressivist conception of literature as being 'the speech, the voice of the heart'. The novel can be seen to participate in the critique of the prevalent 'expressive hypothesis' of emotion and the ideology of the self-sufficient subject which it underpins as formulated by Rei Terada in *Feeling in Theory: Emotion after the 'Death of the Subject'*. Terada questions the widely accepted link between emotion and the subject established through the metaphor of expression: 'The purpose of expression tropes is to extrapolate a human subject circularly from the phenomenon of emotion. The claim that emotion requires subjectivity – thus we can see we're subjects, since we have emotions – creates the illusion of subjectivity rather than showing evidence of it' (11). Subjective schemes of emotional experience depend on 'the disappearance or insignificance of representation' (17). They present the passage from corporeal affect to interpretative emotion as a process of 'representational translucence' by the name of 'auto-affection' (17). As Terada points out, however, auto-affection – the purportedly distortion-free mode of representation of one's own sensations and ideas to oneself – is necessarily second-order. Having no privileged access to our own mental life, 'we have to imagine our way into ourselves' (24).

Theatricality, in other words, is an ineradicable dimension of emotional experience: 'people can feel emotions only through intermediate representations' (18). Unable to circumvent the persistent differentiality of representation, auto-affection cannot make good its promise of self-sufficiency; indeed, 'the very existence of emotive experience assumes the incompleteness of subjectivity' (30).

Though Bill's narrative is crammed with quotations from and allusions to *Hamlet*, the connection to Shakespeare's play, which seemed spurious from the start, becomes altogether untenable following revelations made by Sam shortly before his death. When Sam comes to see Bill in his college quarters after the death of Bill's mother, the latter absurdly expects the former to apologize for the suffering he has supposedly caused: 'He is here (Claudius at his prayers) to atone for his part in my father's death' (154). The real purpose of Sam's visit, however, is to disclose to Bill the secret of his paternity. Sam's contribution to the death of Bill's father turns out to have been fairly minimal: what drove Colonel Unwin over the edge, we are given to believe, was not so much the fact that his wife was having an affair as his discovery that he was not Bill's father. At this point, Bill's conspiracy theory founders, as does his Hamlet identification. He admits as much by declaring Sam's subsequent death – of natural causes – to have removed 'one of the main shaping factors, one of the plots of my life' (6). To Bill's consternation and despair, the revenge plot which has given meaning to his life by holding out the promise of fulfilment is finally exposed as a fanciful projection. Cut off from the prospect of salvation, he exclaims: 'There is nothing worse than Revenge Refuted' (11).

In fact, Bill suspects that the situation may even be one of Revenge Reversed: 'it is Sam who in a posthumous but canny fashion has got his revenge on me' (6). The 'utterly bogus position' in which Bill finds himself, having been appointed to a fellowship at a prestigious university college despite scant qualifications, has put paid to his life-long yearning for 'the real stuff, the true, real stuff' (9). The fellowship in question has been endowed by Sam from the fortune amassed from his plastics business and on the discreet understanding that Bill would be its first beneficiary. Not seeming to mind 'its revered fabric being underpinned by plastic', the college accepted the deal without 'rais[ing] a squeak' at the dubiousness of Bill's candidature (9). Bill interprets Sam's generosity as a sweet but effective means of revenge. After all, having once proudly refused Sam's offer of 'a future in plastic' in the conviction that 'the real stuff of life lay elsewhere' (7), Bill is finally 'turned to plastic', 'born again in plastic' (9) through Sam's doing. Bill's stake in things artificial further increases when a substantial inheritance comes his way after Sam's death, which is experienced by Bill as 'the closing of a trap' (9). Sam has seen to it that Bill, after years of spurning money as an inferior substitute, 'an inescapable second-best' (9), ends up swimming in it. As much as he resents it, the logic of substitution is eventually forced upon him.

Another redemptive narrative which has sustained Bill for the best part of his life and whose validity is finally called into question is romantic love. As a pattern of love which attempts to combine sexual release, affectionate friendship and family functions in a single, life-long relationship, romantic love carries the promise of salvation: once you have found romance, so the story goes, you are saved. Everything will be smooth sailing from now on; or, to quote the traditional fairy-tale ending which gives the novel its title, you will live happily ever after. That this is what is ultimately at stake for Bill is apparent from his evocation of Matthew's love for his wife Elizabeth, which is represented as quelling Matthew's incipient religious doubts and providing him with 'a sense of miraculous, restoring gravitation': 'I choose to believe that at the very first meeting Matthew would have had the overwhelming perception that here, when his thoughts had already shown him how terribly you could go adrift, was the true, sure ground of his life' (103). Bill imagines that Matthew's love for Elizabeth leads him to rediscover the divinity in all things which he had lately begun to doubt – 'Things fit, things have a purpose' – and hence to consider himself a saved man: 'He sees himself, indeed, as "saved" – returned to the sweet, palpable goodness of the world' (108).

The same is true of Bill himself, who finds romantic love while working in a nightclub to finance his studies. He strikes up a relationship with one of the dancers, Ruth Vaughan, a first-year drama student on her way to becoming a famous actress. They get married and live happily ever after – or so we are told – till death does them part: some quarter of a century later, Ruth commits suicide while dying of lung cancer. It is Bill's firm conviction that he has come upon 'the substance of love'; that Ruth and he are 'the real thing' (76), as distinct from the 'substitoot' (149) marriage of Sam and his mother. The narrator's insistence on the originality and the reality of his love appears to be at variance, however, with his awareness that romantic love is basically a cultural construct: 'Romantic love. A made-up thing. A concoction of the poets. Jack shall have Jill. *Amor vincit omnia*' (111). Ironically, true romance is real only to the extent that it successfully imitates an artificial literary model. This paradoxical logic can also be seen at work in Bill's assertion that he did not recognize the reality of his love for Ruth until he had been satisfied as to its compliance with an illusory model: 'And I didn't know I loved her till I'd dreamt of her. I didn't know it was the real thing until an illusion had signalled it' (251). Rather than providing a safe haven from substitution, the phenomenon of romantic love turns out to be a prime example of this practice.

Tracing the literary origins of the concept of romantic love brings out another interesting aspect of Bill's relationship with his wife: its essential self-centredness. It is generally agreed that romantic love has its roots in the ideal of courtly love, which was invented by the troubadours in late eleventh-century France and swept across Europe in the following centuries.[12] Famously defined by C. S. Lewis as 'Humility, Courtesy, Adultery, and the Religion of Love' (2), courtly love identifies a highly stylized form of chivalric courtship, modelled on the feudal relationship between a knight and his liege lord. It requires the lover to pay humble service to his adored lady, who demands that he prove his loyalty by performing valorous deeds and who may or may not reward him for his efforts. The doctrine of courtly love has been seen as reaching out a helping hand to women: by casting woman as a full partner in a relationship involving respect and admiration, this new form of male–female interaction allegedly contributed to women's liberation from their subservient role as sexual object, breeder of children or conveyor of property. This analysis should not blind us, however, to the fundamental fact that, appearances notwithstanding, courtly love is much less preoccupied with the interests of the beloved lady than it is with the concerns of the man who serves her: 'it is men's feelings that are expressed and men's prowess and social standing that are at stake as men practice and profess the art of love even though the adored ladylove stands nominally at the center of the process' (Burns 23). While proclaiming the superiority of women, courtly love actually focuses on men at the expense of women: '*Fin'amor* strives toward a desired but unnamed good, bestowable only by a lady, herself identified only by an emblematic pseudonym: a dialogue without reply, pure song, turning into poetry the movements of a heart contemplating an object whose importance as such is minimal' (Zumthor 15). The worship of woman in troubadour lyric is a means to an end, and that end is the consolidation of male identity. 'Love service' is expected to make the knight a better man and warrior. It is considered to ennoble him, to improve him in every way. The courtly myth of women as revered subjects turns out to be just that: a myth. Despite being raised high atop the metaphorical pedestal of courtliness, woman finds herself reduced to a mere instigator of narcissistic male self-cultivation.[13]

Bill's love for Ruth – allegedly presented with 'an appealing romantic sincerity' (Wall 26)[14] – similarly serves the purpose of shoring up the male subject's fragile sense of self. The narrator is quite self-conscious, for example, about the ploy of peddling self-concern as other-directedness which he used to motivate his decision to become Ruth's manager. Whereas initially he claims to have been guided by 'a desire to protect her' (113), it soon transpires that the need for protection was his rather than hers:

> perhaps only I saw it – this new need of protection. This desire on my part to put my arms irremovably around her, as if I were holding her together, to beg for her a special immunity. . . . it's strange that I say I wished to hold her together, since it was she, after all, who held things together for me, who held my world together. I mean the world that had fallen apart (it did, you see) with my own father's death.
>
> You see, I protected her so she would protect me. (114–15)

Moreover, Bill's representations of women in general, and of his wife in particular, are greatly indebted to traditional descriptions of romantic heroines:

> the days are coming when the poetry will come alive. When the books will turn inside out. When the sighs and raptures and entreaties of all those love-sick bards will no longer seem like wishful thinking. And all those dubious and apocryphal mistresses, all those impossible and enslaving Cynthias, Julias, and Amaryllises, will no longer seem like moonlit phantoms, like paper dreams. (72)

The narrator makes it clear that women, as love-objects, owe their existence to their supposed coincidence with such male fantasies: 'there was this woman who had stepped out of possibility into actuality, as if I had validated her existence' (76). If the courtly lady of troubadour poetry was left 'stranded between the formative mythic paradigms of the self-absorbed Narcissus, on the one hand, and the fetishist Pygmalion, on the other' (Burns 24), the twentieth-century women revered by Bill fare no better.[15]

A rather chilling consequence of Bill's belief that love between a man and a woman is dependent on the woman's compliance with a male-defined dream model is that love is at its most intense when the woman's real existence no longer puts up any resistance to being reduced to a masculine construction, that is, when she is dead. This conclusion is implied by a rhetorical question which Bill asks in relation to Ruth's death: 'Now she has stepped for ever out of her own existence, doesn't she enter, even more readily, even more lovably, the existence of your dreams?' (255). The notion that woman, as a living person, is absent from masculine representations of femininity has been given theoretical credence by Luce Irigaray, who argues that femininity has so far been produced exclusively in relation to the logic of the same, which serves up only false images of woman agreeable to men. The discourses at our disposal are incapable of representing woman other than as an obliging prop for the enactment of man's fantasies:

'In patriarchal culture the feminine *as such* . . . is repressed; it returns only in its "acceptable" form as man's specularized Other' (Moi 134). Woman, for Irigaray, is a point of linguistic absence, the impossibility of a grammatically denoted substance. Within a masculinist language based on univocal signification, woman constitutes the unrepresentable, the undesignatable: she is always 'elsewhere'.

Ever After offers ample evidence of woman's absence from the romantic paradigm invoked to contain her.[16] Whereas Bill claims to have always been attracted to the 'real' Ruth rather than to any of the parts she played – 'It was *her*, it was *her*, you see, never those roles she dressed in' (76) – it is strongly suggested in the text that what he takes to be the real Ruth is already an insubstantial semblance. From Bill's perspective, Ruth appears first and foremost as a guarantor of the meaningfulness of life. Indeed, the notions of presence, plenitude and life are central to his representation of her. However, there are clear hints that this appearance of meaningfulness is no more than a superficial mask behind which lurk absence, emptiness and chaos:

> she proved, not exactly that she could sing, but that she could disguise impeccably the fact that she couldn't sing, could act impeccably the part of a singer; and that she had, moreover, that indefinable, spell-casting quality called (but why don't we all have it, since we are all present?) 'presence'.
>
> I think I saw – and perhaps only I saw – just for a moment, the terror in her eyes, the hidden absence out of which the presence emerged. Then it was gone, she had overcome it, a little internal victory, and I was caught in the spell. (74–75)

In addition to the fact that she cannot sing, Ruth can disguise impeccably the fact that she does not possess presence as an innate quality. Under Ruth's spell, though, Bill tends to forget this state of affairs. He comes to regard her as the embodiment of the fulness of life which he so craves. It is in such terms, for example, that her face is described: 'There was no other word for it: it was full of *life*. So full of life' (118). Again, however, there is some confusion as to the exact status of this fulness. Having asserted its substantial existence as an inherent feature of the 'real' Ruth, the narrator raises the possibility that the fulness of life which he attributes to her is a mere role which she puts on: 'She represented life to me. I know that, now she is dead. She was life to me. And that isn't just vain hyperbole, is it? She was an actress, wasn't she? It was her job: to represent life to people' (120). This passage hinges on the indeterminacy of the verb *represent*, which, in this context, can denote both a substantial relationship (Ruth 'is' life) and a more contingent, substitutive one (Ruth only 'stands in for' life). The question, then, is whether Ruth coincides with what she signifies for Bill, or whether she stands in an arbitrary relationship to the meaning he ascribes to her.

The latter possibility is consonant with the distinctly unromantic view of love offered by Sam: 'You see, I don't believe in this there's-a-girl-for-every-boy-and-a-boy-for-every-girl stuff. It's just who you get thrown against in the trolley-car, and there's more than one trolley-car and more than one ride' (157). Though Bill rejects this view, which undermines his cherished belief that 'the real thing' (his own relationship with Ruth) is categorically distinct from 'substitoot' love (as exemplified by Sam and Bill's mother), he does not cease to be haunted by it. In fact, Bill's suicide attempt, which is generally interpreted as a final confirmation of the impossibility of substitution, may have been prompted by the insight that there is no outside to substitution. The novel's critics tend to explain Bill's suicide attempt as an act of despair motivated by a heightened awareness of his wife's essential irreplacability. According to Del Ivan Janik, 'his suicide attempt was immediately precipitated by his realization after his near-seduction by Katherine Potter that neither she nor anyone else could ever become a "substitoot" for Ruth' ('No End'). In the same vein, John Marsden writes that Katherine's advances force Bill 'to confront the obvious but painful truth that she cannot be Ruth's substitute, that Ruth herself can neither be restored nor replaced' (*After Modernism* 194). In Stephen Wall's opinion, finally, 'one can accept that after Ruth's suicide – and reminded of what he has lost by the sexual approaches of Potter's wife – he should want to follow her example' (26).

These interpretations pass over a moment of textual undecidability which deserves to be examined in some detail. Though it is indeed the case that Bill tries to kill himself after Katherine has been to see him in his room in a vain bid to seduce him, he is less than clear about his reasons for attempting suicide. In fact, he professes his confusion as to whether or not he did it because of Katherine: 'I don't know which is true myself' (88). This admission is immediately followed by a question whose interpretative potential has been overlooked by the aforementioned commentators: 'How can one person take the place of another?' (88). This question, which concludes Bill's reflection on his reasons for wanting to take his own life, is open to a double meaning. It can be – and very often is – read rhetorically, as seeking the reader's agreement that it is simply impossible for one person to take the place of another. The expected answer to this rhetorical question would be: 'They cannot.' However, if we adopt this perspective, the timing of Bill's suicide attempt does not seem to make much sense. After all, the knowledge that his beloved wife was the real thing and is therefore irreplacable is old news for Bill, who has never believed otherwise. If the realization that through Ruth's death he has lost the real thing is enough to push him over the edge, he need not have waited till Katherine's visit to proceed to action. The fact that he does wait so long seems to suggest that some other factor is involved.

The second possible meaning of the question 'How can one person take the place of another?' sheds some light on this matter. In addition to being understood as a rhetorical question insisting on irreplacability, it can also be interpreted as an exclamation of despair at the ubiquity of substitution: 'How terrible that it should be possible for one person to take the place of another!' On this reading, the question does not signal the final defeat but the ultimate triumph of the principle of substitution. What Katherine's advances make Bill realize is not that Ruth is irreplacable but precisely that she *can* be replaced: to his shock and horror, he has found a perfect substitute for his late wife in Katherine Potter: 'It could have been her. It could have been us' (245).[17] His feelings for Katherine, to whom he is undeniably attracted, are perceived as posing a threat to the meaningfulness of his life allegedly guaranteed by Ruth:

> And as for the Ellison Fellow's feelings towards Katherine Potter – to be honest, they involve a good deal of confusion. He reacts before Katherine Potter, in fact, as he has reacted before all new, strange (attractive) women who happen, since a certain event, to have crossed his path. He does not know how to deal with them. He is filled with dismay, a giddy sense of arbitrariness, an apprehension that the universe holds nothing sacred; all of which is only to be stilled by the imperative of loyal resistance. (84)

Bill's attraction to Katherine, which raises doubts about Ruth's uniqueness and irreplaceability, effectively undermines the redemptive romantic ideology which has sustained him for so long. Though Bill – obeying the imperative of loyal resistance – rejects Katherine's advances, he can no longer escape the realization that the function which Ruth performed for him – namely to sanctify his life – can be taken over by another woman. This suggests that Ruth never really coincided with or embodied the meaning he attributed to her, and that the sanctity supposedly conferred by the beloved woman is no more than a groundless romantic fantasy. Ruth is basically a 'cipher', as Nicolas Tredell would have it: a mere placeholder in an artificial scenario serving the illusory purpose of masculine self-aggrandizement. According to this reading, then, the insight which drives Bill to suicide is not that his late wife can never be replaced, but rather that she can and that therefore he has never really had what he thinks he has lost: the fulness of life to which he believed his love for Ruth gave access. It turns out that there is no redemption to be had through romantic love, which sees the logic of substitution reign supreme, giving the lie to all promises of presence and plenitude.

One final metanarrative which Bill resorts to in the hope of recovering the sense of wholeness lost with his father's suicide – and not to be regained by means of either literature or romantic love – is history. Having inherited the notebooks of his Victorian ancestor Matthew Pearce after his mother's death, he sets out to study these historically significant documents – 'a testimony to the effects on a private life of ideas that shook the world' (48) – with an apparent view to publishing them. The actual reason for Bill's interest in Matthew, however, is to be looked for elsewhere: 'You see, it is the personal thing that matters' (49). Indeed, his research has 'nothing of the academic' about it and is 'rather more germane to *me* than the notebooks of Matthew Pearce' (147). Rather than simply editing a scholarly edition of Matthew's writings, as Michael Potter (his rival for the documents) wishes to do, Bill wants nothing less than to bring Matthew back to life: 'to take the skeletal remains of a single life and attempt to breathe into them their former actuality' (90). In so doing, he hopes to be able to turn the past into a source of stable personal identity. As Frederick Holmes points out in his insightful reading of *Ever After*, Bill is driven by the desire to establish 'a historical link to a foundational reality' (26) which is supposed to give meaning and purpose to his life. This mission, however, is 'bedeviled by his awareness that the representation of history is itself a substitute for the real thing, the vanished past' (25) whose reality cannot be captured. Once again, then, the principle of substitution emerges to prevent the fulfilment of Bill's desire for a source of fundamental meaning.

The basic tension which Holmes identifies in the novel is the one between totalizing and detotalizing forces familiar from historiographic metafiction as theorized by Linda Hutcheon. On the one hand, there is Bill's attempt to 'bestow upon his work clarity and an overriding narrative unity achieved through uniformity of theme, symbolism, tone, style, and point of view' (26). On the other hand, there are various 'pressures working against totalization' which 'strain almost to the breaking point Bill's efforts to achieve narrative smoothness and unity' (29). For example, though Bill positions himself as an omniscient narrator *vis-à-vis* his Victorian subject-matter, feigning to have full knowledge of the story's events and of the motives and unspoken thoughts of its characters, he fails to keep up this pretence. At various points in the text, Bill openly acknowledges his fallibility as a narrator. In the following passage, for instance, he interrupts the flow of the narrative to contemplate the strict limitations of his own point of view:

> So, have I got it all wrong? I invent. I imagine. I want them to have been happy. How do I know they were ever happy? I make them fall in love at the very first meeting on a day full of radiant summer sunshine. How do I know it was ever like that? How do I know that the Notebooks, while they offer ample evidence for the collapse of Matthew's marriage, were not also a desperate attempt to keep alive its myth, and that, even when he seems most honest, Matthew, with much display of fine feeling, tender conscience and wishful thinking, only beats about the bush of an old, old story? (212)

Holmes also shows how *Ever After* uses another convention of Victorian fiction only to subvert it: that of the epilogue, the brief synopsis of what will befall the characters in the future beyond the time-frame of the narrative proper:

> Bill's account of Matthew's life after he has left his family and has stopped writing in the notebooks is so replete with questions and highly tentative speculations that it fails to perform the traditionally reassuring function that such passages once had, namely, to satisfy readers' desires for finality and closure. (30)

The narrator's failure to paint the full picture is nowhere more apparent than in his account of the dramatic final confrontation between Matthew and his father-in-law Rector Hunt, who banishes Matthew from his parish when the latter refuses to 'repeat [his] creed' (186) and retract his Darwinian criticism of the doctrine of natural theology. If the numerous extracts from the notebooks inserted into the narrative already carry an implicit recognition that the evidence of the past cannot simply be integrated into a coherent, conclusive story, Bill's struggle to reconstruct this particular episode provides proof positive of the vanity of all such endeavours. Having tried to capture the scene in a prose narrative focalized through the Rector's wife, Bill briefly experiments with another form – the television script – 'as if to acknowledge the inadequacy of his chosen form' (Holmes 31). However, this new form proves even less satisfactory, and Bill suddenly throws in the towel, exclaiming: 'But I do not know, I cannot even invent, what the Rector said. I falter in my script-writing, just as the Rector himself, perhaps, faltered on the verge of his imprecation' (187). Despite using every trick in the book to reproduce the life and times of his forefather, Bill eventually finds himself forced to confront the futility of his quest for stable meaning in the past: the living presence of the past remaining forever out of reach, substitutes are all that is available.

Bill's interest in the Pearce manuscripts is shared by his colleague Michael Potter, an expert in the history of Victorian ideas who smells an opportunity to revitalize his somewhat dwindling academic career. Bill vehemently opposes Michael's attempts to get hold of the manuscripts on the grounds that Michael plans to exploit Matthew's agony for purely selfish reasons. He, in contrast, claims to be driven by a duty which he feels he has to perform towards Matthew: 'I have to revive him' (132); 'I owe Matthew nothing less' (90). Whereas Michael is after recognition, Bill passes himself off as a man of duty who is above such trifles: 'Some of us want recognition, some of us don't. Potter wants it. I can live without it (perhaps I should rephrase that)' (117). The parenthetical remark is an oblique allusion to what Bill likes to refer to as his 'posthumous' condition, but a good deal more rephrasing may be called for here than Bill would have us believe. Indeed, for all his protestations to the contrary, Bill does yearn for recognition, though perhaps not in the usual sense of the word. Warned by his mother against 'the ruinous desire to outwit mortality' (231), which has marred the life of many a vainglorious relative of hers, he takes an ironic distance from 'death-defiers' and 'immortalists' and their 'struggle for *remembrance*' (231). However, he does raise the possibility that, while he may not have a stake in the 'race for posterity' (232), he is engaged in a quest for a different but related good: 'And maybe it's not posterity I seek at all. . . . Maybe for me it is the other way round. Maybe it's anteriority (if such a thing exists) I'm looking for. To know who I was' (235). While he slights 'that all-important stuff: recognition' (49) so desperately pursued by the likes of Michael Potter, Bill is possessed by an equally urgent desire 'to recognize [his] former self' (239). What Bill seeks, then, is not acclaim or renown, but *literal* recognition – which, as we will see, is just another way of maintaining the fiction of his own self-sufficiency and centrality.

Indeed, in turning to the life of an ancestor in his search for a ground, an original core of identity, Bill ironically imitates one of the great death-defiers of his mother's stories: his great-uncle Rupert Rawlinson. A disgraced military officer, Uncle Ratty – as he is known to Bill's mother – seems to have given up on 'the desire to cheat death by the vain quest for distinction' (27), which he thought would confer on him 'a kind of personal invulnerability' (28). However, to compensate for his own ignominy and failure, he starts looking for 'borrowed glory' (29) in the family archives, tracing a dubious lineage to Sir Walter Ralegh and appropriating the great Elizabethan's 'imperishable fame' (29). Bill's genealogical activity, which ostensibly serves some higher purpose than mere egotism, turns out to be no less of a self-interested affair. Just like Ralegh, Matthew is enlisted in a narcissistic project of self-glorification. Trying to recognize himself in Matthew, Bill shamelessly projects his own desires onto him, showing little respect for the singularity of his existence in the process:

> Or that is how I like to see it. That is how I wish it to have happened. I give to Matthew's life that very quality of benign design that he had already glimpsed might be lacking from the universe. I choose to believe that Matthew first met Elizabeth in his father's office in Launceston that same July. And I choose to believe that at the very first meeting Matthew would have had the overwhelming perception that here, when his thoughts had already shown him how terribly you could go adrift, was the true, sure ground of his life. That he would have felt himself falling, sinking, collapsing again, not with that fearful sense of falling into a void, but with a sense of miraculous, restoring gravitation. (103)

Regardless of the available evidence, which leaves open the possibility that his wife was cheating on him, Bill makes Matthew live the dream of perfect marital bliss, as if this putative historical precedent could somehow lend credibility to the narrator's grand claims for his own marriage and take away his nagging suspicion of his own wife's infidelity: 'I want them to have been happy' (212). In turning Matthew into a character in such a self-serving fantasy scenario, Bill can be seen to validate his existence in much the same way as he did Ruth's: 'Let Matthew be my creation' (90). Thus, Matthew too seems destined to fall victim to the imperialism of Bill's voracious self, which seeks to reduce the outside world to its own solipsistic terms.

In this connection, it is quite striking to note that, for all his talk about duty, the one thing which Bill cannot seem to understand is the call of conscience by which his nineteenth-century ancestor claims to have been guided. Indeed, *conscience* is a word which figures prominently in Matthew's writings, where it is invoked to explain the author's crisis of faith and its dramatic outcome, namely his abandonment of his wife and children. It is his conscience which causes Matthew to question his faith on the basis of his readings of Lyell and Darwin, and to face the consequences of his apostasy. He even professes 'to have had a conscience about having a conscience' (52); that is, concerned not to worry his wife unduly by revealing the full extent of his spiritual torment, he decided to keep his religious doubts to himself in the years leading up to the final showdown. Bemused by Matthew's chosen course of action – 'I don't understand him' (132) – Bill inadvertently reveals himself to be a stranger to the call of conscience: 'Who lets a Big Question upset his small, safe world?' (143). Further evidence of Bill's inability to grasp the fact that people can let their world be upset by a Big Question is provided by his reflection on the reasons for his father's suicide, which he cannot conceive to have been anything other than personal: 'And "personal" – his motives for suicide "were personal". What the hell else should they have been?' (177). Soon afterwards, however, Bill learns that his father, who appears to have been involved in the development of the atomic bomb, is likely to have killed himself at least in part because of a guilty conscience about Hiroshima. In reply to his request for clarification about the circumstances surrounding his father's death, Bill is informed by a certain Major Pilkington that Colonel Unwin 'may have harboured, since the final months of the war, a growing aversion, on conscientious grounds, to the nature of his special duties, which, conflicting intolerably with his considerable dedication and ambition, may ultimately have contributed to his suicide' (192).

In contrast with Matthew and his father, Bill cannot be suspected of any moral soul-searching. Too busy nursing his private melancholias to care about anyone else's predicament, Bill appears to be supremely unconcerned about the exigencies of the world which he inhabits. Whereas Matthew is profoundly shaken not only by the scientific discoveries of his time but also by the appalling living conditions of the English working classes,[18] and whereas Colonel Unwin is shocked by the unprecedented havoc wreaked by weapons of mass destruction to whose production he has contributed, Bill is completely unaffected by the Big Questions of his era, such as the Cold War threat of nuclear annihilation: 'When the first Aldermaston marchers set out in the late 1950s on their pilgrimage of protest, what were Ruth and I doing? We were sharing our new-found love-nest . . . Too happy, too busy being happy, to worry about the Bomb' (249). Bill's philosophy of life may be summed up as follows: 'Forget the other stuff. Stick to the love-interest' (220). His adherence to this general rule is explained with reference to the Abdication Crisis which coincided with the moment of his birth. This concurrent event, which is said to have had a lasting effect on Bill's life, imbuing it with 'a sort of fairy-tale propensity', must have been viewed by many, so Bill surmises, as 'a welcome intrusion of Romance, allowing them fondly to forget for a moment Hitler, Mussolini, and Franco. All for Love. Or, The World Well Lost' (57).[19] In fact, Bill's entire life can be conceived as one long drawn-out attempt to make the intrusion of Romance into an enduring reality, entailing permanent oblivion and indifference to the woes of the 'lost' and 'doomed' world 'out there' (256).

Bill's moral narcissism also marks his relationship with his wife, who, as we have seen, is reduced to a prop for the enactment of his self-serving fantasies. It makes itself felt, moreover, in his conception of literature as a way of imposing order and stability on the world. As is apparent from his comments on Ralegh's poem, literature, for Bill, reabsorbs overwhelming, destabilizing experiences by way of the aesthetic, understood in terms of beauty, poise and equilibrium. It domesticates terror and anxiety, which threaten to disturb the subject's complacent self-enclosure, into a reassuring experience of aesthetic pleasure. If, according to Bill, literature thus construed is a way of 'stat[ing] the obvious' (70), this is because it reduces the disquieting impact of the real: in making an unpalatable reality palatable, literature makes the world seem obvious, that is, congenial to one's preset views. An apposite analogy for this appropriative process is provided by the contrast which Bill sets up between the ichthyosaur encountered in the wild by Matthew and the domesticated version held in a museum. Whereas the former, 'the thing itself', makes Matthew's world '[fall] apart' and turns him into 'another person' (101), the latter can be observed with equanimity: museums being 'safe, orderly, artificial places', their exhibits, no matter how distressing in themselves, can be apprehended without 'feel[ing] that much at all' (100). By aesthetically defusing the threat posed to one's self-conception by a traumatic reality, literature can be seen to perform the same museumizing function for Bill.

And yet there are signs that Bill, by the end of his narrative, is not quite comfortable with the path he has chosen. Especially in regard to Matthew, he seems to have some qualms about the selfish schemes to which he has devoted the best part of his life. For one thing, he keeps questioning the exact nature of his perceived duty towards Matthew: 'Why should I hug Matthew Pearce to me and not want to let him go? What is he to me?' (49). Bill is haunted by the question 'why he should matter so much to me. And why things mattered so much to him, when . . . he might have gone on living happily ever after' (49). Just as Matthew is shaken to the root of his being by the encounter with 'things' beyond his customary frame of reference, so Bill is singularly affected by the encounter with a fellow man whom he has to admit he cannot finally make sense of. While he can easily relate to the younger Matthew, to whom he imputes an instinct for 'not looking too far about him, or looking only at what he wishes to see' (98), the later Matthew, who sacrifices his personal happiness for his conscience, totally eludes him. Indeed, critics have often remarked on the incongruence between Bill's and Matthew's respective life-stories. Kirsty Milne, for example, writes that '*Ever After* has something disjointed about it. Swift's drive to yoke past and present seems misplaced in this case: the 20th-century widower and the 19th-century truth-seeker do not complement each other quite as they should. It is as if there are two fledgling novels struggling to get out' (40). Stephen Wall agrees that 'the two men don't really seem to have as much in common as the book's design seems to imply' (26). He feels that 'the different areas of narrative interest disperse rather than concentrate attention. Although its varying strands are conscientiously knitted together . . . they don't seem significantly to cohere' (26).

Rather than being a defect on the part of the novelist, however, this lack of meaningful coherence serves to convey a crucial insight to the narrator. In Matthew, Bill's previously unchecked drive towards narcissistic self-completion runs up against an insurmountable obstacle, a radical alterity putting into question the spontaneous dogmatism of the self which insists on reducing exteriority to its own terms. As a result of the fact that Matthew overflows the frame in which Bill seeks to enclose him, the frame itself disintegrates: the possibility of possession of the other is exposed as a delusion. As Andrew Gibson points out with respect to narratorial modes that challenge the traditional subject–object model, 'An entity deemed to be identical with itself no longer holds the other at bay, at a "knowing" or *scrutinizing* distance. It rather enters into composition with, is invaded by or questioned in relation to this other' (36). Such questioning pervades Bill's narrative, which sees its narrator grapple with the need to understand the nature of his responsibility towards Matthew: 'What is Matthew to me? "What's Hecuba to him or he to Hecuba?"' (143). The latter question, on which the former is modelled, is a direct quotation from Hamlet's second soliloquy, in which the hero berates himself for not pursuing his father's revenge with as much passion as an actor has for something which, presumably, does not concern him in the least:

> Is it not monstrous that this player here,
> But in a fiction, in a dream of passion,
> Could force his soul so to his own conceit
> That from her working all his visage wann'd,
> Tears in his eyes, distraction in his aspect,
> A broken voice, and his whole function suiting,
> With forms to his conceit? And all for nothing!
> For Hecuba!
> What's Hecuba to him, or he to her,
> That he should weep for her? (2.2.545–54)

This sceptical question about why the player would establish an ethical or emotional bond with Troy's legendary grieving mother sparks off a train of thought in Hamlet's mind which results in a plot to 'catch the conscience of the King' (2.2.601) by way of having the players re-enact his father's murder in front of Claudius. Apparently, the player's supposedly gratuitous concern for Hecuba is not 'all for nothing' after all, but may serve to expose a guilty conscience. It is in precisely this way that Bill is affected by Matthew: Matthew trips up Bill's conscience, ruptures his self-complacency and makes him aware of his responsibilities towards others which he has disregarded for so long.

Hamlet's question is also taken up by Levinas in 'La substitution', the fourth chapter of *Autrement qu'être ou au-delà de l'essence* (*Otherwise than Being or Beyond Essence*). Somewhat surprisingly, given his famous denunciation of art and literature as being opposed to ethics, Levinas uses this literary quotation to formulate 'the core question of his philosophy' (Eaglestone 159):

> Pourquoi Autrui me concerne? Que m'est Hécube? Suis-je le gardien de mon frère? – ces questions n'ont de sens que si on a déjà supposé que le Moi n'a souci que de soi, n'est que souci de soi. Dans cette hypothèse, en effet, il reste incompréhensible que le hors-de-Moi absolu – Autrui – me concerne. Or, dans la 'préhistoire' du Moi posé pour soi, parle une responsabilité. Le soi est de fond en comble otage, plus anciennement que Ego, avant les principes. . . .
>
> C'est de par la condition d'otage qu'il peut y avoir dans le monde pitié, compassion, pardon et proximité. Même le peu qu'on en trouve, même le simple 'après-vous-Monsieur'. L'incondition d'otage n'est pas le cas limite de la solidarité, mais la condition de toute solidarité.

> Why does the Other concern me? What's Hecuba to me? Am I my brother's keeper? These questions only have meaning if one has already assumed that the Self has regard only for itself, is only self-regard. On this hypothesis, it does indeed remain incomprehensible that the absolute outside-of-Me – the Other – concerns me. And yet, in the 'prehistory' of the Self put by itself there speaks a responsibility. The self is entirely a hostage, older than the Ego, before principles. . . .
>
> It is thanks to the condition of being hostage that there can be pity, compassion, forgiveness and proximity in the world. Even the little that one finds, even the simple 'after you, Sir'. The uncondition of being hostage is not the limit-case of solidarity, but the condition of all solidarity. (Lévinas 186)

By 'hostage', Levinas means that we are always already responsible for other people. Their very otherness imposes this duty upon us before we are able to deny it: responsibility does not emanate from the initiative of a subject; it chooses us before we choose it. The question why the other concerns me is asked three times in the above passage, and each time it is articulated in a different discourse: that of philosophy, literature and religion respectively. According to Robert Eaglestone, Levinas inadvertently makes a case for the ethical significance of literature through this juxtaposition:

> the question 'what is Hecuba to me?' is a question asked in and of literature, asking how and why literature might have ethical meaning. It requires an answer compatible with the same discourse. If one were to follow the argu-

> ment of *Otherwise than Being* on art, where art is said and supports western ontology, the answer would be that Hecuba meant nothing to me. This is clearly very different to the answer to the other two questions. If the saying, the revelation of 'my ethical exposure to the other' could not take place in art, the question of what Hecuba is to me is meaningless and out of place. If, on the other hand, the question can have an answer that shares a trajectory with the other two questions, not only is it not out of place, but also it suggests that art can be a locus for the saying and that there might be a literary or critical equivalent of the 'reduction' to expose this saying. (159)[20]

It follows that Levinas's relegation of literature to the realm of the 'said' – that is, the linguistic equivalent of the economy of the same; a kind of denotative speech that absorbs alterity into thematization – needs to be reconsidered. Literature, according to Eaglestone, opens up an ethical space in which alterity is registered precisely as it persistently interrupts the closure of the said: 'It is in these moments when our sense of our selves and our relation to the *logos* is interrupted and put into question that the ethics of literature are at their clearest' (175). Indeed, in dissolution, identity yields to the eminently ethical condition of being hostage, of being caught in a responsibility from which there is no release.

This ethically significant abasement of the presumptuous self is evidenced, or at least intimated, in *Ever After*. Instead of confirming the narrator in his identity, Bill's encounter with Matthew puts into question his sense of self and his totalizing tendencies. Relinquishing narcissism, Bill finally abandons his exclusive claim to the notebooks which he had previously been 'so possessive' (49) about. When Katherine comes to see him in the college gardens, where he sits writing, he gives her a copy of the Pearce manuscripts and, with an uncharacteristic display of humility, silently adds: 'Who am I to raise Matthew Pearce from the dead?' (88). Bill can be seen to let go of the narcissistic fantasy that the self-completing object can be had and that the real thing can be seized hold of. Whether pursued through literature, romantic love or history, the promise of plenitudinous presence is exposed as a fallacy, and a harmful one at that. Substitutes being all that is available, the narcissistic search for completion turns out to be a futile and pernicious undertaking. This vital insight appears to be lost, however, on critics like William Pritchard, Ursula Le Guin and Mecklenburg, who object to the sense of artificiality in which the novel is steeped. Pritchard denounces *Ever After*'s 'overwrought atmosphere', calling the novel 'too sheerly fabricated for the good of its own artistic life' (484). Le Guin even feels tempted to speak, with obvious disdain, of 'a substitoot novel' (6), and Mecklenburg, finally, finds *Ever After* to be 'zu weit entfernt von "the real thing" und "the Here and Now", um das es ihm [Swift] erklärtermaßen ja auch in diesem Buch unverändert geht' ('too far removed from "the real thing" and "the Here and Now", with which he [Swift] is explicitly concerned in this book as well', 171), for the text's supposed ethical aims to be readily discernible.

However, the text's ethical import lies precisely in its critique of the notion that substitution can be circumvented and that the real thing – which is indeed the crux of the matter – can be possessed in its full presence. After all, the desire to lay hold of the real thing, which is a function of the will to a complete and self-sufficient identity, leads one to ignore one's responsibility to an irreducible alterity which resists comprehension and puts the self into question. *Pace* Mecklenburg, Wendy Wheeler is right to conclude that, in confronting the necessary elegiac task of substitution, Swift's work is concerned with 'the discovery or invention of ways of being in the world which move beyond the harsh individualism of utilitarian modernity, and towards a different way of accounting for and valuing human needs' ('Melancholic' 65). According to Wheeler, the all-important dissolution of Bill's narcissistic self-enclosure is borne out by the novel's closing sentence, which reads: 'He took his life, he took his life' (261). The ambiguity of these final words – which can be taken to signify both suicide and acceptance of life as it is – is interpreted by her as 'a sort of agreement not to close off, or possess, the meaning of the object' ('Melancholic' 75). This agreement, in turn, suggests 'a desire to tolerate anxiety and ambivalence which is part of the relinquishment of narcissistic melancholia' ('Melancholic' 75). Freed from the compulsions of its narcissistic fantasies, the self is ready to take up its place in a disenchanted world, to negotiate the constant demand of alterity, and to live ethically ever after.[21]

7 'All the Same Underneath'?

Sympathy and Ethics in Last Orders

What costs humanity very dearly is doubtless to believe that one can have done in history with a general essence of Man, on the pretext that it represents only a Hauptgespenst, *arch-ghost, but also, what comes down to the same thing –* at bottom – *to still believe, no doubt, in this capital ghost. To believe in it as do the credulous or the dogmatic. Between the two beliefs, as always, the way remains narrow.*
Jacques Derrida, *Specters of Marx*

Last Orders signalled a new departure for Graham Swift in that it was his first sustained attempt (his debut novel *The Sweet Shop Owner* excepted) to represent a social milieu markedly different from the middle-class environment which he normally portrays. Whereas in his previous books the protagonists and primary narrators had tended to be educated, highly articulate middle-class men (an archivist, a history teacher, a photojournalist, a university don), *Last Orders* presents us with the milieu of upper-lower-class Bermondsey, whose inhabitants include a retired insurance clerk, a grocer, an undertaker, a used-car salesman and a butcher.[1] Using multiple first-person narration, it tells the story of a group of old friends who are preparing to honour the last wishes of Jack Dodds, a deceased butcher, who has asked that his ashes be scattered off the end of Margate pier. In part, *Last Orders* is the story of the men's car journey from South London, through Kent, to the Kentish coast; in part, it is a collection of reminiscences by each of the characters in turn. Critics and author alike have been very dismissive of the class issue in *Last Orders*, which they see as a mere distraction from what they consider to be the novel's central preoccupation with the articulation of a humanist ethics of sympathy.[2] This failure properly to address the issue of class will serve here as a point of departure for a reflection on the ethical dimension of

Swift's novel, and of literature more widely, which will take issue with some of the more established views on the subject.

Critics have been almost unanimous in their praise for Swift's 'virtuoso facility for inhabiting other voices' (Quinn) and for the overwhelming effect of realism and authenticity resulting from this act of ventriloquism, which is said inevitably to elicit an empathic response from the reader. In its insistence on 'the essential dignity of humble people' (Banville), Swift's novel has been perceived as a warm plea for human interconnectedness and sympathy. Melissa Bennetts, for one, reads *Last Orders* as 'a poignant set of variations on John Donne's theme "No man is an island." It is a novel redolent with hope, triumph, and promise, and despite its few drawbacks, it returns the warmth of humanity to the field of literature, which all too often is heartless and barren.'[3] Jay Parini, for his part, asserts that the novel is concerned with 'inventing that most precious of things, a genuine community. As Ray says, "We're all part of each other."' (Ray is one of the characters and the main narrator of the novel.)

The critic who has made this point most forcefully, Susanne Mecklenburg, argues that one of the most noteworthy things about *Last Orders* is the effect it has on the reader, 'der im Laufe des Buches ganz ohne moralischen Zeigefinger von Werten beeindruckt wird, die als selbst heutzutage universell und zeitenüberdauernd begriffen werden' ('who, in the course of the novel, without any moralist finger-wagging by the author, is instilled with values which are conceived as universal and timeless even in this day and age', 174). Mecklenburg depicts Swift as 'einen in religiösem Denken verhafteten Moralisten' ('a religiously anchored moralist', 181), a latter-day prophet with absolute faith in the mainly humanist values – centring round the spontaneous expression of feeling, open interhuman communication and love[4] – which he is allegedly seeking to promote through literature. In all of Swift's works, with the exception of *Ever After*, she discerns one or more characters who display the author's forward-looking ethical attitude, and with each novel or story these 'bearers of hope', as they are called, increase in number, as a result of which Swift's conception of morality is rendered with maximum clarity in *Last Orders*, his then-latest novel: 'In *Last Orders* verwandeln sich alle Protagonisten . . . zu Hoffnungsträgern, die Swifts sonst unveränderte Ethik am eigenen Leibe in ihren Tälern, aber auch in ihren Höhen durchleben' ('In *Last Orders* all protagonists . . . turn into bearers of hope who live out Swift's still unchanged ethics in their personal lives, not only in their downs, but also in their ups', 180).

In the course of the narrative, Mecklenburg argues, all of the characters come to see the error of their ways, get their priorities straight again, and determine to resolve the conflicts which have marred their lives. All of them are said to manifest an 'extreme Sehnsucht nach dem Aufbruch zu neuen Ufern einerseits und dem Ankommen in zwischenmenschlicher Liebe und Harmonie andererseits' ('extreme desire to explore new territory on the one hand and to find interhuman love and harmony on the other', 174). To give but one example of this, by the close of the novel, Ray, Jack's best friend, overcomes his initial selfish impulse to hold on to the substantial amount of money which he has won for Jack, resolving instead to hand it over to Jack's stepson, Vince, who is experiencing financial hardship, and to Jack's widow, Amy, for whom it was originally intended. According to Mecklenburg, Ray's victory over his egotistical instincts is presented as a purifying and heroic act which removes all obstacles for the establishment of a harmonious love-relationship between Amy and himself and for a reconciliation with his estranged daughter, who is living on the other side of the world. Ray thus allegedly comes to embody the ideals of love, interhuman contact and hope for a better world which Mecklenburg locates at the heart of Swift's literary enterprise.

An interview conducted shortly before the publication of *Last Orders* reveals that the notion that literature may serve to inculcate sympathy in people, which underlies Mecklenburg's reading of Swift's novel, is endorsed by the author himself. Asked whether he would define himself as a moralist, Swift at first rejects this label, which he associates with 'rules and discipline', but then goes on to claim that his business as a writer is in fact 'deeply moral' since 'all morality, all real morality, rests on doing what a novelist makes a speciality of – that is, attempting to get inside the experience of others' (quoted in Bernard, 'Interview' 224). Pressed to elaborate, he adds that 'empathy is the beginning of sympathy, sympathy is the beginning of compassion, and compassion is where morality really accrues' (quoted in Bernard, 'Interview' 224).

Some years earlier, in a rare piece of criticism in *The Times*, Swift had already contended that 'the fundamental task of literature is to enable us to enter, imaginatively, experiences other than our own', something which he conceived as a difficult but necessary task: 'The hardest task in the world, against which consciousness stacks insuperable obstacles, is to understand what it is like to be someone else. But if we cannot even attempt that vital mental act, what hope do we have as the social, political and cultural animals we claim to be?' ('Throwing Off'). Class differences do not seem to give him pause in his endeavour to expand the limits of sympathy. Asked, in another interview, 'whether he'd found it hard to go from his customary middle-class voice to that of salt-of-the-earth working man Ray "Lucky" Johnson', Swift answers in the negative:

'No, and I should probably say from the outset that I don't think of class and classification. The characters are human beings – what you have to do as a writer is to get close to them. That's as true whatever the sociology might be' (quoted in Quinn).

However, the notion of an unproblematic cross-class identification underlying this reading of *Last Orders* is challenged by the text itself. Analysing moments when the text draws attention to its artificiality and to the forced nature of the construction of its characters will allow us to establish the novel's awareness of the fact that there is always a certain measure of violence involved in any sympathetic attempt to represent the other, in this case the lower-class other. Indeed, in its desire for direct contact with the other, sympathy suspends the separation between self and other, thereby effectively stripping the other of his or her otherness and reducing him or her to the same. The process of sympathetic identification with fictional characters enacts a scene of recognition in which the writer or reader discovers the 'truth' of him- or herself reflected in the character. This recognition comes at the expense of the otherness of the other, which is denied in a move towards a sympathetic fusion that grants the self a position of security in its own identity. By pretending to know the other fully and comprehensibly, the self assures itself of its own truth and originary status, and refuses the challenge which the other as other might put to such notions. While Swift's novel solicits the sort of sympathetic reading which it has received from the vast majority of critics, at the same time it ironically demystifies the basic assumption informing this reading, namely that sympathy as an ideal is a sufficient ground for the foundation of an ethical community.

In a 1988 interview, Swift comments on his preference for first-person over third-person narration:

> If you're dealing with a particular narrator, then you can't really give that one individual the authority to answer the big questions and to draw the conclusions; that must come from some kind of overview, and I don't really want that overview. Wonderful things have of course been written in the third person, but it always seems to me that in the third person one is above the characters, looking down on them in a rather sort of chess-playing fashion, and I don't want to have that elevated, omniscient role; I'd much rather feel that I am down on the ground with the characters in the sort of thick of things. (quoted in Profumo, ICA *Guardian* Conversation)

Swift asserts his desire to be on the same level with his characters (not to be 'elevated' 'above the characters', but to be 'down on the ground' with them) and renounces an authoritative gaze ('some sort of overview' allowing one to '[look] down' on the characters and to manipulate them like pawns in a game of chess). He thus distances himself from the so-called traditional novel in which the author behaves like an omniscient and omnipotent God who treats his characters like puppets. Swift, in contrast, wants to show maximum respect for his characters by trying to put himself in their place and taking on their experiences.

If the prevailing critical opinion is to be believed, he pulls this feat off brilliantly in *Last Orders*. Whereas, according to Oliver Reynolds, in Swift's previous books one is occasionally aware of the novelist 'attending to the nuts and bolts of the plot or buffing up his themes to the detriment of the independent life of his characters', in *Last Orders* 'the characters live their own lives and the novelist pays them (and his readers) the ultimate compliment: he disappears'. Using neither 'an old-fashioned omniscient narrator' nor 'the modish modern equivalent making an open-palmed avowal of unreliability', Swift resorts instead to 'the alternation of different characters' points of view'. The technical skill required by this disappearing trick is praised by Reynolds as 'a beautiful example of Swift's integrity, of the way he grants autonomy to his own creations'. Anthony Paul similarly connects 'de afwezigheid van iets als een auteursstem' ('the absence of anything like an authorial voice') in *Last Orders* with 'het ruimhartig medeleven en respect dat Swift voor zijn personages voelt' ('the large-hearted sympathy and respect which Swift feels for his characters').

However, Swift's disappearing trick is not quite so successful as these critics claim. If it is Swift's intention to promote fellow-feeling across class boundaries by absenting himself as an authorial presence from the novel, then *Last Orders* can be read as a record of resistance to the textual execution of this project. This case can be made by closely examining the alleged absence of the author in the novel. There are various textual signs which suggest that the 'absence' of the author has in fact led to a displacement of the author-function onto various other ordering and integrating principles: authorial control still haunts the novel as a ghostly presence. Three different versions of the displaced author-function will be considered here: first, the characters' constant sense of being watched and determined by an invisible external authority; second, the section of *Last Orders* narrated by the ghost of Jack's father and the injunction which it contains; and third, the web of linguistic connections established in the novel. While Swift may have intended the 'absence' of the author as a strategy enabling cross-class intimacy, a critical reading of this strategy as executed in the text recovers the class struggle as a struggle over representation.

Parenthetically, it may be noted that Swift's criticisms of the traditional novel and the problems he runs into trying to supersede it strongly recall the work of Jean-Paul Sartre. In his essay 'M. Mauriac et la liberté', Sartre lambastes François Mauriac's novel *La fin de la nuit* – and the complete literary output of most other French writers with it – for violating the freedom of its characters, which, in its preface, the author had vowed to safeguard: 'Ainsi *La Fin de la Nuit*, qui, dans la pensée de M. Mauriac, doit être le roman d'une liberté, nous apparaît surtout comme l'histoire d'une servitude' ('Thus *La fin de la nuit*, which in Mr Mauriac's mind must be a novel of freedom, appears to us above all as a history of servitude', 45). Indeed, Sartre detects a powerful sense of determinism in the novel, which he traces back to Mauriac's use of an omniscient, God-like narrator:

> Il a écrit un jour que le romancier était pour ses créatures comme Dieu pour les siennes, et toutes les bizarreries de sa technique s'expliquent par ce qu'il prend le point de vue de Dieu sur ses personnages: Dieu voit le dedans et le dehors, le fond des âmes et les corps, tout l'univers à la fois. De la même façon. M. Mauriac a l'omniscience pour tout ce qui touche à son petit monde; ce qu'il dit sur ses personnages est parole d'Évangile, il les explique, les classe, les condamne sans appel.
>
> He wrote one day that the novelist is to his creatures what God is to his, and all the oddities of his technique can be explained by the fact that he adopts the point of view of God *vis-à-vis* his characters: God sees the inside and the outside, the depth of souls and bodies, the entire universe at the same time. Likewise. Mr Mauriac is omniscient with regard to everything that concerns his little world; what he says about his characters is the Gospel, he explains them, classifies them, condemns them without appeal. (41–42)

Mauriac's arrogation of divine authority is seen by Sartre to be at odds with the essence of the novelistic genre, which he constructs as the absence of an omniscient perspective: 'dans un vrai roman, pas plus que dans le monde d'Einstein, il n'y a de place pour un observateur privilégié' ('in a real novel, just as in Einstein's world, there is no room for a privileged spectator', 52). Hence, by raising himself above his characters, Mauriac has committed a highly unliterary act: 'M. Mauriac s'est préféré. Il a choisi la toute-connaissance et la toute-puissance divines. Mais un roman est écrit par un homme pour des hommes' ('Mr Mauriac has preferred himself. He has chosen divine omniscience and omnipotence. But a novel is written by a human being for human beings', 52). Interestingly, a similar comment is made by Swift in the interview with Catherine Bernard, in which he declares that he does not want to be a 'defensive' writer, that is, a writer who hides, behind 'cleverness' and 'formal virtuosity', 'even that part the writer has in common with other people and which above all should be exposed': 'I don't want to say "Look at me being clever!" instead of "Look at me as someone like you!"

So I hope I am not a defensive writer' (quoted in Bernard, 'Interview' 229). According to Swift, for a writer to show his or her undefensiveness or vulnerability involves 'dispens[ing] with your self, whatever that actually means in terms of a specific novel. It might mean your ability to enter as one hundred percent as this is possible another character: I mean your ability to see the world through somebody else's eyes and not constantly insist on yourself' (quoted in Bernard, 'Interview' 229).

Just as Swift set out to realize this ambition in *Last Orders*, so Sartre attempted to put his philosophical and literary-theoretical ideas into practice in a series of novels comprising *La nausée*, *Le mur* and the proposed tetralogy of *Les chemins de la liberté*, whose fourth volume he left unfinished. In his doctoral dissertation *Métaphysique et technique dans l'oeuvre romanesque de Sartre*, Gerald Prince analyses the techniques used in Sartre's novels. He concludes that his close examination of narration, structure, time, space and characterization in these texts has revealed a perfect match between Sartre's literary techniques and his philosophical ideas:

> La technique de Jean-Paul Sartre est une d'un bout à l'autre de son oeuvre romanesque. Elle s'adapte à la présentation d'êtres libres dans un monde en devenir, et renvoie ainsi à la métaphysique de l'auteur.
>
> Jean-Paul Sartre's technique is consistent from one end of his novelistic oeuvre to the other. It adapts itself to the presentation of free beings in a world of becoming, and in so doing refers back to the author's metaphysics. (137)

In his chapter on narration, for example, Prince claims that Sartre consistently does away with omniscience in favour of focalization through the characters themselves in a successful attempt to respect their freedom.

However, when we look at the actual textual analyses carried out by Prince which lead him to this conclusion, a far more complicated picture begins to emerge. In each chapter, Prince sets out to show how Sartre's views on a particular topic as expressed in his essayistic writings have been realized in his own novels. While he finds that, generally speaking, Sartre has managed convincingly to translate his theories into textual practice, he repeatedly stumbles upon textual elements that seem to contradict this conclusion. Time and again, comments such as the following interrupt the smooth flow of the argument:

> De notre rapide analyse, il ressort que Sartre a fait un emploi toujours judicieux et souvent brillant de la vision 'avec un personnage', vision qui, d'après lui, doit constituer le point de départ de toute narration. Il convient toutefois de mentionner que, la pratique étant plus difficile que la théorie, il arrive que

> Sartre fasse une infraction à son propre code et que l'observateur hypothétique apparaisse.
>
> From our quick analysis, it appears that Sartre has always judiciously and often brilliantly used the vision 'with a character', vision which, in his opinion, must constitute the point of departure of every narration. It should be mentioned, however, that, given the fact that what is simple in theory is often difficult in practice, it happens that Sartre infringes his own code and that the hypothetical spectator emerges. (35)

Though several instances of this return of the omniscient narrator are recorded, in an equally typical gesture, this phenomenon is dismissed as irrelevant to the overall significance of Sartre's novels:

> Il ne faudrait pas croire que ces quelques infractions au code nuisent à la totalité du roman où elles se produisent. Les apparitions du romancier omniscient sont par trop fugitives pour ébranler vraiment l'identification du lecteur avec le porteur de vision.
>
> One should not think that these few infringements of the code do any harm to the totality of the novel in which they occur. The appearances of the omniscient novelist are far too fleeting actually to thwart the reader's identification with the bearer of vision. (35)

No sooner is the ghost of authorial determination called up than it is conjured away again by some such neutralizing comment.[5]

Another (though not unrelated) way in which Prince tries to accommodate potentially disruptive elements is by providing aesthetic grounds for their presence in the text. Indeed, the passage just quoted continues as follows: 'Parfois, les "fautes" de Sartre lui permettent de très beaux effets d'ironie et d'objectivation . . .' ('Sometimes, Sartre's "mistakes" allow him to achieve very beautiful effects of irony and of objectification . . .', 35). To give another example, earlier on in his study, Prince contends that the world evoked in Sartre's novels is in perfect harmony with the author's philosophical beliefs, that is, marked by contingency and free of determinism. Any remaining traces of necessity are said to be 'merely' aesthetic:

> l'univers du roman sartrien est un univers de contingences, un univers dans lequel l'existence précède l'essence. On peut évidemment partir d'un tel univers pour arriver à une solution unique mettant fin à toutes les questions, un peu comme dans certains romans de Mauriac où le héros est délivré de l'incertitude par la grâce. Mais ce n'est pas le cas dans les romans de Sartre: si rien au début n'y est acquis, tout y est encore possible à la fin; et la seule nécessité qui se dégage des événements présentés est une nécessité interne, une nécessité esthétique.

> the universe of the Sartrean novel is a universe of contingencies, a universe in which existence precedes essence. One can of course start from such a universe to arrive at a unique solution putting an end to all questions, somewhat like in certain novels by Mauriac in which the hero is delivered from uncertainty by grace. But that is not the case in Sartre's novels: if at the beginning nothing is fixed there, everything is still possible at the end; and the sole necessity which can be extracted from the events presented is an internal necessity, an aesthetic necessity. (14)

By reducing the aesthetic or the specifically literary to an essentially superfluous category, or at best an element of marginal interest which does not affect the overall meaning of a text in any significant way, Prince disregards what is most proper to these texts as literature. In his eagerness to do away with any jarring notes (either by simply minimizing their impact or by reducing them to ornamental frills) so as to be able to provide a conclusive interpretation of Sartre's novels – which would no doubt be much to the author's liking – Prince in fact throws away the baby with the bathwater. What Prince's study reveals, in the end, is that literature does not lend itself willingly to the sort of cleansing project promoted by Sartre.

Nor is it quite at ease with the aims which Swift has set himself. To return now to our analysis of the displaced author-function in *Last Orders*: the first important feature of the novel to be noticed in this regard is the sense, shared by all the characters, of an all-powerful and all-seeing but invisible authority looking down on them from above and determining the course of their lives – exactly the sort of authority, in fact, which Swift abdicates in the above quotation. Throughout the novel, instances of seeing without being seen are recorded by the various narrators, and often an element of sadistic pleasure or depreciation on the part of the seer is in evidence, as is the case in the following descriptive passage about Canterbury Cathedral: 'It's a big building, long and tall, but it's like it hasn't stretched up yet to its full height, it's still growing. It makes the cathedral at Rochester look like any old church and it makes you feel sort of cheap and titchy. Like it's looking down at you, saying, I'm Canterbury Cathedral, who the hell are you?' (194). Another example is to be found in the passage recounting the aftermath of the fight between Lenny and Vince, which represents the absolute lowpoint of the journey to Margate. In this case, the subject of the gaze is the urn containing Jack's ashes, which is referred to as a 'badge of authority' (108) by one of the characters:

> It's like the reason we're out here in this field is because the jar's gone and made a bolt for it and we've had to run after it and catch it. It's all the jar's fault. Except we know it aint, it's the other way round. It's all our fault. Fighting over a man's ashes. And the jar's sitting there in Vince's hands like

> it's shaking its head at us all, like Jack's inside there peeping out and sighing over us . . . It's as though we're all wondering whether we should press on with this exercise or quit now on the grounds of not being up to it. Two detours, one fight, a piss-up and a near-wetting. (180)

The characters are pictured as objects of the gaze, not as subjects of perception. Jack, Ray and Lenny all had dreams beyond the barriers of class or parental expectation, but failed to realize their ambitions. This failure is attributed to a general lack of vision: 'if we could all see and choose . . . If we could choose. And you'd be riding Derby winners and Lenny'd be middleweight champ. And I'd be doctor Kildare. . . . If we could all see. . . . If we could all see and choose' (283–84). Instead, the characters feel as if they have been fixed in their places by a superior power. This becomes apparent, for example, in Lenny's account of Jack's homecoming after demobilization from the Second World War: 'when it came to being back in Civvy Street, he didn't know nothing better, like most of us, than to stick like glue to what he knew, like there was an order sent down from High Command that he couldn't ever be nothing else but a butcher. That shop was his bleeding billet, it's a fact' (132). Similarly, having disgraced himself by picking a fight with Vince over Jack's ashes, Lenny himself reflects: 'It's the way you're made. It's hard fighting against your own nature when it's in your nature to fight' (176). The alleged intimate authenticity of Swift's portrayal of his characters thus appears to come at a price: authorial manipulation is no sooner abandoned than it re-emerges as an extra-authorial authority naturalizing the author as its ghost-writer. Indeed, the author's decision to withdraw from the text does not so much set the characters free as turn them into truly ideologized subjects, while the author himself is reduced to a passive mediator of ideology.

Another displaced return of the 'absent' author can be witnessed in the one section of the novel narrated by the deceased, or rather the deceased's father. Fatherhood is, after all, an ancient trope for authorship: the author as the progenitor of the fiction he creates. As has already been mentioned, the narration in *Last Orders* is delegated among several characters, who each in turn recount events in the narrative present – mainly to do with the day's outing to Margate – or recall moments in the past when their lives intersected. By using this device, Swift manages to impress the reader with a sense of direct, immediate contact with the characters. As Michel Morel puts it,

> le lecteur se trouve comme projeté devant la réalité de fiction qui se donnerait dans une sorte d'immédiateté clinique: plus de récit, seulement de l'agir, de

> l'agir qui se prétend brut et non interprété. Le résultat de cette première procédure paraît alors être une sorte de voyeurisme exacerbé.
>
> the reader finds himself thrown before the fictional reality which seems to offer itself up with a kind of clinical immediacy: no more text, only action, action which pretends to be raw and uninterpreted. The result of this first procedure appears to be a kind of exacerbated voyeurism. ('Le récit orphelin' 83)

However, as Morel goes on to point out, the editing work that has gone into the production of the novel is not totally concealed, as a result of which the reality effect is undermined. This is especially the case when, in the section under discussion, the reader is confronted with the voice of the ghost of Jack's father. Clearly, this does not fit into the naturalizing framework that has been set up, and hence raises serious questions about the status of the narrative:

> Inversement, un malaise demeure, en particulier lorsque, de fragment à fragment, s'impose la brisure d'un montage qui n'est plus naturalisé par l'imitation des faits de visualisation réels comme dans le film. Ici, au contraire, et surtout quand le fragment n'entre pas directement dans la diégèse latente – comme lorsque le lecteur tombe de façon totalement inattendue sur la voix du père de Jack au milieu de fragments narratifs se rapportant tous de près ou de loin à la chronique immédiate du voyage – l'arbitraire de ce montage est mis en évidence. Soudain le lecteur, qui l'instant d'avant pouvait pouvait [sic] se laisser aller à 'croire' tout son saoul, se pose avec effroi la question de l'origine, de l'intention, et de la possibilité même de la construction narrative.
>
> Inversely, a malaise remains, particularly when, from fragment to fragment, the break imposes itself of a montage which is no longer naturalized by the imitation of the real facts of visualization like in a film. Here, in contrast, and especially when the fragment does not enter directly into the latent diegesis – as when the reader totally unexpectedly stumbles upon the voice of Jack's father in the midst of narrative fragments related from near or from far to the immediate chronicle of the journey – the arbitrariness of this montage is in evidence. Suddenly the reader, who only a moment ago could rest assured that he could 'believe' whatever he pleased, anxiously asks himself questions about the origin, the purpose and the very possibility of the narrative construction. ('Le récit orphelin' 83)

The inclusion of a dead man's impossible speech act into the text constitutes a radical departure from the verisimilitude which the novel had seemed so anxious to preserve. The novel thus calls the reader's attention to the fact that what he or she is witnessing is not raw reality but mediated reality, a representation carefully crafted by the author. The characters whom the reader is so eager to identify with are not authentic lower-class people, but the author's imaginings of what such people might be and act like.[6]

Looking at what is actually said in the section under analysis, we find that, in classic *Hamlet* style, the ghost of Jack's father – who, like Jack, was a butcher – lays an injunction on his son. Once again, we have a character being restrained and kept in check by an extra-authorial authority filling the place left empty by the 'absence' of the author. Jack is enjoined by his father to avoid wastage, and warned that failure to do so would 'cost [him]': 'Whole art of butchery's in avoiding wastage. . . . You got to keep a constant eye on wastage, constant' (285). This passage lays down the guiding principle of a self-sufficient private economy, which needs no input from the outside to keep going. Beyond the economic realm, however, it can be understood metaphorically as sanctioning an integrated, closed community with no use for outsiders.

Before developing this point in some more detail, I will bring in a third locus of the displacement of the author-function, namely the level of language. The fragmentation resulting from the absence of an authorial narrator is counteracted by the establishment of intertextual networks within and between the narratives of the various characters, linking them together in a seemingly organic whole. As Morel writes, 'Les échos, correspondances, reprises, et prolongements qui unissent les personnages à leur insu, établissent une sorte de transversalité qui lie tout à tout' ('The echoes, correspondences, repetitions and continuations which unite the characters without their knowing establish a kind of network connecting everyting with everything', 76). Elaborate metaphorical chains and clusters are set up in the course of the novel, accumulating ever more meanings, connotations and associations through being taken up and further developed by different narrators. The integrative function traditionally associated with an authorial narrator is thus transferred to language. As John Marsden points out, 'the world of *Last Orders* is tenuously held together by a shared language' ('After Modernism' 190). Nodal points in this shared language are words which function as badges of lower-class identity, such as 'meat', 'motors' and 'beer'. This common language, shot through as it is with clichés, received expressions and folk wisdom, constitutes a 'collective *doxa*'[7] which restricts the possibilities of thought for the characters to the point of complete determination:

> La pensée ordinaire n'est pas à concevoir en dehors de ces reprises du discours collectif, la langue parlant l'individu autant que ce dernier la langue. C'est

du moins l'impression qui s'impose à la lecture de *Last Orders* qui fraie en ce domaine un chemin nouveau dans l'oeuvre de Graham Swift.

Ordinary thought cannot be conceived outside these repetitions of the collective discourse, language speaking the individual as much as the latter speaking language. Such is at least the impression one gets from reading *Last Orders*, which in this regard breaks new ground in the work of Graham Swift. (Morel, 'Le récit orphelin' 78)

A good example of a passage in which the speaker derives the legitimacy of her speech from the collective discourse of the group is to be found in Amy's evocation of the moment of the conception of her mentally disturbed daughter June:

Things come together in this world to make things happen, that's all you can say. They come together.

But you'll never know, June, that that was how you came together. Or not quite together, not quite. Like Jack won't ever know it was the sight of that gypsy. The things that do and don't get told. You'll never know, you never had the chance, about warm August nights and colanders. You'll never know, you'll never need to and maybe you're better off as you are, how one thing leads to another. If you lead a man to water, he'll drink. And there you are with your bellyful, trying to tell yourself that you're no more to blame than he is, but feeling anyhow, you can't help it, that you've got him on a rope, saying, I do, I will, in a borrowed suit, with the rest of them looking on like butter wouldn't melt. Hitched, they call it. (238)

The fact that individual voices can only express themselves by mimicking the language of the group leaves the reader with a 'puissant sentiment d'inévitabilité et d'irréversibilité' ('strong feeling of inevitability and irreversibility'): 'Le recours à l'adage légitime la parole individuelle tout en montrant qu'il n'y a rien à inventer en termes de conduite de vie' ('Recourse to sayings legitimates individual speech, revealing in the process that there is nothing left to invent in terms of conduct of life'; Morel, 'Le récit orphelin' 79).[8] In this way, a closely integrated textual world is constructed on the level of language itself.

In fact, it can be argued that, read uncritically, all the displacement strategies that we have considered contribute to the creation of an integrated community. Not only does the language spoken by the characters bind them together as members of a tight, consensual community, but the voice of the ghost of Jack's father addressing his son and the various instances of an authoritative gaze surveilling the characters also constitute them as belonging to a particular class and consolidate the supposed integrity of their class identity. The vision of a unified community thus projected is naturalized by the delegation of authorial authority to a locus of impersonal power. The result of this operation is that the vision apparently cannot be attributed to anyone in particular but seems to coincide with the way things are, with the natural order of things. As we have seen, the great majority of critics are enchanted by this vision. They commend the author for the alleged authenticity of the portrayal of his characters, who are seen to make up a 'genuine community' (Parini) which they promote as a model worthy of imitation in the socio-political world of today.

Some critics, however, have expressed reservations about the vision which the novel puts forward. Adrian Poole, in his review of *Last Orders* for the *Guardian*, registers a certain claustrophobic quality in the novel – which, however, does not disturb him in the least; in fact, he considers it as a credit. Yet, Poole's description of the community which *Last Orders* depicts as a 'tribal milieu', and of the reader's response to the novel as a 'sense of a tightening embrace, with no easy exits or escape-routes' leads one to suspect that something more sinister may be involved ('Hurry Up'). This troubling element, so obvious that it is easily overlooked, is the almost complete absence of outsiders, of people of a different race, culture, sexuality or class, in a text purporting to be an authentic representation of contemporary London life. This point has been made very emphatically by Ruth Pavey:

> Swift is justly celebrated for his ability to create an encompassing feeling, a sense of his novels existing in their own special air. His Bermondsey is certainly a hermetic place; a tight community of small tradesmen, some struggling, but with scarcely a hint of what they are struggling against. The supermarket that is driving Jack out of business gets a mention. But it's almost inconceivable that such a group of oldies would not have attributed blame to another factor: the incursion of outsiders.
>
> During the 1980s, the ex-docking community of Bermondsey, with its back against the wall, showed a marked distaste for incomers of the wrong colour, the wrong class, or the wrong sexual orientation. That none of this shows up in *Last Orders* is a choice that Swift is perfectly entitled to make in a novel. But it is fair to say that, without it, this view of Bermondsey is a very partial one in both senses of the word. Yes, Swift has again created a bewitching impression of place, but it is an imaginary one. If it ever existed, this old, tough, wise-cracking, united, fathers-and-sons community has long been more a Bermondsey of the heart than of actual experience.

Another critic who is deeply troubled by 'the selectivity of the novel's vision' is Kate Flint, who takes Swift to task for incorporating the reader into 'a certain form of nostalgia for a fading way of life':

> Swift's South London, or at least the South London of his characters, seems self-protectingly free of all possible multiculturalism. 'Abroad' is primarily where they fought in the war; their recollections of this, and their visit to the Navy's memorial obelisk at Chatham help, as in culture more widely, to generate and consolidate memories that provide powerful nationalistic integrative forces even in peacetime. (40–41)

Blatantly excluded from the celebrated vision of an integrated community which *Last Orders* projects is the multicultural other. Apparently, sympathy, which binds the lower-class community of Bermondsey together in a sense of a shared identity, does not extend to him or her. Indeed, what the multicultural other, through his or her invisibility, makes visible are the limits of sympathy as an ethical ideal. Sympathy is driven by a yearning for unity, which can harden into a denial of what escapes that unity. Confronted with unassimilable otherness, the sympathetic imagination turns into an aggressive rejection and exclusion of the other.

The few (missed) encounters with the multicultural other which the novel does record are cases in point. A clear example of rejection of alterity is provided by the section of the text in which Vince reveals the virulent hostility which he feels towards Mr Hussein, the wealthy Arab whose custom he desperately needs to ward off bankruptcy. Not only does Vince greatly resent this dependence, but he is especially distressed by the fact that his daughter Kath, whom he had dangled as bait before Mr Hussein when the latter first showed up, has gone to live with Mr Hussein and might soon be dumped by him. The caricatured portrayal of Mr Hussein as a deceitful, lecherous, calculating interloper taps into a long-standing orientalist tradition which, as Menno Spiering argues, gained new ground in Britain in the 1970s, a decade of oil embargoes, dramatic Palestinian attacks on Western and Israeli targets, and high-profile Arab purchases of 'Western' properties:

> it is undeniable that to some extent a sense of menace and fear strongly coloured British sentiments towards 'the Arabs' when, in the course of the postwar period, Middle Eastern petro-dollars began to flow into the failing British economy. Consequently, an image caught on of blackmailing oil sheikhs who were out to buy up, and probably Islamize, all that was dear and native. (37)

Mr Hussein is seen to thwart the establishment of a self-contained communal identity enacted in the novel, which is why Vince silently threatens him with physical violence and wishes him back to 'that stinking, flyblown heat-trap he'd be at home in' (165).

No less of a challenge to the vision of a consensual, homogeneous community evoked by the novel is posed by 'Romany Jim', the gypsy whom Amy felt sexually attracted to as a young woman picking hops in Kent. This encounter – which never actually takes place – is equally overlaid with a tradition of projection, prejudice, longing and suspicion. Amy portrays Romany Jim – to whom she never speaks a word – as an exoticized figure of mystery, adventure and romance, and attributes to him a carefree existence transcending social and institutional constraints:

> The gypsies came with their caravans and horses, needing the hopping just like us, but made their camp separately, over by the wood, eyeing us like we were the ones who'd pitched up where we shouldn't, and I used to envy them because they were a stage further at being outlaws than us and because they were professionals at it and we were just amateurs and when we were back again in Bermondsey, all bricked up and boxed in, they'd still be wandering the woods and lanes. (235)

As Katie Trumpener points out, this utopian invocation of a gypsy life seemingly beyond the reach of the authorities echoes a traditional Western gypsy fantasy:

> Decades after the persecution of the Gypsies under the Third Reich, Gypsy life remains in the popular imagination as a carefree, defiant, disruptive alternative to a Western culture at once humanized by its history and restrained by the discipline of its own civilization. Moving through civil society, the Gypsies apparently remain beyond reach of everything that constitutes Western identity . . . outside of historical record and historical time, outside of Western law, the Western nation state, and Western economic orders, outside of writing and discursivity itself. . . . Despite their self-containment, paradoxically, the Gypsies' wildness is highly contagious, as their arrival in a new place initiates and figures a crisis for Enlightenment definitions of civilization and nationalist definitions of culture. (860)

Trumpener also calls attention, however, to 'the historical reality of Gypsy life, a story over the last millennium of persecution, expulsion, and prison sentences as much as carefree wandering' (853). This sort of treatment is indicative of the other of 'the two halves of the post-Enlightenment ideology of Gypsy alterity – feared as deviance, idealized as autonomy' (854). Beyond any social integration, the gypsy has often been perceived as posing a dangerous threat to the existing social order, to be contained by all possible means, including violence. The tension between the two dimensions constitutive of the mythology of gypsy life – 'exemplary autonomy, feared alterity' (857) – can also be detected in Amy's narrative. After all, Amy, though fascinated by the spirit of freedom and transgression which the gypsies seem to embody, resists the temptation to become romantically involved with Romany Jim, resolving instead to stay on more familiar ground. Repressing her desire for the gypsy, she begins a relationship with a boy from her own neighbourhood: 'And I didn't, though I might've. I played with Jack Dodds instead, Jack Dodds from the other end of Bermondsey' (235), even though she did not 'fancy him, not that much, not so much' (237). Catching sight of Romany Jim during a walk with Jack, Amy suddenly agrees to make love to Jack, as if to seal their union in the face of an uncanny power that might disrupt the bond between them and unsettle the secure sense of identity which it provides. Amy and Jack's union, which is at the centre of the web of relationships woven in the novel, is thus founded on an originary act of exclusion of a discomforting alterity.[9] In the integrated community projected by *Last Orders*, there is simply no place for otherness.

Whether implicitly or explicitly, both Pavey and Flint associate Swift's novel with a dubious reactionary politics sanctioning such exclusions.[10] Yet, *Last Orders* can be read precisely as a critique of any sympathy-based and hence exclusionary ideology. A critical reading of the authorial displacement passages that we have considered shows that, instead of naturalizing a vision of a fully integrated community, *Last Orders* exposes such naturalization as the ultimate ruse of ideology. Where a naive or innocent reading sees a sympathetically portrayed, authentic organic community, a critical reading reveals ruthless determination, violence and exclusion trying to hide themselves from view.[11] This procedure is in evidence in the displacement of the author-function onto an impersonal external gaze which locks the characters up in an essential class identity. It can also be seen at work in the delegation of authorial authority to the voice of the ghost of Jack's father. The unifying and integrating impulse behind the injunction which it lays on Jack is undermined by the very spectrality of the speaker, whose incongruity shocks the reader into an awareness of the artificiality and arbitrariness of a narrative construction passing itself off as an authentic representation of the lower-class other. The integration achieved by the linguistic connections binding the characters together, for its part, is subverted on the one hand by the arbitrary and excessive nature of these connections, but also by the literary associations evoked by the final destination of *Last Orders*' journey towards interconnectedness: the town of Margate. After all, Margate owes its – admittedly marginal – claim to symbolic status to T. S. Eliot's *The Waste Land*, which has the following lines: 'On Margate Sands. / I can connect / Nothing with nothing' (300–2).[12]

On this reading, Swift's novel does not promote but rather critiques the noble gospel of sympathy, revealing the unholy assumptions upon which it is founded. As a reproductive, mimetic faculty, the sympathetic imagination tends to subsume alterity within traditional categories of knowledge, reducing it to an already familiar truth. Otherness is refused a chance to interrupt or disturb the discursive patterns within which the self is at home. This counter-reading of *Last Orders* exposes sympathy as a self-serving strategy with little or no concern for the singularity of the other: 'sympathy acts as an incentive to egoism, rather than as its corrective' (During 77). What it is concerned with is shoring up the self and confirming it in its identity in an essentially self-fulfilling gesture. The self is closed off for and unaffected by the otherness of the other and the claim which he or she makes upon the self. The ability of alterity to alter the self and render it responsible for the other is flatly denied in sympathy's unchecked drive for self-realization.

If this second reading can be seen to deliver a fundamental critique of the notion of sympathy as the ultimate ethical ideal, this is not to suggest that the first, sympathetic reading is thereby invalidated. Both readings, though they cancel each other out, are simultaneously valid. The ethical moment in *Last Orders* (and perhaps in literature at large) is to be situated precisely in the experience of undecidability between these two mutually exclusive readings. What this means is that the novel continues to advocate sympathy as an ideal worth pursuing, but at the same time urges the reader to adopt a critical attitude towards this ideal by exposing its limits. Despite the violence that is shown to be one of its constitutive features, sympathy is not simply done away with. After all, the violence inherent in sympathy, which it is of paramount importance to be constantly aware of, can never be completely avoided in an encounter with the other. As Derrida observes in 'Violence and Metaphysics', his seminal first essay on Levinas, the irreducible alterity of the other, which puts the other beyond the reach of my cognitive powers, can only be respected as an intentional phenomenon, that is, as a representation. The fact that the other has to appear to me, that respect for the other cannot circumvent intentionality, is the necessary violence – called 'transcendental violence' by Derrida – from which no encounter with the other can free itself:

> To return, as to the only possible point of departure, to the intentional phenomenon in which the other appears as other, and lends itself to language, to *every possible language*, is perhaps to give oneself over to violence, or to make oneself its accomplice at least, and to *acquiesce* – in the critical sense – to the violence of the fact; but in question, then, is an irreducible zone of factuality, an original, transcendental violence, previous to every ethical choice, even supposed by ethical nonviolence. (125)

The suggestion, then, is not that there is an alternative for sympathy which would not commit violence against the other, but that an unproblematic valorization of sympathy ignores this violence and in so doing disavows responsibility for the other who calls upon the self to open itself up to alterity and change.

Critics like Mecklenburg, who in their search for moral content and values in literature repress the element of undecidability complicating any such endeavour, miss precisely what it is that literature *as literature* can contribute to our political and ethical thinking and acting. Mecklenburg's reading practice relies on a notion of expression in which the verbal component of the text is a means of access, but also a barrier to a stable, autonomous core of meaning. The aim of literary reading as she sees it is to overcome the materiality of the sign so as to reach a prediscursive essence of meaning. In the case of *Last Orders*, this essence of meaning, the ultimate truth of the novel, would be the moral value system which the author is seen to promote – a value system, moreover, which, as Mecklenburg readily admits, has nothing peculiarly literary about it:

> Dabei geht die hier als Moralismus bezeichnete Werthaltung nie über ein festes ethisches Konzept mit den überwiegend in christlichem Denken wurzelnden Größen der Nächstenliebe, der Rücksichtnahme und Menschenwürde hinaus.
>
> The disposition which is labelled moralism here never goes beyond a fixed ethical concept consisting of the values – mostly rooted in Christian thought – of charity, considerateness and human dignity. (3)

This solid moral core comes dressed in a fancy postmodern narrative outfit: 'Diese bisher unübertroffen deutliche literarische Darstellung seiner [Swifts] Lehre' ('This literary representation of his [Swift's] doctrine which is of an as yet unsurpassed clarity') is achieved 'durch eine beeindruckend souveräne Handhabung der postmodernen Technik einer summierenden Nebeneinanderstellung von Versatzstücken' ('through an impressively superior application of the postmodern technique of an enumerative juxtaposition of set pieces', 180). Thanks to the supposedly postmodern narrative strategies which the novel employs,[13] the author's 'ganz geradlinige moralische Botschaft' ('very straight moral message') is 'behutsam genug eingebettet . . . um von einem großen Publikum als bildend angenommen zu werden' ('embedded cautiously enough . . . to be accepted as instructive by a large reading public', 183). In Mecklenburg's view, then, the formal properties of the text are nothing but ornaments, means to get a message across which leave the message itself intact. They are mere pieces of trickery needed to sugarcoat a moralist pill which a sceptical and incredulous contemporary reading public would otherwise find hard to swallow.

By establishing such a rigid separation between form and content of a literary text and locating the ethical dimension of literature solely in the latter aspect, Mecklenburg not only misconstrues the specific nature of the literary work as a textual object, but also disregards the distinctive contribution which it can make to ethical thought. As Derek Attridge points out,

> *form is always already meaning*; as an act of signification a literary work is meaning in motion, and there is no moment, not even a theoretical one, at which it is possible to isolate a purely formal property – at least not without turning the literary text into something else. . . . The effect of this mobilization of meaning by formal properties is that it can never close down on a represented world, can never become solely the reflection of or pointer to a set of existents outside language. The question of meaning and reference is kept alive as a question; referentiality is enacted – but not simply endorsed – in every literary act. . . . Literary form therefore produces (in conjunction, of course, with the assumptions and conventions of the literary institution which govern reading) a suspension of linguistic instrumentality, which we can think of as *blocking* the aesthetic urge to separate form from content and to assign content alone to the domain of ethics and politics. ('Literary Form' 247–48)

In our reading of *Last Orders*, the opposition between form and content is suspended and replaced by a friction between the understanding of the text as a gospel preaching universal sympathy and the reading of the textual constellation as a crisis of foundational meaning. The instances of textual resistance to the assignment of determinate meaning that we have analysed highlight the permanent, irresolvable tension between these two strictly incompatible interpretations. The intimation of a critical ethics which the literary work offers through the undecidability at its very heart may well be the most valuable contribution that literature as literature can make to ethical theory and practice.[14]

8 Adieu

Stepping into The Light of Day

It doesn't look like journey's end . . .
Graham Swift, *Last Orders*

The pursuit of redemption, a major focus of attention in *Last Orders*, is again placed under critical scrutiny in *The Light of Day*, which was published seven years after its Booker Prize-winning predecessor. The novel's plot revolves around a murder case with which the narrator, George Webb, a disgraced policeman turned private detective, has become intimately involved. Over the course of a November day in 1997, George ruminates on the events of exactly two years earlier, when his client Sarah Nash, a well-off language teacher and translator, knifed her husband just after he had permanently sent his refugee girlfriend back to Croatia. On this second anniversary day, George leaves his Wimbledon office to lay flowers on the dead man's grave and to visit Sarah in prison, as he has been doing on a twice-monthly basis for more than eighteen months. He is in love with Sarah and patiently waits for her release in eight or nine years at the earliest. As he goes along, George also reflects on elements from his personal history, including the secrets his father harboured in an otherwise happy marriage, the case that got him thrown off the police force, his wife Rachel's decision to leave him, and his late-blossoming relationship with his lesbian daughter Helen, whose friendship brings him comfort after Rachel's departure.

The Light of Day has been widely recognized by reviewers as an unusually optimistic book. Sven Birkerts, for example, calls the novel 'unexpectedly redemptive'; Soumya Bhattacharya writes that the book is 'touched with the hope of redemption'; and O'Mahony characterizes *The Light of Day* as 'perhaps the least "drizzly" of Swift's works' on account of 'its perversely contented central character'. The author himself agrees with this assessment:

> dit is zeker mijn meest positieve roman. Dit is een optimistisch boek, ondanks de duistere elementen erin. Het heet 'Het volle daglicht': het is vol licht en warmte, vol betekenis en zin. Het is verbazend rijk aan goede dingen, hoewel dat op het eerste gezicht niet meteen duidelijk is.
>
> this is certainly my most positive novel. This is an optimistic book, despite its dark elements. It is called 'The Light of Day': it is full of light and warmth, full of meaning and sense. It is surprisingly rich in good things, though this is not immediately apparent at first sight. (quoted in D'hoker)

Though the narrator, as Swift points out, has plenty of cause for sorrow – a failed career and a failed marriage – he ends up being offered 'een grote nieuwe kans in het leven' ('a great new chance in life', quoted in D'hoker).[1]

The great crises in George's life occur in 1989, eight years prior to the time of the narrative, when he is dismissed from the police force for intimidating a witness. Out of an honest desire to see justice done in a case involving a racist stabbing, he had made a witness sign a statement that was true but that the witness had not actually uttered. This professional crisis is compounded by a personal crisis when his wife abandons him soon afterwards. His daughter – with whom he has always had a troubled relationship – having already left the parental home, George is left alone with his misery and grief, a situation thoroughly familiar from Swift's earlier novels, most of which feature a protagonist who is confronted with identical or very similar problems. One is reminded, in particular, of *The Sweet Shop Owner*'s Willy Chapman, whose wife Irene has died and who is alienated from his daughter Dorothy; *Waterland*'s Tom Crick, who loses both his job and his wife Mary (to madness); *Out of this World*'s Harry Beech, whose wife was killed in a plane crash and who is estranged from his daughter Sophie; and *Last Orders*' Ray Johnson, who has lost touch with his daughter Susie and been abandoned by his wife Carol.

However, while these characters either do not progress beyond the crisis situation in which they find themselves (Willy Chapman) or at best face an uncertain future (Tom Crick, Harry Beech and Ray Johnson), the protagonist of *The Light of Day* is quite unequivocally put back on track. He is saved from despair by Helen, who unexpectedly comes to his rescue after Rachel has left him and effectively puts his life, which has 'fall[en] apart' (123), 'back together again' (127). The daughter's return home, an event that is without precedent in Swift's earlier works – where it is either vainly hoped for (most poignantly in *The Sweet Shop Owner*) or surrounded with question marks (as in *Out of this World*) – is definitively realized in *The Light of Day*. Thanks to Helen, George recovers his balance, successfully embarks on a new career as a private detective, and later even enters into a love relationship with another woman. The novel closes with a lyrical evocation of the eagerly awaited moment when Sarah will finally be released from prison and step out into 'the clear light of day' (244) to be (re)united with her lover. If *Last Orders* ended on a redemptive note, with Ray looking forward to a possible resumption of his relationship with Amy and a possible reunion with Susie in Australia, this note swells and grows in power in *The Light of Day*, a novel buoyant with hope and anticipation that strongly suggests that past losses can be effectively redressed.

No less significant than the sheer fact of this unabashed hopefulness are the explicitly religious terms that the novel uses to frame its redemptive vision. The subject of religion enters the text through the character of Rachel, who, unlike George, received a deeply religious education. At the age of seventeen, however, Rachel rebelled against her family ('one of those strict peculiar lots'), saying '[s]he didn't believe in it any more' (90), ran away from home and was disowned by her parents. George's memories of his ex-wife trigger off a train of thought that sums up the role of religion in *The Light of Day*:

> I wasn't brought up like Rachel. But you pick things up about God. You pick up his scent, like the smell of church. I remember some passage being read out somewhere, that there's no sinner so bad, so worthless, that God will ever let them slip through the net of his love. . . .
>
> And whether he's up there or not, and whether he's got a net, I don't know. But I think that's how it ought to be just among us. There ought to be at least one other person who won't let us slip through their net. No matter what we do, no matter what we've done. It's not a question of right or wrong. It's not a question of justice. . . .
>
> No matter what we do, no matter how bad. If we're found to be corrupt. Even if we do the worst thing ever, even if we do what we never thought it was in us to do, and kill another person. Even if that other person was once the person for whom we were holding out a net. (136)

George is referring, of course, to himself ('found to be corrupt') and to Sarah ('kill another person'). In both cases, what 'ought to be', is. Indeed, both characters are caught in their fall by a loving person: George by Helen and Sarah by George.

The imagery of falling – which is repeatedly invoked in both *The Sweet Shop Owner* and *Ever After* to describe the impact of trauma – dominates George's memories of his expulsion from the police force and his abandonment by Rachel: 'And I still remember the feeling – until then I hadn't had it, even if the ground had been opening up – of falling. Just falling, in the way you fall when you know there's nothing to land on, endlessly falling, the way people must fall in outer space. . . . Falling. Off the edge, off the cliff of life' (49). George's professional and marital fall from grace result from his having become the victim of a double scapegoating exercise. About his dismissal, he is told – or imagines being told – by his superiors: 'Look at it this way, they said – or I could read it in their eyes – you're being sacrificed for the good of the Force, a bigger thing than you, for the sake of its reputation, for the sake of keeping its grubby face clean. . . . Not just a cop who'd overstepped the mark. I'd sinned' (134). Distrusted by the public and suspected of corruption, the police force seizes on George's transgression as an opportunity to polish its sullied image. By heaping all the blame for police malfunctioning and corruption upon him – even though, as George points out, he has never misused police powers to further his own ends or to put an innocent man behind bars – and eliminating the black sheep from the fold, the police force hopes to restore its tarnished reputation in the eyes of the public. The Manichaean logic informing this purifying ritual also underlies Rachel's decision to leave her husband. Rachel regards George's disgraceful dismissal as clinching evidence that he is solely responsible for whatever has gone wrong in their marriage: 'But now she had the chance to make it all my fault. The taint *was* me. Not Mr Right but Mr Wrong. And not my wife, my judge' (135). What Rachel's self-righteousness and judgementalism shows, according to George, is that, for all her declared apostasy, she 'never really gave up her god' – or, at least, 'the big stern daddy part of him' (135).

The seeds of the narrator's rejection of this Old Testament version of God – God as a vengeful and authoritarian ruler – in favour of the New Testament notion of God as unconditional love were already sown in *The Sweet Shop Owner*, where the same conflict is suggested – albeit much more implicitly – through the etymology of Dorothy's name and through intertextual references to *The Merchant of Venice*. However, whereas in Swift's first novel the gift of love (understood as disinterested, non-reciprocal generosity) remains all but unthinkable, his latest novel is filled with uninhibited displays of love. To begin with, there is Helen, who, unlike her mother, 'didn't clear out. Right or wrong' (94) when George had fallen into disgrace. Putting their differences behind her, she comes home to visit George and to take his side. In marked contrast also with *The Sweet Shop Owner*'s Dorothy, Helen readily forgives her father for his mistakes – or so George surmises: 'She never forgave Rachel but I think she forgave me, pretty quick, even when I was still putting my hand up to say it was all my fault, I shouldn't have done it, blame me' (48). Staying within the religious sphere, George describes his daughter's surprise return – '[t]he strangest thing' (49) – as nothing short of a miracle: 'The mercy, the miracle that, after everything, she and I should be friends' (94). In his relationship with Sarah, George seeks to repeat this miracle by casting himself in the role of the saviour. While society has written Sarah off completely, George starts paying her regular visits in prison and 'forgive[s] her': 'Thousands wouldn't, but I have. A thousand times' (153). Clearly, he sees himself as the saviour holding out his net for her: 'But I'll be there, I'll be there, sweetheart, to catch you' (244). Religious overtones are also apparent in George's concluding vision of Sarah stepping out of the darkness of her imprisonment into the clear light of day.[2] Indeed, this passage draws on the Christian symbolism of the divine light dispelling the darkness, which is used throughout the New Testament to indicate God's salvation of His people.[3]

The insistent presence of these intimations of the intercession of God's grace calls attention to an aspect of Swift's work that has only recently begun to be fully appreciated: its engagement with religion. Though Swift's religious interest only comes into full view with *The Light of Day*, it is present also in *Last Orders*, and traces of it can be detected in *The Sweet Shop Owner*, *Waterland* and *Ever After*. While several critics mention Swift's use of religious motifs in passing, Pamela Cooper and Lynn Wells make a case for religion to be considered as an essential ingredient of his work. In *Graham Swift's* Last Orders*: A Reader's Guide*, Cooper argues that Swift's work as a whole is marked by a tension between rationality and faith, between 'human systems of knowledge' on the one hand and 'faith, revelation, and miracle' on the other:

> The importance of the miraculous to Swift's vision of modern life can hardly be overstated. His fiction is preoccupied with the limits of rationality – the failures of human knowledge – and the mysterious possibilities of intuition and spiritual insight. Rationality and faith debate with each other as alternate ways of knowing in Swift's work. (36)

In *Last Orders*, a novel with a 'subtly religious tone' (40), faith is suggested, according to Cooper, by the weird luck of Ray 'Lucky' Johnson, which makes him 'a figure not just of hope, but of the possibility of miracles. With his extraordinary good fortune as a punter, Ray embodies the chance that resurrection and new beginnings might manifest themselves on this side of the grave, not only for the dead but for the living' (47). Cooper reads Ray's luck as an expression in the novel of 'God's mysterious grace, which is, for Swift, as deeply rooted in the world and human life as suffering, loss, bewilderment, and death' (47).[4] In her reading, the possibility of renewal is also implied by the image of 'winged ash' with which the novel ends: 'This imagery, bringing together flight and ash, expresses the fervent hope for regeneration and new life – for beginnings discovered within endings – which pervades *Last Orders*' (46).[5]

According to Cooper, this is just one of many such images in Swift's fiction: 'Images of resurrection abound in his work' (13). Though she claims to discern a spiritual undercurrent in the author's oeuvre in its entirety, the only other novel that she briefly considers in this light is *Waterland.* Her reading of this text turns on the messianic overtones surrounding the death of Tom Crick's brother:

> In *Waterland,* Swift's strong sense of the limitations of knowledge and ratiocination meets a deep longing for spiritual comfort which emerges clearly in his characters. The suicide of Tom's brother Dick at the end of the novel is portrayed as a mythical, semi-religious return to the primeval waters of both birth and death. His departure effaces the historical determinism that has both tempted and frustrated Tom. Dick's death is sacrificial; it suggests the possibility of salvation and the incipience, in the everyday world, of miracle. (12)[6]

Waterland is interpreted along the same lines by Wells, who offers an in-depth analysis of the novel in the third chapter of *Allegories of Telling: Self-Referential Narrative in Contemporary British Fiction.* Like Cooper, Wells attaches great importance to *Waterland*'s '"miraculous" subtext' (81), which, in her reading, serves as a constant corrective to what she takes to be the narrator's 'narrowly pessimistic attitude towards history as a whole' (86). Regarding history as 'circular rather than truly progressive' (85), Tom allegedly 'rejects the possibility of any forward movement whatsoever' (85–86). However, this negative view of history, which 'essentially rules out historical redemption' (86), is said to be subtly counteracted by a messianic pattern of death and rebirth which manifests itself at various points in the text. The conflict between these two perspectives recalls Cooper's tension between rationality and faith: 'Tom's tale thus accommodates two seemingly contradictory existential points of view: on the one hand, death is final, but on the other, the dead *may* come back to life in ways that defy ordinary comprehension' (Wells 86).

Wells finds evidence for this claim in the symbolically interrelated stories of Mary and Dick, which 'conjoin to form a pattern based on Christian typology, a tropological cycle of universal salvation in which children are born, sacrificed, and then promised to return' (84–85). She argues that Mary, who is associated in the text with the Virgin (after whom she was named), becomes the mother-figure to a sacrificial child (the aborted foetus) which reappears (as the baby stolen from the supermarket) to redeem the world. In Wells's reading, Mary's taking of the baby fulfils 'the possibility of merciful rebirth latent in the narration of her youth' (91). Even though the stolen infant is immediately taken away from her, its brief presence as Mary's 'child' allegedly 'establishes the figurative possibility of new life where only incontrovertible loss had existed before' (91). Hence, the incident may be understood as 'a step in the regenerative sequence, leaving open the potential for future opportunities at which the past could be recovered' (91). Wells goes on to contend – in a similar vein to Cooper – that this messianic pattern of sacrifice and projected salvation is also at work in the story of Dick, Tom's mentally disabled brother who is predestined by his (grand)father Ernest Atkinson to save the world. While conceding that Dick's retardation makes him 'patently unfit for activities of Messianic consequence' (93), Wells yet maintains that we should look beyond the 'manifest failure' of Ernest's redemptive plans – which result not in salvation but in pointless suffering and death – to 'the potentially positive implications of Dick's sorry demise' (94). After all, Dick's supposedly fatal plunge into the water, which recalls his earlier dive in the contest for the right to look at Mary's genitals, need not be fatal at all: given Dick's extraordinary swimming skills, it is conceivable that he has not drowned and will simply reappear much later. Like the aborted foetus which returns as the baby Mary abducted, Dick could eventually emerge from the river in a 'miraculous rebirth': 'If realized, this promise of new life . . . would mean that he has fulfilled his role as saviour through sacrifice, bringing about the absolution of humanity's sins and its rescue from eternal death' (94). Thus, 'the divine plan leading to ultimate salvation' (95) remains operative. According to Wells, the 'latent hopefulness' apparent in the stories of Mary and Dick carries over into Tom's own narration, which likewise conceals a 'positive potential' (95). Indeed, Tom is said to redeem the death of his child by symbolically adopting his pupil Price as his son. Moreover, the fact that his retirement coincides with Easter further inscribes Tom in the messianic sequence of death and rebirth (95).

The ringing endorsement of the miraculous that Cooper and Wells attribute to Swift's fiction needs to be qualified. While it is true that religious imagery and symbolism pervades Swift's work, Cooper and Wells fail to take sufficient account of the bitter irony implicit in many of these references. Especially in *Waterland*, a novel that is preoccupied with the apocalyptic consequences of ideological obfuscation, there is a strong sense that religion is part of the problem rather than the solution. Indeed, what history teaches us, according to the narrator, is precisely 'to avoid illusion and make-believe, to lay aside dreams, moonshine, cure-alls, wonder-workings, pie-in-the-sky – to be realistic' (W 108). History teaches us 'no short-cuts to Salvation, no recipe for a New World, only the dogged and patient art of making do' (W 108). This realistic art of making do, which the narrator puts forward as a way of breaking out of the destructive cycle in which human history appears to be caught up,[7] requires a sustained commitment to the questioning of grand narratives pushing towards finality.

Only by cultivating our innate curiosity, by engaging in inquiry and keeping open the question Why, can we hope to avoid the bloodbaths, holocausts and Armageddons periodically demanded – or so it seems – by history (W 141). As Damon Marcel Decoste points out in the course of an incisive reading of *Waterland* similar in some respects to the one presented here, the kind of inquiry that the novel advocates is radically anti-eschatological in nature: questioning persists in the face of any proffered answer; the question Why 'remains restless, never satisfied or content but constantly able to trouble and dissect narratives making claims to definitiveness' (395):

> What inquiry subverts is the claim to know, once and for all, where we are headed, the claim, built out of narrative, of certainty as to our proper destination. What it undermines, then, is the drive to apocalypse that so typifies, and so often bloodies, history as narrative. As the text's principle of endlessness, inquiry is anti-eschatology and thus the best hope for a future, for proving wrong Price's dire, if not novel, diagnosis of imminent ending. (396)

Seen from this perspective, the story of the narrator's brother appears not as a triumphant reaffirmation or reinstatement of the Christian narrative of redemption, but as evidence that such narratives, for all their promises of salvation, may well take us down the royal road to hell. As Tom tells us, Dick is '[n]ot a saviour of the world. A potato-head. Not a hope for the future. A numbskull with the dull, vacant stare of a fish . . .' (W 242). Dick even becomes 'an instrument of terror' (Decoste 393), murdering Freddie Parr and thereby setting off a fatal chain of events that results in Mary's abortion, his own suicide, Mary's attempted baby-theft and institutionalization, and Tom's dismissal as history teacher. Rather than being a figure of hope and possibility, then, Dick 'embod[ies] totalizing narrative's apocalyptic conclusion in the void of the real' (Decoste 391). Or, as Del Ivan Janik puts it, Dick serves not to provide the text with a saviour, but to reveal how 'the world cannot afford saviors' ('History' 87). It is worth mentioning, in this connection, that Swift himself is extremely reluctant to recognize a religious dimension to his work. Asked, in a 2002 interview, whether he is 'een religieus auteur' ('a religious author', D'hoker), Swift replies: 'Ik ben zelf niet religieus en het was dus zeker niet mijn intentie om deze roman [*Het volle daglicht*] een religieuze boodschap mee te geven' ('I am not religious myself, so it was certainly not my intention to put a religious message into this novel [*The Light of Day*]', quoted in D'hoker).

Though it rejects the metanarrative substance of institutionalized religion, Swift's work is profoundly marked by an allegiance to a certain religious spirit. While it disbelieves in short-cuts to salvation, it does not give up on the *idea* of salvation. Its principled repudiation of narrative closure proceeds from a desire to salvage the future. By ceaselessly subverting the false certainties of utopian programmes that claim to deliver the one and only end for history to pursue, it works towards an extension, rather than end, to history. This commitment to an indeterminate and indeterminable future aligns Swift's fiction with Derrida's recent writings on religion, which attempt a reconceptualization of the idea of messianic hope. In texts such as 'Faith and Knowledge', *The Gift of Death* and *Specters of Marx*, the notion of *messianicity* (or *the messianic*) figures as an important building block in Derrida's reflection on ethics and politics. While Derrida clearly draws his inspiration from religion, the discursive field in which this notion originates, he insists that messianicity as he understands the term stands apart from religious messianism insofar as the latter awaits a specific event or particular revelation: '*The messianic dimension does not depend upon any messianism, it follows no determinate revelation, it belongs properly to no Abrahamic religion* . . .' ('Faith' 17). This messianicity without messianism – 'without content and without identifiable messiah' (*Specters* 28) – '*would be the opening to the future or to the coming of the other as the advent of justice, but without horizon of expectation and without prophetic prefiguration*' ('Faith' 17).

In *Philosophy and the Turn to Religion*, Hent de Vries argues that the rearticulation or redeployment of religion in Derrida's work revolves around the – originally Levinasian – figure of the *adieu*, which evokes at once a gesturing towards God and a leave-taking from God. According to de Vries, Derrida recasts our understanding of the ethical and the political by exposing these concepts to that of the religious tradition, a procedure that involves a double movement: 'The procedure of this turn to religion forces these concepts into a relation of simultaneous proximity with and distance from a phenomenon that they are thus said to both generalize (or universalize) *and* to trivialize, if only by stripping it of its ontological and axiological privilege and substance' (24). This doubleness is captured by the ambiguous phrase *à Dieu* or *adieu*, which designates both 'a movement toward God, toward the word or the name of God' and 'a no less dramatic farewell to almost all the canonical, dogmatic, or onto-theological interpretations of this very same "God"' (24). The same balancing act can be witnessed in Swift's writing, which stubbornly tries to hold on to a sense of religiousness without lapsing back into a reactionary pre-modernism. Religion as the final answer is challenged by religion as a process of incessant questioning opening up the possibility of the future.

Cooper and Wells might or might not agree with this characterization of Swift's engagement with religion: what renders their work problematic is precisely its lack of clarity on the particular conception of religion that they ascribe to Swift's fiction. They seem to waver between an undetermined messianicity and a more substantial messianism, without ever clearly distinguishing between the two. Both Cooper and Wells discuss the religiously inspired desire for renewal apparent in Swift's work in fairly general terms (for example, 'open-ended hope for regeneration' (Wells 85)), but ultimately this desire seems to remain firmly grounded in a robust metaphysical theology: it is subservient to 'the divine plan leading to ultimate salvation' (Wells 95) or to 'a possible counter-narrative of eternity' (Cooper 55). Cooper and Wells's inattention to the critical dimension of Swift's work, which they either ignore or make light of, can be adduced as further proof of a residual allegiance to a pre-deconstructive, undifferentiated notion of religion.

Rather than warranting a simple return to metaphysics, Swift's work elaborates a post-metaphysical religiousness conducive to the production of a new Enlightenment, one that would be enlightened about the limits of the old one. While this is at its clearest in *Waterland*, the distinction between the two conceptions of religion is less pronounced in *Last Orders* and *The Light of Day*, novels in which the element of critique recedes into the background. In *Last Orders*, however, the religious allusions are for the most part so veiled that the messianic hope that they inject into the text is too elusive and indeterminate to be reduced to the Christian metanarrative of salvation. *The Light of Day*, by contrast, wears its religious inspiration on its sleeve, and, moreover, appears to give free rein to the drive towards redemption. While this may seem to suggest that Swift has finally seen the light (of day), in the sense of having capitulated to the seductions of metaphysics, anyone tempted to jump to this conclusion would do well to give some thought to the peculiarity of the narrative set-up.

One of the more conspicuous features of *The Light of Day* is its explicit thematization of the attempt to write in a literary, quintessentially Swiftian manner. Though not exactly a *Künstlerroman*, *The Light of Day* does recount the story of a man who is learning to write. Before he met Sarah, George, a self-confessed 'man of action' (205), 'never used to think much about words – hold them up to the light' (131). Words 'weren't [his] thing' (90); they were 'just something floating in the air' (72). However, all this has changed since Sarah asked him to bring 'homework' on each visit, written accounts of daily life that allow her imagination to roam outside the prison walls: 'Write it down for me, George, what it's like out there. Bring the world in here' (188). George sets himself to this task – a continuation of his earlier surveillance mission involving Bob and Kristina – with great devotion: 'I try to lift Sarah from where she is, I try to be her eyes' (53). During each visit, George hands in his report, but also collects Sarah's corrections of his previous piece of work, a routine that earns him the nickname of 'The Schoolboy' or 'The Teacher's Pet' among the prison wardens (115). Sarah is indeed George's teacher. What she expects from him is not just any old piece of writing, but properly literary prose: 'Not like a police report, you understand?' (188). She is, after all, a college lecturer and translator: 'words were her thing' (160). To make sure she gets what she wants, Sarah teaches George, who was '[n]ot much good on paper, till now' (132), to become a writer: 'The truth is she's taught me to say things, to say all this, to put things down in words. It's been an education, really' (8). Through her, George learns to 'take words seriously' (168), to pay attention to linguistic subtleties and nuances, and comes to recognize that the language of which he used to be so negligent has real substance: 'She taught me to look at words. . . . Strange English words. Their shape, their trace, their scent' (188).

The Light of Day bears ample testimony to the fact that George has taken Sarah's lessons to heart. As narrator, he is acutely aware of the hidden depths of meaning contained in simple words and phrases – words and phrases, moreover, which he literally tastes on his tongue. About his dismissal from the police force, for instance, he says: 'The word that got used was "corrupt". A strangely physical word. A black taste welling in your throat, a thickness on your tongue, as if you have a disease. As if they've rooted out some foul stuff inside you and it's you, it's yours now, you're stuck with it for good' (36). Every word tells in *The Light of Day*. George's narrative brims with clichés and casual phrases – such as 'crossing a line', 'watching over someone', 'something came over me', 'you never know what's in store', 'all her own fault', 'how do we choose?' – which acquire a definite weight as they are repeated and reworked across tens of pages, gathering ever more shades of meaning. These echoes and antiphonies, which function as hinges between ostensibly unrelated situations, characters and relationships, give the novel a distinctly poetic quality.

The narrator – 'a sleuth with Wittgenstein's penchant for semantics', as Russell Celyn-Jones puts it – forces the reader to reflect on the meaning of the most innocuous of words by introducing an element of ambiguity. A good example of this procedure can be found in the passage in which George expresses his regret that he cannot be with Sarah to '[hold] her hand' (155) – that is, to comfort her – while she relives the moment of the murder exactly two years after the event. The phrase 'holding her hand' crops up again a couple of sentences later, as George reflects that he was not with her either two years earlier: 'But I can't be with her when it happens. Holding her hand' (155). Its meaning, however, has changed. The words no longer denote a gesture of consolation, but rather refer to George's wish that he could have restrained Sarah – or, perhaps, the exact opposite: that he could have assisted her in planting the kitchen knife in her husband's heart. Another expression that is rendered ambiguous is 'to keep mum', which, in the following passage, can mean both 'to stay silent' (about the adultery of George's father) and 'not to lose mother': 'Before we reached the tee I'd already made my decision: that I'd have to pretend – so Mum would never know. Keep mum. That was my mission now' (99).[8] At one point, George declares his adherence to the following 'sound principle': 'make a little do for a lot' (66). This principle, which he later describes as 'the only rule' (104), not only defines his general attitude towards life, but also applies to the compositional method of the narrative itself: out of the limited resources of colloquial speech, George spins a peculiarly rich and meaningful texture.

This intense interest in mining the poetic potential of everyday language is, of course, a familiar feature of Swift's work. As D. J. Taylor points out in his review of *The Light of Day* for the *Times Literary Supplement*:

> From a very early stage in his career – the tendency could be glimpsed as far back as *The Sweet Shop Owner* – Swift's work has been characterized by its attempts to improvise a fugitive lyricism out of the patterns of 'ordinary' speech, to weave together a skein of clichés and fragments of late twentieth-century demotic in such a way as to make them resonate. (21)

In interviews, the author himself has identified these resonances as a key characteristic of his poetics:

> Ik werk vrij veel met herhalingen om lezers te dwingen over de betekenis van bepaalde courante zinnen en uitdrukkingen na te denken. In dat opzicht komt mijn proza dicht bij poëzie. En ben ik misschien een hoeder van de taal.
>
> I often work with repetitions to force the reader to reflect on the meaning of certain common phrases and expressions. In this respect, my prose is close to poetry, and maybe I am a guardian of the language. (quoted in Hemmerechts 5)

Swift does not shrink from holding up his own position as the norm for literary writing *tout court*: 'The real art is not to come up with extraordinary clever words but to make ordinary simple words do extraordinary things. To use the language that we all use and to make amazing things occur' (quoted in O'Mahony). What is remarkable about *The Light of Day*, then, is not so much its poetic aspect *per se* as the self-consciousness with which it is approached and the sheer emphasis that is placed upon it.

Through the rather unlikely ploy of a poorly educated ex-cop who is being taught to write like Graham Swift by a literary-sensitive convicted murderess, *The Light of Day* manages at once to affirm its status as a typical

Graham Swift novel and to make the novel's plot appear faintly ridiculous. What the reader is served up in *The Light of Day*, so it seems, is a performance of Swift's writing practice rather than the thing itself. The peculiar *Bildung* story played out in the novel introduces an element of structural irony that appears to put the entire textual constellation under erasure – including, that is, the redemptive vision projected by the narrator. Ultimately, then, Swift's most straightforwardly redemptive novel, like its predecessors, is marked by a measure of confusion: doubt is cast – no matter how obliquely – on the direction in which the text seems to be moving.

In fact, *The Light of Day* not only makes a show of its compliance with Swift's trademark stylistics, but also overtly rehearses numerous other aspects of the author's previous works. In terms of characters, narrative technique, setting and themes, for example, *The Light of Day* closely resembles Swift's earlier novels. The brooding elderly narrator-protagonist recalling past misfortunes, the use of multiple time frames, the conspicuously ordinary suburban setting, and the preoccupation with loss, broken connections and the hope of redemption unmistakably mark *The Light of Day* out as a Graham Swift novel. Moreover, *The Light of Day* literally incorporates its predecessors in the sense that specific motifs and plot elements of Swift's other novels recur in this text. The bright and sunny day on which the action takes place, the rigorously circumscribed setting, and the protagonist who runs a business on the main shopping street, who used to be a poor student and who does 'homework' for the woman he loves, strongly recall *The Sweet Shop Owner*. George's decision to keep his father's adultery secret from his mother and not to disclose the full details of Bob's drive home from Heathrow either to the police or to Sarah echoes Prentis's determination to suppress 'needless painful knowledge' in *Shuttlecock*. Some of the concerns prevalent in *Out of this World* enter the novel through George's reminiscences about his father, who was a High Street photographer. George and Sarah's fascination with the Empress Eugénie, whose biography Sarah is translating, mirrors Bill Unwin's obsession with his nineteenth-century ancestor Matthew Pearce in *Ever After*. The one-day car journey and the stops along the way, finally, recall the commemorative ritual enacted in *Last Orders*. Taylor is right, therefore, to call *The Light of Day* 'a kind of boiled-down version' (21) of the author's earlier books. In his assessment, the novel is 'like nearly everything else that Swift has written, only more so' (21).

It is this 'more so' element that gives the novel a subversive aspect: *The Light of Day* is overdoing the act of being all that a Graham Swift novel can be to the point of becoming a parody of itself. Its excessive indulgence in repetition can be seen to undermine the text's effort finally to bring to full fruition the redemptive promise never quite realized in the author's previous works: the (literal) apotheosis of Swift's literary endeavour is undercut by a subtle comic irony belying the novel's apparent high seriousness.

Interestingly, the notion of farcical repetition enters the text through the character of Napoleon III. Louis Bonaparte's presence in the novel is explained by the fact that he ended up living as an exile in George's native Chislehurst following the collapse of the Second Empire. Moreover, his wife Eugénie, who outlived him by nearly fifty years, becomes an inspirational figure for Sarah: she embodies the possibility of starting a new life after the death of one's husband. According to George, the story of the Empress is what has 'kept us afloat. A raft: the three of us. Her, me and the Empress Eugenie. Not forgetting Eugenie's old Emperor husband. The four of us' (139). Though the Emperor is mostly treated by George as something of an afterthought, there is indeed a very good reason why his presence in the text should not be forgotten. His name has become indissolubly linked, in the cultural imagination, with Karl Marx's *The Eighteenth Brumaire of Louis Bonaparte*, a historical study that ironically and unflatteringly compares Louis Bonaparte's *coup d'état* of 2 December 1851 with that of his uncle, the great Napoleon Bonaparte, which took place on 9 November 1799 – the 18th Brumaire, according to the French Revolutionary calendar. One of the themes that run through the heart of Marx's book is the way in which political events in France in 1848–51 repeatedly parodied the events of the revolutionary decade from 1789. In fact, Marx famously announces this theme in the first sentence of the first chapter: 'Hegel remarks somewhere that all great world-historic facts and personages appear, so to speak, twice. He forgot to add: the first time as tragedy, the second time as farce.'

Marx sets up an opposition between authentic revolution, seen as the gateway to salvation, and inauthentic or farcical repetition (as exemplified by the grotesque masquerade of the 1848 revolution and its aftermath), which makes a mockery of the redemptive pretensions of the real revolution. The status of the first French Revolution is that of an authentic prefiguration of the great proletarian revolution on which Marx pins his hope. The reason why he speaks of tragedy in this connection is that, given the historical conditions in which it unfolded, the revolution of 1789, though a noble effort, could not but fail to bring about ultimate salvation – conceived, by Marx, as the establishment of an ideal, stateless, propertyless and classless society with no oppression or exploitation and general abundance and freedom. The aim of *The Eighteenth Brumaire*, however, is to raise the prospect of a revolution that will do just that.

According to Marx, this fully authentic revolution will turn away from the past rather than imitate old models, as did all previous revolutions:

> The social revolution of the nineteenth century cannot take its poetry from the past but only from the future. It cannot begin with itself before it has stripped away all superstition about the past. The former revolutions required recollections of past world history in order to smother their own content. The revolution of the nineteenth century must let the dead bury their dead in order to arrive at its own content. There the phrase went beyond the content – here the content goes beyond the phrase.

With content surpassing phrase, Marx's revolution has no need, apparently, for the poetry of the past. However, Marx does not succeed in establishing a neat division between a fully liberated revolutionary language (in which content wins out over phrase) and the enchanted discourse of former revolutions (which is haunted by ghostly allusions and echoes of the past). In a thoughtful analysis of the role of allusions and 'scare quotes' in *The Eighteenth Brumaire*, Martin Harries points out that this passage, which posits the radical dumping of recollections of past world history, paradoxically borrows a key phrase – 'let the dead bury the dead' – from one of the most influential world-historical myths of the West, namely the New Testament (Matt. 8.22):

> It is at the moment that Marx stresses the need for the revolution to come to its own content that he borrows from the New Testament: may one say that 'here the content goes beyond the phrase'? It seems that it is not so much that content goes beyond the phrase but that the phrase recalls the difficulty of even imagining any place stripped of superstition and the poetry of the past. (87)[9]

Ironically, Marx's commandment to forget the past turns out to rely on borrowed language, which 'provides an indirect inducement to excavate a historical source for that language' (Harries 88). The prospect of a true revolution which would bring final redemption is gently mocked, so it seems, by this phraseological reminder of the apparent inevitability of repetition.

The Light of Day, in its yearning for metaphysical consolation, is equally haunted by the spectre of Louis Bonaparte. The ironies of repetition expose the true revolution which the novel enacts – the redemption of a tragic history through religion – as a premature attempt to close the book on the past. The revolutionary language of *The Light of Day* manifestly fails to abolish its origins, bust its ghosts and let the dead bury their dead. The purported victory of content over phrase is belied by the insistent return of the phrase, signalling the tenacity of a history that will not be suppressed and throwing into confusion the redemptive programme embraced by the narrative. Thus, twenty years on from *Waterland*, Swift still persists in his critique of short-cuts to salvation: the particular short-cut that we are served up in *The Light of Day* ends up becoming a question unto itself, deconstructing the very notion of salvation.

Conclusion

A Pathless Path

Caminante, no hay camino,
se hace camino al andar.
Antonio Machado[1]

In an interview with Lidia Vianu, Swift defines his 'basic position as a novelist' as a renunciation of authority. He deals in questions rather than in answers, and above all wants his works to be true to 'the confusion of life':

> I may be an author but I don't think of myself as any kind of 'authority'. I don't have answers to things – though I have plenty of questions (*Waterland* is full of them) and plenty of doubts. There are a good many people who profess to have answers, to know things, to tell us what is so or what we should do, but this is not what novels are for or why I'm a novelist. An American writer once said we all lead lives of quiet desperation. Perhaps, but I think we all lead lives of quiet confusion. The novel is a form in which you can be true to the confusion of life. I'm not different from my readers and I certainly don't want to have power over them. I'm confused too, I'm in the same boat. (quoted in Vianu)

This is only part of the story, however. Though his desire is to 'share' his confusion with the reader, Swift does not want to do so 'directly' or 'unconstructively'; his ultimate aim is not simply to convey confusion but to 'redeem' it through a kind of story-telling that manages to avoid the pitfall of denial:

> I think of the relationship of writer and reader as one of sharing. I want to share confusion – but not directly and, I hope, not unconstructively. So I offer the confusion of my characters who are nonetheless trying to steer some kind of sustainable and hopeful course through their confusion. That course is story-telling. I believe good story-telling can, without denying or misrepresenting the actual confusion of life, redeem it. (quoted in Vianu)

Wary of easy explanations and simple solutions, Swift does not promote confusion for its own sake, but presents it as a state of perplexity and incomprehension that one has to pass through in order to come up with better answers.

This tension between questions and answers, between the insistence on confusion and the wish to redeem it, represents an eminently ethical predicament. As Geoffrey Galt Harpham points out, ethical discourse is characterized by 'a struggle between questions and answers'; it is '[a] relentless drive toward the necessary answer, conjoined with the equally relentless generation of yet more preliminary questions' (*Shadows* x). The straightforward answers of morality need the confusing questions of ethics, because decisions achieved without a passage through undecidability represent 'mere blindness and brutality' (*Shadows* 30). Ethics, for its part, is no less dependent on morality, since without decision, ethics would be 'condemned to dithering' (*Shadows* 30). Swift's writing practice thus appears to be suspended between the principled irresolution of ethics (articulating confusion) and the precise prescriptions of morality (guiding the confused). In trauma-theoretical terms, this translates roughly as the tension between the disorientation and unsettlement of acting-out, which may lead to paralysis, and the concrete rebuilding efforts of working-through, a process that continually risks lapsing into denial.

These concepts, which recur with different emphases and in various configurations throughout the novels, are at the centre of Swift's literary endeavour. His work can be seen to proceed from a prevalent concern with denial in *The Sweet Shop Owner* and *Shuttlecock*, through an intense preoccupation with acting-out in the middle-period novels, to a liberating insistence on working-through in *Last Orders* and *The Light of Day*. However, to suggest that the story of Swift's literary evolution is one of smooth, linear progress would be somewhat misleading. The trajectory of his novelistic career can also be described as a pendulum movement in which more 'questioning' texts, which are generally regarded as gloomy or despairing, and more 'affirmative' ones, which typically work towards some kind of happy ending, alternate and balance each other.[2] The former category would comprise *The Sweet Shop Owner*, *Waterland* and *Ever After*, novels that are characterized by a profound scepticism about redemptive discourses; the latter *Shuttlecock*, *Out of this World*, *Last Orders* and *The Light of Day*, novels that push towards resolution. According to this description of the internal dynamic of Swift's work, each successive novel (with the exception of *The Light of Day*) either challenges the unwarrantedly optimistic conclusions of its immediate predecessor or, alternatively, imagines a viable way out of the impasse diagnosed in the previous novel. While this circular narrative of Swift's literary evolution provides a welcome counterweight or supplement to the linear narrative, it should be stressed that the distinction between the two types of texts is far from absolute. Indeed, one of the main objectives of the readings undertaken in the preceding chapters has been to show that the 'questioning' novels affirm regenerative possibilities and that the 'affirmative' ones raise questions about the redemptive programme they are made to enact. The aporetic tension between questions and answers is ultimately at the heart of each individual novel.

This frequent recourse to structural undecidability or aporia – a term which literally means 'blocked path' or 'non-passage' – does not make Swift's literary enterprise an apology for resignation, fatalism or apathy. As Derrida points out in *The Other Heading*, the experience of aporia, of not knowing what path to follow or of coming to a point where no path can be found, is a necessary precondition for responsible action:

> I will even venture to say that ethics, politics, and responsibility, *if there are any*, will only ever have begun with the experience and experiment of the aporia. When the path is clear and given, when a certain knowledge opens up the way in advance, the decision is already made, it might as well be said that there is none to make: irresponsibly, and in good conscience, one simply applies or implements a program. Perhaps, and this would be the objection, one never escapes the program. In that case, one must acknowledge this and stop talking with authority about moral or political responsibility. The condition of possibility of this thing called responsibility is a certain *experience and experiment of the possibility of the impossible*: *the testing of the aporia* from which one may invent the only *possible invention, the impossible invention.* (41)

The value of Swift's work lies in its relentless denunciation of clear and given paths, short-cuts to salvation that time and again turn out to be blind alleys. Having no predetermined destination, the aporetic journey on which his novels are engaged leaves room for the impossible invention of a future beyond the end of history.

Notes

Introduction: Walking Wounded

1 'There is not enough space, and yet one has to talk about the Swiftian traumas.' I have made the English translations of all French, German, Spanish and Dutch quotations in this book.

2 The publication history of Swift's work across the Atlantic is a different story. In the United States, Swift's first two novels – *The Sweet Shop Owner* (1980) and *Shuttlecock* (1981) – and his short-story collection *Learning to Swim and Other Stories* (1982) were only published in 1985, following the success of *Waterland* (1983). Since then, however, the US and Britain have kept pace: all of Swift's later novels – *Out of this World* (1988), *Ever After* (1992), *Last Orders* (1996) and *The Light of Day* (2003) – have come out more or less simultaneously in both countries.

3 In fact, Miquel is citing the author here, who is himself (approvingly) quoting a description of him which he claims to have found in 'un compte-rendu de *Last Orders*' ('a review of *Last Orders*') by 'un critique anglais' ('an English critic', 131) – presumably Adrian Poole, who calls Swift 'a master of the terminal' in his review of *Last Orders* for the *Guardian*.

4 The only exceptions to this quasi-general rule are the short stories 'Hide and Seek' and 'Learning to Swim', which use third-person narration, and *The Sweet Shop Owner*, in which third-person narration predominates over first-person narration. For completeness' sake, it should be added that the first-person narrators of some of Swift's other novels (*Waterland*, for example) also occasionally resort to the third person for short stretches of text.

5 In another interview, Swift is quoted as saying: 'I write a great deal about the past catching up with the present. It [sic] I have a dominant theme, maybe that is it' (quoted in Smith).

6 According to Bényei, the fact that *Last Orders* is not as preoccupied with trauma as some of Swift's earlier novels is apparent from the more composed and unadorned speech of its characters, which contrasts sharply with the uncontrolled, exuberant narration of *Waterland* and *Ever After*: 'The muted language of *Last Orders* avoids the sense of creating an ineffable secret centre around which the verbal world of the novel is orbiting' (53).

7 Most of the eleven stories making up *Learning to Swim and Other Stories* were written before his first novel, even though the collection itself was not published until 1982, that is, after *The Sweet Shop Owner* (1980) and *Shuttlecock* (1981). Since then, Swift has been remarkably single-minded in his dedication to the art of the novel: as far as I am aware, his non-novelistic post-1982 writerly ventures can be counted on the fingers of two hands. These are 'My Canterbury Tale' (2002), an article in which the author marvels at seeing *Last Orders* made into a film; the short story 'Our Nicky's Heart' (2000); 'Fishing, Writing and Ted' (1999), an article in which Swift reminisces about his fishing trips with the late Ted Hughes; 'I Never Pretended My Novel Owed No Debt to Faulkner' (1997), a *Times* feature in which he defends himself against half-hearted accusations of plagiarism in *Last Orders*; '1974' (1993), an autobiographical account of the year he spent in Greece; 'Looking for Jiří Wolf' (1990), a journalistic report on his search for and meeting with a dissident Czechoslovakian writer; and 'Throwing Off Our Inhibitions' (1988), a piece of criticism in which he outlines his views on literature. (This list excludes the advance publications of chapters from *Waterland*, *Ever After* and *Last Orders* in *Granta.*) 'Hide and Seek' is a story that appeared in an Arts Council anthology in 1982 and was not included in *Learning to Swim.* The only uncollected pre-1982 short story by Swift that I know of is 'The Recreation Ground' (1976).

8 John Marsden writes that *Learning to Swim and Other Stories* 'offers us an index of Swift's subsequent work. Here, we are introduced to many of the themes and techniques that the novels bring into sharper focus . . .' (*After Modernism* 16). Similarly, Pamela Cooper claims that 'several of the stories isolate interesting aspects of Swift's technique that work together in an integrated way in his novels' (*Reader's Guide* 11).

1 What Went Before: A Swift Survey

1 These include, besides *PMLA* 114.1 (January 1999), *Philosophy and Literature* 22.2 (October 1998), *Style* 32.2 (1998) and *EJES* 7.2 (2003). The articles in the *Philosophy and Literature* special issue respond to an article by Richard Posner entitled 'Against Ethical Criticism', which had appeared in the same journal a year earlier. A concluding reflection on the debate – in which, besides Posner, Martha Nussbaum and Wayne Booth took part – was offered by Simon Stow in 2000.

2 Another useful introductory essay on the subject of ethics and literary criticism by the same author appeared in the ninth volume of *The Cambridge History of Literary Criticism*, which came out in 2001.

3 As distinct from 'undergraduate pedagogy', at which level traditional Arnoldian-Leavisite ethical criticism 'has continued on among us alive and well' (Parker 1).

4 In this article, which is framed as a response to a virulent attack on ethical criticism delivered by Richard Posner in an earlier issue of *Philosophy and*

Literature, Nussbaum is careful to confine her argument to 'a narrow group of pre-selected works, all of them novels' (346). Such reservations were largely absent, however, in *Poetic Justice*, whose claims frequently seemed to pertain to literature – or, at least, to the novel genre – as a whole.

5 As Harpham points out, 'the overriding law of perception' active in Nussbaum's work also determines her account of literature as 'a verbal structure that exhibits, elicits, and tests the perceptual – rather than, say, the interpretive – powers of author, narrator, character, and reader' (*Shadows* 230).

6 Felman is acutely aware of living and working in a 'post-traumatic century, a century that has survived unthinkable historical catastrophes' (1); Caruth routinely talks about our 'catastrophic age' (*Trauma* 11); and Kirby Farrell characterizes the dominant cultural mood of the 1990s as being essentially post-traumatic: 'In contemporary culture, . . . trauma is both a clinical syndrome and a trope something like the Renaissance figure of the world as a stage: a strategic fiction that a complex, stressful society is using to account for a world that seems threateningly out of control' (2).

7 For a comprehensive overview of the history of the concept of trauma, see Ruth Leys's *Trauma: A Genealogy*.

8 Published in 1995, this volume brings together (revised versions of) essays that had originally appeared in 1991 in two issues of the journal *American Imago* devoted to 'Psychoanalysis, Culture and Trauma'.

9 Caruth's conception of reality as fundamentally traumatic, inaccessible, incomprehensible and all but unrepresentable bears more than a passing resemblance to the Lacanian notion of the Real, which plays a crucial role in the political-philosophical work of Slavoj Žižek. However, see Linda Belau's 'Trauma and the Material Signifier' for an attempt to articulate some basic differences between deconstructive and psychoanalytic understandings of trauma.

10 Caruth and Felman's version of trauma theory has been described as 'an intricate displacement and disguise of the de Manian variant of deconstruction', with the key notion of unreadability now being construed in terms of trauma (LaCapra, *Writing* 107 n.20). Indeed, trauma theory in Caruth and Felman's rendering may strike one as the reinvention in an ethical guise of an embattled paradigm struggling to refute nagging accusations of indifference and irrelevance to 'what goes on in the real world'. As Michael Roth observed in 1999, 'Many of the people who were doing deconstruction ten years ago are talking today about testimony and witnessing and trauma. This is, for them, a path back to talk about ethics.'

11 *Waterland* came out to rave reviews – as David Leon Higdon points out, 'reviewers vied with one another in finding ways to praise [it]' ('Unconfessed' 186) – and was nominated for the prestigious Booker Prize. The novel established Swift as 'a novelist of authority and range', and 'more than justified' his inclusion in a controversial but strangely prophetic list of the twenty best young British novelists drawn up by the Book Marketing Council and

published in *Granta* in 1983 (Tredell). Writing in 1991, Higdon called *Waterland* the author's 'most accomplished work', 'a truly extraordinary novel, as significant for the 1980s as *The French Lieutenant's Woman* was for the 1970s' ('Double'). Instantly canonized as a modern classic, *Waterland* is still widely regarded as Swift's finest novel – though *Last Orders* has emerged as a close contender for that title.

12 The disproportionate amount of attention accorded to *Waterland* has been remarked upon by, among others, John Marsden and Geoffrey Lord. Marsden notes that critical responses to Swift's work 'have been limited almost exclusively' to *Waterland* (*After Modernism* 10); Lord confirms that *Waterland* 'has received far more critical attention than any other work by Swift' ('Graham' 5).

13 Though Hutcheon selects her examples from many different national literatures, British fiction appears to be exceptionally well represented among them. The other books by British writers that Hutcheon discusses, besides the aforementioned novels, include Peter Ackroyd's *Hawksmoor*, D. M. Thomas's *The White Hotel*, John Fowles's *A Maggot* and *The French Lieutenant's Woman*, Angela Carter's *Nights at the Circus* and *The Infernal Desire Machines of Doctor Hoffman*, Alasdair Gray's *Lanark* and Salman Rushdie's *Shame*.

14 Bernard later condensed her study – which we will have occasion to return to in chapter 4 – in an article entitled 'Dismembering/Remembering Mimesis: Martin Amis, Graham Swift'. The only other published monographs on Swift's work that I was aware of while writing this book are Susanne Mecklenburg's *Martin Amis und Graham Swift: Erfolg durch bodenlosen Moralismus im zeitgenössischen britischen Roman* and Pamela Cooper's concise reader's guide to *Last Orders*. Other book-length studies that I had come across are Alan Hickman's, John Marsden's and Wendy Wheeler's doctoral dissertations. Wheeler's dissertation served as the basis for a number of articles on Swift, two of which – 'Melancholic Modernity' and 'After Grief?' – were later incorporated, with slight modifications, in her book entitled *A New Modernity? Change in Science, Literature and Politics*. As I put the finishing touches to this book in the autumn of 2004, it appears that the world of academic publishing has begun to make up for lost time. Not only has the last year seen the publication of three new monographs on Swift's work – Jakob Winnberg's *An Aesthetics of Vulnerability: The Sentimentum and the Novels of Graham Swift*, David Malcolm's *Understanding Graham Swift* and François Gallix's *Graham Swift: Écrire l'imagination* – but three more full-length studies (not counting the present one) are reported to be forthcoming: a volume on Swift by Peter Widdowson is to be published shortly in Northcote House's Writers and Their Work series, Anastasia Logotheti's *From History to Storytelling: Confession and Redemption in the Novels of Graham Swift* is coming out from Sussex Academic Press, and Daniel Lea is completing a Swift monograph for Manchester University Press's new Contemporary British Writers series. In addition to full-length studies, there have been, of course, numerous reviews of Swift's

works and a fair number of articles scattered through academic books and journals or published on the Internet. A scholarly publication that deserves special mention is *Graham Swift ou le temps du récit*, a collection of essays by researchers associated with the University of Nancy 2 that was put together by Michel Morel. In fact, one of the more remarkable facts about the field of Swift criticism is its internationalist character: an author who 'travels well', Swift appears to have attracted a strong academic fan-base outside the Anglo-Saxon world, especially in France and Germany.

15 Though it is obviously not the case that the historiographic-metafictional approach to Swift's work has simply left the stage to give way to trauma-theoretical interpretations, the idea of a chronological succession need not be abandoned completely: whereas the former type of inquiry manifested itself with particular intensity in the late 1980s and early 1990s but appears to have spent most of its force by now, the latter type has stood its ground (albeit with far fewer practitioners) since it emerged around the middle of the 1990s.

16 Further on in his text, the 'obsession' with truth and referentiality that drives Hutcheon's mode of inquiry is claimed to be 'literally irrelevant' to *Waterland* (van Alphen, 'Performativity' 209).

17 With his 1997 book *Caught by History: Holocaust Effects in Contemporary Art, Literature, and Theory*, van Alphen follows in Felman's footsteps by investigating the ways in which artistic practices can contribute to working through the trauma of the Holocaust, a duty imposed by history, which in his judgement, however, historiography is ill-equipped to meet owing to its predominant focus on epistemological issues:

> History brings with it more responsibilities than only knowing and remembering the facts, especially when that history concerns the Holocaust. Other responsibilities that are poignantly imposed on us involve the working through of the traumatic intrusion of an unimaginable reality, and the foregrounding of the cracks and tears that are concealed by the coherence of the stories being told. It is in relation to those responsibilities that the imaginative discourses of art and literature can step in and perform functions that, though historical, cannot be fulfilled by the work of the historian. (37)

18 For another insightful reading of *Waterland* in terms of the crisis of paternity, see Botting 97–140.

19 As Swift points out in a 1996 interview, the inheritance motif in his work is linked, in some ways, to being 'antitradition' (quoted in Bernard, 'Interview' 224). He speaks of 'a sense of contradictory connection' to do with 'going against the grain', 'going against the received notions, against the received pattern' (quoted in Bernard, 'Interview' 224).

20 A similar claim is made by Bertrand Westphal, who describes Swift's novelistic output as 'sa contribution au grand oeuvre de déconstruction de l'Idée, entrepris après Auschwitz et Hiroshima' ('his contribution to the great work of the deconstruction of the Idea, undertaken after Auschwitz and Hiroshima', 53).

21 Swift allegedly satisfies '[d]ie harmoniefixierten Sehnsüchte seiner Figuren' ('[t]he harmony-oriented desires of his characters') by integrating 'Vorstellungen der englischen Romantik' ('ideas of English Romanticism') into his work:

> Die ursprünglich romantischen Motive des Wanderns, der zwischenmenschlichen Vereinigung und der Verwurzelung in der Natur erleben somit bei diesem Autor eine Art zeitgenössischer Renaissance.
>
> The originally romantic motifs of wandering, of interhuman union and of rootedness in nature undergo some kind of contemporary renaissance with this author. (Mecklenburg 114)

2 Burying 'Undying Memories': Traumatic Denial in *The Sweet Shop Owner*

1 For a fairly comprehensive overview of formal and thematic similarities between *The Sweet Shop Owner* and these two modernist classics, see Marsden, *After Modernism* 52–58.

2 This particularity is also remarked upon by David Leon Higdon, who yet insists that the protagonist manages to arrive at 'minimal enlightenment' ('Unconfessed' 184) by an alternative route: 'In most retrospective fiction, the act of looking back and telling the story in some way transforms the person doing the telling. Because he is not consciously telling his story, Willy Chapman's case is more problematic and open, depending as it does on the reader's comprehension of symbolic connections' ('Unconfessed' 183). The one example of this procedure which he adduces is the juxtaposition, towards the end of the novel, of scenes from Willy's walk across the Common, which is instrumental in precipitating his death, and the 1931 mile run for his school, which Willy either narrowly won from or lost to Irene's brother Jack. It is not at all clear, however, how the connection suggested between these two events is indicative of Willy 'finally understand[ing] the grotesque joke Irene has played upon him and on her family' and 'wish[ing] to escape from the patterns she and life have imposed upon him' ('Unconfessed' 183). What is clear, though, is that, for all the 'heart trouble' (19) his marriage has given him, Willy remains very assertive throughout the novel about the essential rightness of Irene and his views and reproachful of Dorothy for having failed them.

3 Though third-person narration clearly predominates, first-person narration is not completely absent from the novel. Passages in which the third-person narrator uses Willy as a focalizer often alternate with first-person passages in which Willy directly addresses his absent daughter. Another first-person narrator who puts in a brief appearance is Irene, in the passage referred to above. Nor is it the case that the extradiegetic narrator focalizes exclusively through Willy: some passages are focalized through Mrs Cooper and Sandra, his employees at the sweet shop.

4 The assumption that Willy's way of life is in need of some critical reassessment

is not shared by Alan Hickman, who concludes his otherwise incisive close reading of the novel with the curious assertion that Willy's way of life is vindicated in the end: 'The third part of the novel . . . vindicates him for both his treatment of Dorry and his subservience to Irene' (49). Hickman maintains that 'the picture' is 'complete' for Willy, the only character in the novel to '[stand] in a correct relation to the past', and that 'salvation' awaits him (despite 'the many ways he may be judged to have failed his obligations to others') – though why this should be so is not made clear (52).

5 In some ways, *The Sweet Shop Owner* leaves off where *Ever After* begins. Telling the story of a failed suicide, *Ever After* can be read as a prolonged, tortuous attempt by the narrator to break free from the unreflective, narcissistic way of life which led up to his desperate act and to move towards a more viable and sustainable ethos. The protagonist of *The Sweet Shop Owner*, however, appears to be stuck in a state of incomprehension and frustration with no possibility of redemption this side of the grave. The relationship between the two texts is construed in a similar fashion by Wendy Wheeler. Having argued that *The Sweet Shop Owner* offers a diagnosis of 'Romantic "failure"' (*From the Sublime* 114), Wheeler goes on to suggest that 'the question which *Ever After* will ask is what forms of symbolization are appropriate, or can be formulated, in order to acknowledge the impossibility of the Romantic notion of fully, transcendentally, seizing hold of reality' (*From the Sublime* 116).

6 Or, to quote Jenny Edkins: 'States abuse citizens on the battlefield, in captivity, in concentration camps. The modern state cannot be assumed to be a place of safety, any more than the patriarchal family can. Political abuse in one parallels sexual abuse in the other. Both give rise to what we call symptoms of trauma.' The connection between militarism and sexual oppression, first posited by Virginia Woolf in her famous essay *Three Guineas*, is also taken up by Judith Herman, who points out the 'commonalities' 'between rape survivors and combat veterans, between battered women and political prisoners, between the survivors of vast concentration camps created by tyrants who rule nations and the survivors of small, hidden concentration camps created by tyrants who rule their homes' (3), and by Kalí Tal, who insists on the 'connections' between 'the Holocaust, the Vietnam War, and sexual abuse of women and children' (3).

7 The traumatic event is designated by the words 'all right, now', which are frequently invoked in the novel to mark key climactic moments, such as the instant of Willy's death (222), the decisive moment in the mile race (198) and the taking of a picture during the Harrison family's photo shoot (74). In each case, someone is struck, in one way or another, by the overwhelming force of the present; he or she is either 'stabbed', 'wounded', killed or 'captured by the moment'. It is tempting to read the phrase 'all right, now' as a prefiguration of *Waterland*'s more fully theorized notion of the 'Here and Now', which is defined as 'that which we seldom glimpse unscathed – for it appears more often . . . dressed in terror' (W 51); a 'knife blade' which punctures the 'thin garment'

of history (W 36) and whose 'surprise attacks' announce that 'time has taken us prisoner' (W 61). Indeed, according to Wendy Wheeler, 'The "Now" in *The Sweet Shop Owner* is clearly, like the "Here and Now" in *Waterland*, the moment of danger in which the Real erupts' (*From the Sublime* 115). The relationship between photography and trauma cautiously suggested in *The Sweet Shop Owner* is pursued at greater length in *Out of this World*. As 'an instant which occurs once and once only' and yet 'remains permanently visible' (OW 205), the photograph can be seen to condense the particular temporality of trauma, which is described in the following terms: 'what is over in an instant just goes on happening' (OW 109).

8 The same ambivalence is apparent in another comment Willy makes on the nature of his wife's illness. Having posited that 'She could never get enough air', he goes on to voice a suspicion that the opposite was the case: 'Or was it that air assailed her?' (218).

9 In fact, Willy specifies later on that the only thing Irene ever divulged to him about her past was where the money came from which had allowed her family to start up the laundry business: 'She never talked about the past, but she told me about the money . . .' (222).

10 The meaning of this notion of 'nothing happening' undergoes a radical change in the transition from *The Sweet Shop Owner* to *Waterland*. Whereas in the former novel it is used to characterize a life of routine and habit deliberately removed from the chaos of the outside world, in the latter work it functions as a figure for the intrusive traumatic reality which both invites and defies such forms of evasion. *The Light of Day* reverts to the earlier model. As in *The Sweet Shop Owner*, the notion of nothing happening is invoked there to describe the ostensibly safe, peaceful and unexciting world of affluent suburbia: 'This home-and-garden land, this never-never land where nothing much is ever meant to happen' (LD 19); 'The lights of houses through trees, quiet streets where nothing happens' (LD 215). Like Swift's debut novel, *The Light of Day* highlights the discomforting fact that this peace, however carefully maintained, can suddenly be disturbed by an eruption of violence: 'Something happens' (LD 3); 'It happened here' (LD 203). Irrespective of the terminology in which it is couched, however, the basic tension between the forces of order and disorder, of trauma and post-traumatic defence, is a constant concern in all of Swift's novels.

11 The notion of pattern-making in *The Sweet Shop Owner* anticipates that of story-telling in *Waterland*, which serves roughly the same purpose, namely 'making sense of madness' (W 225) and thus throwing up a bulwark against an essentially unbearable reality: 'As long as there's a story, it's all right' (W 63). Moreover, in both texts a naive investment in the redemptive power of pattern-making or story-telling is exposed as a recipe for personal and historical disaster.

12 Though this sentence is taken from a passage focalized through Willy, Mrs Cooper herself later confirms the accuracy of Willy's assessment of her.

Daydreaming about marrying her employer, she imagines that 'they'd sell the shop. They wouldn't need it anyway, with all the money (she'd find out how much it really was) *Mrs* Chapman had left. They'd simply stop work. And they'd take, at last, that holiday. That long, long holiday . . .' (157–58).

13 As the narrator of *Ever After*, another suicide (albeit failed), well knows: 'People die when their world will no longer sustain them' (EA 24).

14 The fact that Mr Harrison, Willy and Irene all die from a heart condition is highly significant. Often disavowed by their owners – Mr Harrison, for instance, 'swears there's nothing wrong with him' (82) – defective hearts can be seen to function as a metaphor for the sheer heartlessness of the characters' utilitarian way of life, that is, its failure to create a healthy sense of self and community.

15 In a way, Irene's traumatic experience of being reduced to a sexual object by Hancock is mirrored by the objectification suffered by Dorothy, who is treated as a commodity in an essentially economic exchange between her parents. Both characters are perceived as presents waiting to be unwrapped: in assaulting Irene, Hancock acts like 'a man unwrapping a parcel' (52), and as a newborn baby, Dorothy strikes Willy as 'a little thing, wrapped like a gift' (10) when he comes to visit his wife in hospital.

16 On her wedding night, for example, Irene undresses 'as if she were unwrapping a gift, as much as to say: "There, see the reward you have got. And do you think such a reward will not ask certain things in return?"' (30). Even her smiles she only ever gives to her husband as a form of payment for services rendered: 'She only took and squeezed his hand now and then and gave him those short, quick smiles that were like small coins thrown without fuss to someone who has done a service' (29).

17 A similar sentiment informs another question which Willy puts to his absent daughter: 'And did you feel: whatever I do, she will have predicted it; whatever I do, it will not be my own?' (116). Having first given birth to Dorothy in fulfilment of a contractual obligation, Irene now seems to expect her daughter's life to unfold according to a predictable pattern.

18 As a matter of fact, images of imprisonment and confinement abound in *The Sweet Shop Owner*, underlining the characters' immobility and isolation. As a teenager, Irene 'cowered inside [her] looks like a captive' (50), a simile which recurs in the description of a picture which Mr Harrison took of his three children: 'The developed photograph would show her like some captive between two vigilant sentinels' (69). Many years later, Irene strikes Phil the paper boy as 'someone trapped in a glass case' (185) the one time he sees her, standing behind the window of her house as he comes round to deliver her papers. Irene's brothers, for their part, are said to 'have the looks of statues, trapped in immovable poses' (51), and Mrs Cooper is pictured as 'an animal in a cage' (158), as is Willy (214). Moreover, lying in bed, Willy is compared to 'a toy in its box' (11), and going out of his shop, he only walks into 'the hot envelope of the street' (160).

19 Irene's out-of-hand dismissal of Dorothy's attempt to discuss this explosive

topic with her parents recalls the reaction of Irene's family to her suggestion that Hancock 'was not good to [her]' (52): 'What nonsense' (52, 53).

20 Clearly, this scene contains the germs of the obsession with the prospect of nuclear annihilation which haunts Tom Crick's students in *Waterland.*

21 Though Willy might have smelt a rat after seeing the play, he comes away from it none the wiser, as he 'didn't understand' (145) the lines spoken by the actors. Nor does he recognize his own predicament in a line from Keats's 'Ode on a Grecian Urn' which he reads over Dorothy's shoulder: 'Bold lover, never, never canst thou kiss . . .' (147). Though the connection between Keats's 'cold pastoral' – or, for that matter, the china shepherd and shepherdess on the dressing-table who, being 'for ever on the point of flying into each other's arms' (10), faithfully re-enact this Keatsian scene – and his own loveless marriage is fairly obvious, Willy is totally bewildered by these 'lines of verse . . . which I didn't understand' (147).

22 Interestingly, Jessica's rejection of parental control, like Dorothy's, is inscribed in her name. 'Jessica' has been traced back to Hebrew *Iscah*, which Elizabethan commentators glossed as meaning 'she that looketh out' (Dobbins and Battenhouse 108). This meaning is reflected in Jessica's looking 'out at window' (2.5.40) for her lover's coming. In doing so, she disobeys her father's repressive decree that she stay inside the house and close the shutters on the outside world (2.5.28–36). In a similar fashion, Dorothy attempts to look beyond the predictable bounds of immobility and economic exchange in which her parents seek to enclose her.

23 According to Gary Rosenshield, criticism of *The Merchant of Venice* has taken 'three basic paths' in the last century (38 n.31). The first interprets the play as a 'romantic comedy', seeing the Venetians as embodiments of 'love, friendship, joy, and sacrifice' (38 n.31). The second is 'ironist' in that it interprets the values which the characters ostensibly embody as 'superficial, more often than not the means to disguise more selfish motives' (38 n.31). The third, finally, understands *The Merchant of Venice* as 'a hybrid, combining significant romantic and ironic elements', which create the play's 'many problems for interpretation' (38 n.31). *The Sweet Shop Owner* allows for a similar variety of interpretations, due to the unresolved tension between economic/static and aneconomic/dynamic forces at play in the text.

24 In his silent address to his daughter, Willy confirms his faith in the validity of Irene's – as opposed to Dorothy's – foresight: 'But you never looked closely at that face, into those blue-grey eyes, because if you had you would have seen how much more she knew than you' (116).

3 Getting Rid of 'Needless Painful Knowledge': Problem *Dis*solving in *Shuttlecock*

1 To be fair, in the course of her reading of *Out of this World*, Wheeler does note, albeit in passing, that in *Shuttlecock* too 'there is a sense . . . of something closed too soon, and of a too quick and easy resolution in which quite evident dangers are repressed' (*From the Sublime* 136).

2 To mark the distinction between Dad's Shuttlecock and Swift's identically titled novel, underlining will be used for the former, italics for the latter.

3 This is one of several passages connecting Prentis with the spiteful and self-hating narrator of Dostoevsky's *Notes from Underground*, a thoroughly disagreeable character who is similarly motivated by contradictory impulses. Another prominent intertextual presence in *Shuttlecock* is Kafka: not only do the frustrating bureaucratic impasses that Prentis encounters at the office clearly point in this direction, but the notion of the burrowing animal also specifically recalls the mole-like narrator of Kafka's short story 'The Burrow' – another Underground Man.

4 Earlier on in the narrative, Prentis recalls this period as one of pure bliss and fulfilment in harmony with nature: 'do you know what I felt when each of them [Martin and Peter] came into the world? I felt: life is very simple and complete. And there was a time even when the boys were small, when Marian and I used to make love, quite spontaneously, in the open air – in fields, amid ferns, in secluded parts of beaches – when we went out at weekends' (76).

5 To anticipate the argument that follows: the novel's final phrase, 'a piece of nature', which ostensibly celebrates Prentis's successful return to the pure state of nature, effectively undermines this entire undertaking. If 'nature' were indeed a state of plenitude and undivided unity, the notion that 'a piece' can be isolated from it would be impossible to conceive, as it suggests that nature is internally differentiated and fragmented. The very use of this term thus implies that nature does not exist as absolute presence but is always already marked by difference, always already alienated from itself.

6 In fact, the *Critique of Judgement* can be and has been read as the diagnosis of a failure. According to Garrath Williams, for example, 'Kant finds no theoretical bridge across that "great gulf fixed" between free and sensible realms . . . Kantian judgment fails to cross this barrier, to discern reason and freedom in the world of appearances' (118).

7 Moretti uses the phrase 'classical *Bildungsroman*' to denote 'the narrative model created by Goethe and Austen', as distinct from 'the *Bildungsroman* genre as a whole' (229 n.1).

8 In O'Donnell's reading, the artificiality of the novel's cheery ending is compounded by the counterfeit nature of the setting: 'Even when Prentis and his wife make love in the dunes of a nearly deserted beach at the close of the novel, "nature" is portrayed in the form of a cliche, a Hollywood backdrop against which Prentis' successful entrance into adulthood and authority is played out.' The final scene's reliance on overused cinematic conventions has also been remarked upon by Donald Kaczvinsky, who describes it as 'a scene from the repertoire of romance novels and films' (12).

9 In the case of Dad, this is, of course, the spectacular escape from the Château Martine, which he recounts in the final chapters of his memoir as the crowning glory of his career as a secret agent in occupied France. The cells at the castle, which are located half below ground level, bear a close resemblance to the

basement office in which Prentis works, and which he refers to as a 'dungeon' (17). His escape is to the above-ground office occupied by Quinn and to the apparent safety of the dunes where he finally realizes his ambition of becoming a burrowing animal.

10 In positing these two alternatives, Prentis is in fact echoing his father, who reflects, in a passage from his memoir which the narrator quotes at a later stage in the text: 'Perhaps there is much about my days at the Château which I simply do not remember. They say that you only recall what is pleasant. Or perhaps the truth is that certain things defy retelling' (139).

4 'To Be Realistic': Close Encounters of a Traumatic Kind in *Waterland*

1 For some examples of this approach, see the analyses of *Waterland* by Catherine Bernard, John Brewer and Stella Tillyard, Pamela Cooper, Andrzej Gasiorek, Linda Hutcheon, Robert Irish, George Landow, Alison Lee, Sean Murphy, Ansgar Nünning, John Schad, Richard Todd and Elisabeth Wesseling. Some of these analyses are briefly discussed in chapter 1.

2 This reading takes issue with Jean-Jacques Lecercle's startling description of *Waterland* as a totalizing narrative which frantically closes itself off to anything that might exceed known frames of reference:

> Ce n'est pas un texte ouvert à l'événement, à l'inconnaissable, à la mauvaise forme, au radicalement nouveau. C'est au contraire un texte obsessionnellement construit en une totalité fermée: les généalogies, mais aussi la chronologie, mais aussi la complexité de l'entrelacs de la narration, en sont la preuve.
>
> It is not a text open to the event, to the unknowable, to the unshapely, to the radically new. On the contrary, it is a text obsessively constructed as a closed totality: the genealogies, but also the chronology, but also the complexity of the interlaced narration, are proof of that. (45)

In Lecercle's opinion, not even the abortion scene deserves the label of 'événement' ('event'): 'ce spectacle insupportable' ('this intolerable spectacle') is not only 'trop bien entouré pour faire événement' ('too well surrounded to amount to an event'), but it is also 'trop prévisible, trop préparé pour émerger véritablement comme ce non-sens qui permet l'élaboration du sens' ('too predictable, too well-prepared really to emerge as that non-sense which allows for the elaboration of meaning', 46). *Pace* Lecercle, this chapter argues that bearing witness to a traumatic reality is precisely the novel's overriding concern.

3 This particularity of trauma is captured in a phrase that is repeatedly used in the novel to describe the condition in which its traumatized characters find themselves: 'For them life had stopped, though they must go on living' (228). In this quotation, 'them' refers to 'the broken-minded soldiers' of the First World War (228), but the same phrase is used with reference to Mary, whose life is brought to a halt by her teenage abortion (122), to Tom's mother Helen Atkinson, because of her involvement in an incestuous relationship with her

father (228), and to all those who seek the companionship of Tom's ancestor Sarah Atkinson, who loses her wits after being knocked on the head by her husband and who is revered by the people of Gildsey as a local deity (118).

4 For all its mythological overtones (see below), there is an effective deflationary mechanism at work in this passage. Having explicitly distanced himself from the trite and superficial talk of the populace to penetrate to the depth of a traumatic reality, Tom unexpectedly ends his reminiscence with a tiresome cliché which ill befits the high seriousness of his subject matter: 'It all comes out in the wash.' To anticipate the argument developed below: the occurrence of this phrase at this precise moment may be adduced as evidence of the necessarily incomplete success of the attempt to gain access to trauma through poetical language. Tom's bid to grasp the elusive reality of the aborted foetus – which is presumably beyond the reach of ordinary language – by metaphorizing it as 'a red spittle' is ironically undermined a couple of sentences later, when the poetical imagination is shown to produce a depressingly shallow, hackneyed cliché.

5 As Bernard shows, the use of the present tense can also serve other purposes. In some cases it ironically recalls the literary past (more specifically, it can be seen to parody the scenic method beloved of Victorian novelists like George Eliot); at other times the present tense is used simply to present facts more vividly than the past tense would allow, or to draw attention to the moment of enunciation (*La parole chronique* 80–85).

6 A similar conclusion is reached by Jean-Louis Picot, who seizes on the slippage between homodiegetic and heterodiegetic narration to argue that

> A la perspective linéaire proposée par Tom Crick narrateur second [Tom as homodiegetic narrator], la structure du texte, recomposée par Tom Crick narrateur premier [Tom as heterodiegetic narrator], oppose sa propre perspective kaléidoscopique. C'est en effet la logique de l'association d'idées que privilégie le narrateur-auteur dans son travail de remémoration.
>
> To the linear perspective put forward by Tom Crick as second narrator [Tom as homodiegetic narrator], the structure of the text, reconstructed by Tom Crick as first narrator [Tom as heterodiegetic narrator], opposes its own kaleidoscopic perspective. In fact, it is the logic of the association of ideas that the narrator-author privileges in his memory work. (36)

7 In fact, at a certain point in her introduction Bernard herself groups realism and metaphorization together as related strategies of denial. Having first presented them as opposite ways of representing reality, she points out that both models offer up a domesticated version of reality, which is to be distinguished from the noumenal reality that escapes and transcends our attempts to impose meaning:

> A la logique réaliste de la métonymie s'oppose, selon Swift, celle, plus poétique, de la métaphore. De même, contre la réalité apprivoisée par les codes

romanesques – ou par la métaphore – se dresse une réalité plus brutale, qui ouvre de brusques failles dans le continuum lisse des jours et des mots.

The realist logic of metonymy contrasts, according to Swift, with the more poetic one of metaphor. Similarly, against a reality domesticated by novelistic codes – or by metaphor – stands a more brutal reality, which causes abrupt ruptures in the smooth continuum of days and of words. (*La parole chronique* 8)

8 Unlikely though it may sound, in the 1992 film adaptation of *Waterland* directed by Stephen Gyllenhaal, the Greenwich scenes – together with the Charlton and Lewisham scenes – have been transferred to Pittsburgh. This change of setting, which appears to have been inspired by purely commercial motives, is to be regretted, since the setting of a Graham Swift novel is never a mere background but always also functions as a repository of cultural meaning. In the case of *Waterland*, an apprehension of the constant tension between the ordering impulse traditionally associated with a place like Greenwich and the chaos and disorder epitomized by the Fens is indispensable to a viable interpretation of the novel.

9 Of course, Mary's reluctance to narrativize her traumatic experiences can also be seen as a sign of (non-narrative) repression. This would mean that her alleged penchant for realism is actually largely a projection by the narrator – a state of affairs of which he may not be entirely unaware, as his somewhat hesitant phrasing seems to suggest.

10 Ronald McKinney similarly understands *Waterland*'s concept of progress as an ongoing battle between 'the absolutist pretensions of artificial history and the perpetual curiosity of human nature' (828–29). He explains the analogy between progress and land reclamation as follows: 'fictions help create islands of accumulated silt in the middle of floods, but they also need to be dredged out themselves from time to time when they start to clog the waterways due to their absolutist pretensions' (828). Discerning a muted sense of optimism in the novel's reflections on history and progress, McKinney credits *Waterland* with inventing a viable 'postmodern political philosophy' (832). In the same vein, Damon Marcel Decoste, in an insightful reading of *Waterland* indebted to McKinney's, describes the novel as 'a text deeply committed to Enlightenment, to the refusal of that Kantian "immaturity" which seeks out paternal Answers, to that Enlightenment spirit of ceaseless critique that Swift, with Jacques Derrida, declares "must not be renounced"' (398).

11 A revised version of humanism is also what Raphaël Ingelbien believes *Waterland* to endorse. He sees a 'negative humanism' grow out of what he calls Swift's 'nihilistic sublime' (45): the author's alleged vision of England as a void. According to Ingelbien, this 'universalist humanism', which is opposed to identity politics and nationalism, 'remains essential to any genuinely progressive world-view' (45).

5 Cathartic Fables, Fabled Catharses: Photography, Fiction and Ethics in *Out of this World*

1 The pervasiveness of the photographic metaphor in the main narrators' reminiscences and confessions is remarked upon by Patrick Parrinder: 'What they remember, what they look forward to, and the way in which they project their lives, are all, in effect, a series of visible scenes: still photos, or moving pictures, captured from a particular standpoint (their own), fixed and developed, and then stored as if in some psychic album' (17).

2 Michel Morel similarly interprets *Out of this World*'s appeal to photography as a way of reinforcing the realist illusion:

> Le texte semble alors s'approprier l'effet photographique par une sorte de dérivation hypertextuelle, cette dérivation lui conférant la force persuasive de la plaque photographique marquée par la trace matérielle de l'événement vécu. . . . Comme si l'écriture cherchait à s'effacer devant un effet de réel supérieur, effet quasiment mimologique.
>
> The text seems to appropriate the photographic effect by some sort of hypertextual derivation which confers upon it the persuasive force of the photographic plate marked by the material trace of the lived event ... As if the writing were trying to efface itself before a superior reality effect, an almost mimological effect. ('Le romancier' 24)

3 The notion that technological advances are taking us back to square one instead of leading us forward into a bright and radiant future also underlies Harry's wry comment on the fact that some of the astronauts on the Apollo missions 'got religion' (13): 'The irony of it. That we should have spent centuries shedding superstition and actually evolving the means that would get us up into Heaven. Only to discover that, all along, *He* was there first' (14). Harry's bleak assessment of the current state of the world is shared by the author himself, who argues in a contemporary interview that 'there's plenty of evidence for a lack of real progress in the world, real improvement, despite obviously a lot of technical improvement' (quoted in Profumo, ICA *Guardian* Conversation). Significantly, however, Swift refuses to be classified as a fatalist. Confronted, in another interview, with 'explicit' and 'implicit' statements which he has allegedly made to the effect that 'there is no future' and that 'the future is already the past', he responds rather sharply that 'I'm not sure that I've made those statements rather than characters in my novels, particularly in *Waterland*' (quoted in Bernard and Menegaldo 15).

4 In a further parallel, both *Out of this World* and *Camera Lucida* centre around the discovery of a photograph of a dead mother. *Camera Lucida* was prompted by the death of Barthes's mother, which led him to search for an image of her that would keep alive her memory. He finally settled on an image of his mother at a time when he could never have known her, when she was still a child. Similarly, *Out of this World* began with Harry's discovery of a photograph of his mother '[f]rom a time before [he] existed' (205). Indeed, as Swift has revealed in an interview, the first thing that 'got into [his] mind' when he

started on *Out of this World* was 'a specific scene which actually, it appears at the end of the novel as its, in its finished state, of a young boy discovering a particular significant photograph which had been locked away' (quoted in Profumo, ICA *Guardian* Conversation).

5 Rony Brauman, one of the makers of the controversial 1999 documentary film *Un spécialiste* (*The Specialist*), based on original footage of the Eichmann trial, claims to have wanted to demonstrate the exact same thing: 'Eichmann n'a pas le visage du SS ivre de violence et de sang. Mais il est monstrueux par son caractère ordinaire . . .' ('Eichmann does not have the face of a violence- and blood-thirsty SS officer. But he is monstrous because of his ordinary nature . . .', quoted in Bouniot). In *Éloge de la désobéissance*, the book accompanying the film, Brauman and co-author Eyal Sivan write that they set out to show that Eichmann 'ressemble en effet à tout le monde' ('in fact resembles everyone', 98). This sense of familiarity is meant to tempt the viewer to identify with the main character, an identification which may 'frôler la compréhension' ('border on understanding') but ultimately produces 'la peur' ('fear') rather than 'l'indulgence' ('indulgence', 99). Like Brauman and Sivan, whose aim is to provoke 'ce sentiment d'effroi' ('this sense of dread', 99) in the viewer, Harry hopes to discomfort the public with his images. We will have occasion to return to the Eichmann trial – an event conspicuous by its absence from *Out of this World* – later on in this chapter.

6 That the post-war world has largely evaded the hard task of coming to terms with a harrowing past is evidenced by the reconstruction of Nuremberg, a city which had been laid waste during the war. According to Harry, post-war Nuremberg seems designed to excise the historical events of 1940–46, taking tourists back to a pre-war fantasy and drawing attention away from the key historical events which took place there:

> Since 1946 this intricate product of the centuries has been rebuilt. It is not real, of course. It is a modern reconstruction, but it has been painstakingly done – so I am told – as if to re-conjure a world before certain irreversible historical events had happened. Now, Nuremberg is one of the chief tourist towns of Germany. People go for these picturesque reconstructions, mixed with genuine remnants of the old, for the fairy-tale spires and gables. The one-time site of Nazi rallies and the scene of the War Trials are of secondary interest. (103)

As Paul Smethurst points out, in thus providing an easy escape from history, the reconstructed city of Nuremberg represents 'an exercise in post-traumatic defence against the past by a whole people' (277).

7 A rather misleading phrase which, understandably, has created a great deal of confusion. As Seyla Benhabib explains, 'The phrase the "banality of evil" was meant to refer to a *specific quality of mind and character* of the doer himself, but neither to the deeds nor to the principles behind those deeds' (74).

8 An argument explicitly rejected by Arendt, who, in an imagined address to Eichmann, points out that 'there is an abyss between the actuality of what you did and the potentiality of what others might have done' (278).

9 *Out of this World* is mentioned by Nigel Leigh in his discussion of the impact of the Falklands War on English fiction as one of very few 'literary' novels to engage with the conflict, if only through 'passing references' – the dominant mode of dealing with the issue, as it turns out (124). Overall, Leigh writes, 'the Falklands has had only a limited effect on British writers and their literature' (127). As far as *Out of this World* is concerned, however, the Falklands War is more than a passing reference. Indeed, as a powerful instance of the dangers attendant on the resurrection of discredited mythologies, its presence in the text adds greatly to the poignancy of the novel's ethical vision.

10 See also Swift's comments on the Falklands War in the passage quoted in the opening paragraph of this chapter.

11 *Out of this World* holds the dubious honour of having received the worst reviews of all Swift's novels to date – which is not to say that the novel was trashed by the critics across the board, only that it was generally greeted with distinctly less enthusiasm than Swift's earlier and later offerings.

12 Bernard goes on to detect a sense of spatial and referential indeterminacy in *Out of this World*, but this minor point does not warrant the sweeping conclusion she draws from it:

> Dispersées au fil de la narration, ces notations rompent le lien référentiel, ou du moins contribuent à le dissoudre, à le précariser. Un voile descend sur le récit, en trouble la transparence et l'opacifie.
>
> Scattered across the thread of the narration, these notes break the referential link, or at least contribute to dissolving it, to threatening it. A veil descends over the narrative, obscuring its transparency and rendering it opaque. (107)

13 Reservations about the viability of the solution proposed in the novel have also been expressed by Wendy Wheeler: 'As with *Shuttlecock*, there is a sense in *Out of this World* of something closed too soon, and of a too quick and easy resolution in which quite evident dangers are repressed' (*From the Sublime* 136).

14 Many critics have expressed their dismay with the novel's excessive use of cliché at the level of characterization. These complaints tend to centre on the attractive young woman who is rushed in to rescue Harry from his dark memories. Jenny stands accused of inspiring such 'unconvincing writing' that 'one would really rather have seen Harry slog it out alone, on the road to reconciliation' (Duchêne 275). In the same vein, Adrian Poole denounces the 'emergency treatment' administered by the 'unusually conventional figures' of both Harry's dream-girl and Sophie's analyst ('Mourning After' 161).

15 Ironically, the character who seems most committed to life as a bad movie is singled out by Mecklenburg as the true moral hero of the piece. Indeed, Mecklenburg presents Sophie's husband Joe as the only character in the novel never to swerve from the much-vaunted principles of love, hope and communication:

> Als einziger Charakter benötigt Joe keine Fluchtwege 'out of this world', da er in seiner sensiblen, unbeirrt geduldigen und Sicherheit bietenden Liebe zu

> Sophie und den Kindern verwurzelt ist und die Hoffnung nicht aufgibt, sie als Quelle für ein mögliches gemeinsames Glück zu betrachten.
>
> Joe is the only character not to need any escape routes 'out of this world', because he is rooted in his sensitive, unwaveringly patient and safety-giving love for Sophie and the children and does not give up the hope to consider it as the source of a possible shared happiness. (158)

In other words, in a novel which already realizes Swift's alleged moral agenda to the utmost extent possible, the character of Joe is held to embody the undiluted essence of that programme. What Mecklenburg fails to notice, however, is that this purported torch-bearer of unflinching moral courage has a penchant for giving reality the slip and embracing irresponsible dreams and fairy-tales. The desire to get 'away from it all' (15) is deeply ingrained in him, as we learn from both Sophie and Harry, but also from Joe himself in the one section of the novel which he narrates. Anxious always to preserve a semblance of happiness and good cheer, he shuts himself off from any kind of unpleasantness that might pose a threat to this fantasy: having 'opened the wrong door and seen something terrible', he only wants to 'step out quickly. Quick! Shut the door! Quick!' (137). If this attitude causes him to lose touch with reality, Joe does not seem to be too bothered: 'maybe that's how I like it now' (151). In identifying the moral centre of *Out of this World* with this devotee of escapism, Mecklenburg unwittingly exposes the falseness and hollowness of the sense of moral optimism which she claims the novel projects.

16 The spectre of Harry and Sophie's envisaged reunion being thwarted by a plane crash is also raised by Peter Widdowson in the course of an argument about the 'tentative and oblique' nature of any signs of 'possible redemption through love' in Swift's work (219). Widdowson points out that, both characters being on a flying trip as the novel ends, 'potentially both father and daughter could fall out of the sky: literally "out of this world"' (219).

17 The fact that an apparent leap into the future can actually entail a step backwards is also a major concern in *Waterland.* In fact, one of the examples Tom Crick gives of 'great so-called forward movements of civilization' bringing with them 'an accompanying regression' is precisely 'the invention of the aeroplane', which, as he goes on to point out, 'led to the widespread destruction of European cities along with their civilian populations during the period 1939 to '45' (W 135–36). For all its (literally) uplifting technological advances, the twentieth century appears to be stuck in the mud: 'Who will not know of the mud of Flanders? Who will not feel in this twentieth century of ours, when even a teenage schoolboy will propose as a topic for a history lesson the End of History, the mud of Flanders sucking at his feet?' (W 19).

6 When Mourning Comes: *Ever After*, or The World Well Won

1 Bill's professed simultaneous adherence to expressivism and aestheticism seems to be a highly unlikely combination of two fundamentally opposed posi-

tions. Historically, the doctrine of 'art for art's sake' as formulated by Théophile Gautier and Charles Baudelaire in France in the 1840s and by Oscar Wilde and Walter Pater in England towards the end of the nineteenth century was precisely a reaction to the then-dominant paradigm of expressive realism. However, as we will see, Bill's embrace of these apparently incommensurable tendencies can be explained by reference to the common ground they share at a deeper level. As understood by Bill, both expressivism and aestheticism feed and are fed by the notion of the self-sufficient subject which he is anxious to safeguard.

2 The precise extent to which Bill is aware of his own predicament is often hard to determine. Though Bill comes to see the error of his narcissistic ways in the course of the narrative, his views remain highly ambivalent right until the end. Indeed, he occasionally slips back into a distinctly melancholic discourse whose demise he openly acknowledges elsewhere. While he appears successfully to have negotiated the irrevocable loss of his wife, for example, Bill can be seen to regress into his former absolutist mode at a fairly late stage in the narrative: 'You see, nothing else will do. No simulations, fabrications, biographical conjurations. ... Nothing else. Only the exact filling of the exact space. Only the actual reversal of nature' (255–56). One conclusion to be drawn from this is that the interpretation of the novel presented here, while a necessary supplement (in the Derridean sense of the word) to existing readings, is not without its own unresolvable resistances.

3 Though Mecklenburg apparently encounters no such problems in trying to fit Swift's other novels into her grand scheme, her interpretations of these texts reveal an extraordinary amount of hermeneutic violence, as is shown elsewhere in this book.

4 A word on whose centrality to *Ever After* Swift has commented in a 1996 interview with Catherine Bernard (222–23).

5 While the lesson of substitution is one which Bill badly needs to learn, a distinction has to be made between the essentially Levinasian notion of substitution at work in Bill's narrative and the ideology of substitution propagated by Sam. Substitution as defined by Levinas refers to a certain non-coincidence of the self with itself which can be traced back to the confrontation with alterity. It is the movement whereby the self dispossesses itself, empties itself of its being, turns itself inside out in response to the demand of the other. Indeed, Levinas explains 'la substitution de moi aux autres' ('the substitution of myself for the others', 181) as 'sujétion à tout' ('subjection to everything', 185). From this perspective, subjectivity consists in being literally subjected to, or held hostage by, the other:

> Le soi est Sub-jectum: il est sous le poids de l'univers – responsable de tout. L'unité de l'univers n'est pas ce que mon regard embrasse dans son unité de l'aperception; mais ce qui de toutes parts m'incombe, me regarde dans les deux sens du terme, m'accuse, est mon affaire.
>
> The self is Sub-jectum: it is under the weight of the universe – responsible for

> everything. The unity of the universe is not that which my gaze embraces in its unity of apperception; but that which from everywhere imposes itself upon me, regards me in the two senses of the word, accuses me, is my business. (183)

This conception of the self as traversed by alterity is in no way shared by Sam, whose awareness of the enigmatic elusiveness of the real thing leads him not to call the self's mastery over the universe into question and to accept finitude but to adopt a crude utilitarian belief in the malleability of reality. Hence, though originally a reaction to the metaphysics of presence and its premise of the fundamental comprehensibility of the world, Sam's philosophy of substitution actually amounts to a metaphysics of presence to the second degree.

6 The prominence of gold in Bill's evocation of Paris – a city bathed in a sunshine 'made up of countless particles of irreducible, eternal gold' (24) – is significant in this respect, especially since the difference between noble and baser metals acquires symbolic meaning in the course of the novel, becoming associated with the governing opposition between the real and the artificial.

7 On the importance and the ramifications of the distinction between absence and loss, see Dominick LaCapra's 'Trauma, Absence, Loss' (*Writing* 43–85).

8 According to Michael Ewans, the importance of this pattern was first argued by Kitto, whose interpretation of *Hamlet* as a religious drama he considers to be 'flawed' and 'excessively moralistic' (450). At the same time, however, Ewans commends Kitto for providing 'an essential counterweight to the Bradleyan tradition of humanistic, secularized, and psychological readings of Shakespeare' (450). For our purposes, the interpretative merits of the type of reading promoted by Kitto and others are of less concern than the implications of *Ever After*'s possible dependence upon it, which is why its validity will not be discussed here.

9 *Hamlet* is also invoked as a crucial intertext in Swift's short story 'Chemistry' (included in *Learning to Swim and Other Stories*), where it performs a very similar function. In this story, the ten-year-old narrator sets out to take revenge on his mother's lover Ralph for disturbing the 'delicate equilibrium' (LS 124) which had characterized his life together with his mother and grandfather before this newcomer appeared upon the scene. He concocts a plan to disfigure Ralph by throwing acid at him, in the hope that, his face spoilt, he would no longer be attractive to his mother. With Ralph out of the way, the narrator imagines he could regain 'that old impregnable domain which Ralph had not yet penetrated' (LS 125). In this narrative too, then, it is the redemptive promise of Shakespeare's play which captures the protagonist's fancy – though, as in *Ever After*, nothing comes of it.

10 Or, to be precise, 'not grief itself . . . but a nagging, self-pitying, self-accusing emotion born of the guilt at not feeling grief (how could I sigh over young sylphs in tutus when my own father was dead?) and out of a mood of redundancy, which it occurred to me my father must have felt too' (63). Thus it transpires that the authenticity and spontaneity of this supposedly original

pang is no less questionable than that of the vengeful passion which it prompted.

11 The dependence of emotion on representation is again raised as a possibility later on in the text: 'And surely, in the end, as we all know, poetry is one thing and life is another. These big, sonorous, laden words, how inflated and archaic they sound, as if they *could* only belong to literature: heartache; sorrow; grief' (84).

12 Courtly love was not, however, invented *ex nihilo*, but arguably shows the influence of the Hispano-Arabic and classical Mediterranean traditions. This larger perspective legitimizes Bill's illustration of romantic love with a quote from Virgil: 'Amor vincit omnia.'

13 The gender politics of courtly love have been reconsidered somewhat in recent years. As E. Jane Burns points out in a survey article of feminist work on the courtly love tradition, the standard feminist reading, which has just been outlined, has lately been supplemented by a significant body of what might be termed queer readings. These have detected 'forms of resistance to the amorous status quo' which 'point toward the possibility of more flexible subject positions than we have previously allowed' (26):

> Indeed, despite its heteronormative veneer and its tendency to displace and occlude women as subjects, courtly love, when taken as the full range of amorous scenarios staged between elite heterosexual couples in a court setting, offers models for love relations that disrupt the binary and exclusive categories of male and female and masculine and feminine used typically to structure the Western romantic love story. (48)

14 A sentiment widely shared by the novel's critics, as witness many of the obligatory glowing reviews quoted on the book's cover. *Ever After* is hailed as nothing less than 'the most beautiful love story in contemporary literature', 'a luminous testimony to the power of love' and 'a book of immaculate sensitivity and tenderness'. Interestingly, a dissenting note is sounded by Nicolas Tredell in the entry on Swift in the *Dictionary of Literary Biography*: 'The chief weakness of *Ever After* . . . lies in its perfunctory characterization of Unwin's late wife, Ruth, and its failure to make their relationship sufficiently convincing.' Though this relationship is supposed to be 'an intense love match', according to Tredell this 'does not come across', Ruth being 'little more than a cipher'. While Tredell's observations are very much to the point, the negative evaluation he attaches to them is unwarranted: what he considers to be a flaw is actually an integral aspect of the text's design.

15 Other women besides his wife whose existence the narrator 'validates' include the ballerinas 'worshipped from afar' (73) during his childhood stay in Paris, who are described as 'poised, living sculptures' (19) and 'sugar-plum fairies' (20).

16 This textual approach to the issue of gender in *Ever After* contrasts with the traditional type of 'images of women' criticism met with elsewhere. While Pamela Cooper is right to observe that 'gender is seldom treated as a theme in

critical examinations of Swift's fictions' (*Reader's Guide* 81), this dimension of Swift's work has been subjected to scrutiny by Mecklenburg and Alan Hickman. Both these critics adhere to a rather simple form of content analysis when confronted with the literary text, leading Mecklenburg, for example, to accuse the author of promoting 'ein extrem traditionalistisches Frauenbild' ('an extremely traditionalist image of womanhood'):

> Eine weibliche Figur, die familiäres Glück mit anderen Formen der Selbstverwirklichung, namentlich einer eigenen Berufsausübung, vereint, ist zwar innerhalb der übergeordneten moralischen Zielsetzung dieses Schrifstellers durchaus denkbar, allerdings bisher nicht einmal in Ansätzen ausgeführt.
>
> A female character who combines domestic happiness with other forms of self-realization, namely the pursuit of a profession of her own, while always thinkable within this author's overarching moral scheme, has been depicted not once until now. (170)

Not only does *Ever After* present itself as a counter-example to this claim – professional success apparently going hand-in-hand with domestic bliss for its main female protagonist – but the way in which the text exposes patriarchal constructions of women also suggests that a re-evaluation of Swift's gender politics is in order.

17 It should be noted, in this context, that Katherine is portrayed in the same terms as Ruth. Like Ruth, she seems to Bill 'like life itself. Like life itself' (87) – albeit that this time round the relationship is presented more cautiously as one of resemblance rather than identity. Also, her representation can be seen to depend on plenty of references to art and literature, including Eve, the Lady of the Castle (80), pastoralism, Ophelia and Botticelli (87). Finally, both women are perceived to have a face which occasionally falls apart and needs to be put back together again (77, 241).

18 Matthew expresses his concern about this issue as follows: 'These toiling masses of our mine-workers trouble me. . . . by what perverted definition of common humanity do we pronounce that they are brutes and not we?' (218).

19 Ironically, in view of the foundational and exemplary status which this royal romance is assigned by Bill, it has emerged that Wallis Simpson was conducting a secret affair during the 1936 Abdication Crisis. On 30 January 2003, the BBC reported: 'Wallis Simpson took a car salesman as her lover while she was in a relationship with Edward, Prince of Wales, secret government files on the 1936 abdication crisis reveal' (P. Reynolds). The 'fairy-tale propensity' with which Bill's life was supposedly imbued thus appears to have been blighted from the start.

20 Other arguments which Eaglestone adduces in support of his claim that Levinas's understanding of literature as pre-eminently 'said' is fundamentally contradictory include the potential literary status of Levinas's own writings and the fact that literature, being made up of language, cannot but comprise both the 'saying' and the 'said' allegedly present in all language (157–63).

21 The preceding interpretation of *Ever After* bears some resemblance to Keats's critique of the Wordsworthian 'egotistical sublime' (Keats, 'Woodhouse' 836). Though Keats immensely admired Wordsworth, he had reservations about the subjective and didactic qualities of his predecessor's poetry. In Keats's view, Wordsworth appears as a 'virtuous philosopher' ('Woodhouse' 836) who only ever stamps his own fixed self on the world. Keats himself, in contrast, claims to be a 'camelion poet' who 'has no Identity', 'has no self' and 'is every thing and nothing' ('Woodhouse' 836). Whereas Wordsworth seeks to subject the world to his own preconceived notions, the true 'poetical Character' ('Woodhouse' 836), according to Keats, is marked by a mode of openness and attentiveness to an alterity which it has no intention to master. Wordsworth's self-obsession bespeaks a lack of what Keats calls '*Negative Capability*', that is, the ability to endure 'being in uncertainties, Mysteries, doubts' with a concomitant suspension of 'any irritable reaching after fact & reason' ('Keats' 831). *Ever After*, while certainly no stranger to the egotistical sublime, is animated by this spirit of negative capability, which promotes an explorative but non-dominative subjectivity willing to suspend itself in defamiliarization or doubt.

7 'All the Same Underneath'? Sympathy and Ethics in *Last Orders*

1 Delineating class boundaries is a notoriously murky business. The term 'upper lower class' is employed here as a sort of in-between category, to avoid having to use either of two equally unsatisfactory alternatives: 'working class', which suggests wage labour and as such would seem to exclude Swift's shopkeepers, and 'lower middle class', which implies a degree of financial security and a relatively uncomplicated lifestyle unavailable to most inhabitants of the deprived London borough in which the novel is set. In light of the fact (which we will return to later on) that sympathy is more easily felt towards people resembling ourselves than towards complete strangers or outsiders, the fact that Swift chooses to portray upper-lower-class people – who aspire to middle-class respectability – rather than lower-lower-class characters is not without significance in itself.

2 This dismissal of class-based analysis as irrelevant to an understanding of *Last Orders* is symptomatic of the critical neglect which the concept of class has suffered following the collapse of communist and socialist regimes in Russia and eastern Europe. Attention within literary studies seems to have shifted to the social markers of gender, sexuality and race, though there are indications – amongst other things, special issues of *PMLA* (January 2000) and *Modern Fiction Studies* (Spring 2001) devoted to class – that the tide is turning again and that class as an analytic category may be regaining some of the ground it had lost.

3 Significantly, one of the novel's alleged drawbacks is 'the impression', which Bennetts calls '[s]omewhat disconcerting', 'that this is how an intellectual writer imagines the working class perceives things – how they think, talk and act – rather than an accurate representation of their speech and lives'.

4 'Mittels der konstanten, sich gegenseitig bedingenden Trias des spontanen Auslebens von Gefühlen, der offenen, zwischenmenschlichen Kommunikation und der Liebe zeigt der Autor seinen Charakteren und Lesern einen stets ähnlichen Weg aus möglichen Schwierigkeiten' ('By dint of the constant, mutually presupposing triad of the spontaneous display of emotion, open interhuman communication and love, the author shows his characters and readers a way out of possible difficulties which is always similar', Mecklenburg 181).

5 Just to show that this is not an isolated incident, here is another example of a passage in which this conjuring trick is performed. It deals with the use of accelerations, a phenomenon which Sartre had strongly condemned in his essay on Mauriac for foregrounding the author at the expense of his characters ('Il n'est peut-être pas, dans tout le livre d'erreur plus grave que ces lésineries' ('There is perhaps, in the entire novel, no worse error than this stinginess', 48)):

> En dépit de ses efforts, Sartre n'a d'ailleurs pas réussi à masquer toutes ses interventions: il y a dans ses romans des raccourcis où l'on peut déceler la présence de l'auteur. Sans doute n'est-elle pas aussi évidente que dans les raccourcis de *La Fin de la nuit*, tellement critiqués par Sartre, mais elle est quand même indéniable. . . . Cependant, les raccourcis sont relativement rares dans l'oeuvre romanesque de Sartre, et jamais outranciers: ils ne sont opérés que sur de petits morceaux de durée. Aussi se font-ils très vite oublier, et c'est le temps des personnages qui triomphe en définitive.
>
> Despite his efforts, Sartre has not managed to mask all of his interventions: there are accelerations in his novels in which one can detect the presence of the author. No doubt it is less apparent than in the accelerations of *La fin de la nuit*, so severely criticized by Sartre, but it is nevertheless undeniable. . . . Still, accelerations are relatively rare in Sartre's novelistic oeuvre, and never extreme: they are only used for short stretches of time. Moreover, they are very quickly forgotten, and it is the characters' time which wins out in the end. (79)

6 Morel claims that the contradiction revealed by the incongruity of the insertion of the voice of Jack's father is ultimately resolved by the reader in a return to the fictional contract demanding a willing suspension of disbelief:

> en fin de compte notre désir l'emporte de croire quand même que ces êtres, dont nous savons bien qu'ils sont de fiction, sont en quelque sorte rendus plus fiables d'être ainsi fragilisés. Ici au moins, pas de narrateur, serions-nous tentés de dire. Et je ne suis pas sûr que ce ne soit pas cette position seconde de retour du contrat ordinaire de fiction qui l'emporte, malgré toutes les contradictions, tant est fort notre désir de croire.
>
> at the end of the day our desire to believe anyway that these creatures, whom we know full well to be fictitious, are somehow made more reliable by being thus fragmented carries the day. Here, at least, no narrator, we would be tempted to say. And I am not sure that it is not this second position of return to the ordinary fictional contract which carries the day, despite all the contradictions, so strong is our desire to believe. ('Le récit orphelin' 83)

However, a critical reading of the novel should not attempt to cover over this contradiction but rather take it on board and explore the interpretative possibilities which it affords.

7 'les paroles intérieures sont légitimées par l'appui qu'elles prennent sur la *doxa* collective, en particulier sur les expressions reçues' ('the interior monologues are legitimated by their dependence on the collective *doxa*, particularly on received expressions'; Morel, 'Le récit orphelin' 78).

8 The conclusion arrived at here would seem to leave little or no space for 'the sense of the characters gaily speaking their own minds and leading their own lives' which Oliver Reynolds attributes to the novel in his thoroughly sympathetic reading of it (25).

9 Or, as Heike Hartung-Brückner puts it, 'The gypsies are constructed as the "other" against which Amy perceives her own – and her group – identity.'

10 Particularly outspoken in her criticism is Flint, who detects a 'smug' and 'narrow-minded parochialism' in *Last Orders* (41), and accuses the author of promoting static and reactionary images of the nation (40).

11 Fred Schepisi's moving film version of *Last Orders* does not allow for this type of counter-reading. Indeed, there are hardly any traces left of the various elements on which the alternative interpretation of the novel offered here is based. The authoritative gaze has all but disappeared, Mr Hussein and Romany Jim have been tucked away, and the integrative role of language is much less pronounced in the film than in the book. Moreover, the ghostly intrusion of the voice of Jack's father is neutralized by being rendered as just another flash-back attributable to Vince: most of the injunction lines are spoken by Jack in a scene which finds the latter lecturing Vince at the abattoir while an older man – presumably Jack's father, though he is not identified as such – is standing by. While Schepisi's adaptation has been justly celebrated as a work of art in its own right, largely thanks to the extraordinary performances by its star-studded cast, Peter Bradshaw is right to remark that 'you need a bit of a sweet tooth for Cockney nostalgia' to appreciate the film – Cockney nostalgia which, as he goes on to point out, 'runs quite close to reactionary sentimentalism'.

12 As if to add to the irony, Margate became the scene of several far-right National Front demonstrations against asylum-seekers in 2000.

13 The alleged postmodern nature of *Last Orders*' narrative technique is a questionable point. Indeed, as John Marsden points out, 'In its shifting perspectives and its provision of information whose meaning and relevance is illuminated elsewhere in the text, the structure obviously owes a debt to the modernism not only – *pace* John Frow – of Faulkner, but of Joyce, Woolf, T. S. Eliot and others' ('After Modernism' 189). John Frow is an English professor at the University of Queensland who, in March 1997, caused something of a stir in the British press by suggesting that the (numerous and obvious) thematic and technical similarities between Swift's Booker Prize-winning novel and Faulkner's modernist classic *As I Lay Dying* were just a little too apparent. For

some background on this controversy – or, rather, storm-in-a-teacup – see Cherry Norton's 'Swift's Booker Winner "Borrowed" from Faulkner's Masterpiece', Swift's 'I Never Pretended My Novel Owed No Debt to Faulkner', Ian Murray's 'Booker Winner Denies Plot "Theft"' and Frow's 'Parallel Texts and a Fictional Life', all published in *The Times* and the *Sunday Times* between 9 and 15 March 1997; as well as Stuart Millar's 'Literati Back "Plot-Lifter" Swift' and Stephen Moss's 'A Classic Reworked in an Original Way', which appeared in the *Guardian* on 10 March 1997.

14 For another attempt to rescue *Last Orders* from reduction to a simplistic conception of ethics, see Wheeler, 'Melancholic' 76–78 or 'In the Middle' 148–51. Wheeler argues that 'Swift's purpose is not to argue simply for community, or "immediate ethical experience in place of the risks of critical rationality", as Gillian Rose puts it' ('Melancholic' 78). Taking her cue from Rose, she maintains that the characters of *Last Orders* 'follow the commands of love, not as desire, but rather as a kind of acknowledgement of obligations' ('Melancholic' 76). The work of mourning in which they engage is said to be linked to 'the work of mutual recognition and obligation which is love (*caritas*) as work in the social and political commitments and activities of the day to day – "activity beyond activity" as Gillian Rose puts it, and the bindings-up of labouring communality' ('Melancholic' 76).

8 Adieu: Stepping into *The Light of Day*

1 The upbeat tenor of *The Light of Day* appears to reflect a change in the author's general outlook on life. Swift nowadays claims to be 'an optimist in many ways' (quoted in Birnbaum), whereas in a 1988 interview – entitled 'The Attraction of the Pessimistic View' – he confirmed the interviewer's suspicion that he regards the world pessimistically: 'In a strict philosophical sense, I do. I'm actually quite a happy person, and I'm certainly lucky, lucky to be doing what I'm doing. But, looking around and thinking, one inclines to a pessimistic view – or I do. Simply by keeping one's eyes open' (quoted in Profumo, 'Attraction').

2 This jubilant ending is a far cry from the darkness, desolation and despair dominating the final pages of *The Sweet Shop Owner*.

3 For example: 'But ye are a chosen generation, a royal priesthood, an holy nation, a peculiar people; that ye should shew forth the praises of him who hath called you out of darkness into his marvellous light: Which in time past were not a people, but are now the people of God: which had not obtained mercy, but now have obtained mercy' (*Bible*, 1 Pet. 2.9–10); 'Then spake Jesus again unto them, saying, I am the light of the world: he that followeth me shall not walk in darkness, but shall have the light of life' (*Bible*, John 8.12); 'Giving thanks unto the Father, which hath made us meet to be partakers of the inheritance of the saints in light: Who hath delivered us from the power of darkness, and hath translated us into the kingdom of his dear Son' (*Bible*, Col. 1.12–13); 'For ye were sometimes darkness, but now are ye light in the Lord: walk as children of light' (*Bible*, Eph. 5.8).

4 In support of Cooper's claims about the 'Christly properties' (47) clinging to Ray, one could also point to the fact that the horse that Ray backs in an effort to redeem Jack's debts is not just named 'Miracle Worker' (as Cooper notes (48)), but is running at odds of thirty-three to one – thirty-three being, of course, the presumed age of Christ at his death.

5 The religious dimension of *Last Orders* has also been remarked upon by Wheeler. One of the most interesting things about the novel, she suggests, is

> the way in which – beneath the ordinary Bermondsey voices and lives, and embedded in both the pilgrimage form and the allegory names of so many of the characters (Victor, Vince, Ray, Amy and the death-bed nurse Joy) – another language surprisingly emerges: the symbolic language of the spirit and the soul. No elevated language here, but, nonetheless, a glimpse of the sacred and the enchanted. ('In the Middle' 149)

In the entry on Swift in *The Literary Encyclopedia and Literary Dictionary*, Wheeler even goes so far as to claim that 'Swift is essentially a religious writer in secular clothes'.

6 Cooper already hinted at this interpretation of *Waterland* in her 1996 article 'Imperial Topographies', in which she suggests that Dick's suicide is 'potentially a prelude to his miraculous resurrection' (388). Another critic who considers the narrator's brother as a Christ figure is John Schad, who contends that Dick dies in the place of the 'guiltier' Tom: 'Thus, in diving into the water Dick . . . finally becomes the sacrificial "saviour of the world" that his grandfather always predicted he would be' (915).

7 Contrary to what Wells and Cooper claim, the narrator does not fatalistically accept this cycle as an inevitable reality but is driven by a determination to end it, as was shown in chapter 4.

8 Other such effects are Sarah having '[i]nvolved' a detective ('Involved!') (221), Bob getting home 'safely' on the night of the murder ('If "safely" wasn't an unfortunate word') (196), Sarah being 'dressed – don't say it – to kill' (161), and the fateful day being remembered with '[a] stab' (182).

9 Harries's comments on this particular passage are consistent with his overall argument that while Marx announces himself as 'a critic of enchantment' in *The Eighteenth Brumaire*, his engagement with the supernatural turns out to be 'an inextricable entanglement' with it: 'At moments, . . . it seems as if Marx can imagine a positive counterforce to reenchantment only in enchanted or magical terms. The words he uses to describe what he detests, the reactionary coup, for instance, are not wholly opposed to those he uses to picture what he desires, revolution' (57).

Conclusion: A Pathless Path

1 'Wanderer, there is no path, the path is made by walking.'

2 A similar pattern is discerned by Wendy Wheeler, who writes that 'The move between *Out of this World* and *Ever After* repeats the shift noticeable between *Shuttlecock* and *Waterland*' (*From the Sublime* 137).

Bibliography

1. Primary Sources

1.1. Fiction

Swift, Graham. 'The Recreation Ground.' *London Magazine* 16.1 (April/May 1976): 62–85.
——. *The Sweet Shop Owner*. London: Allen Lane, 1980. London: Picador, 1997.
——. *Shuttlecock*. London: Allen Lane, 1981. London: Picador, 1997.
——. 'Hide and Seek.' *New Stories 7*. Ed. Alan Ross. London: Hutchinson, 1982. 29–45.
——. *Learning to Swim and Other Stories*. London: London Magazine Editions, 1982. London: Picador, 1998.
——. *Waterland*. London: Heinemann, 1983. London: Picador, 1992.
Profumo, David, and Graham Swift, eds. *The Magic Wheel: An Anthology of Fishing in Literature*. London: Heinemann, 1985.
Swift, Graham. *Out of this World*. London: Viking, 1988. London: Picador, 1997.
——. *Ever After*. London: Picador, 1992.
——. '1974.' *21 Picador Authors Celebrate 21 Years of Outstanding International Writing*. London: Picador, 1993. 19–27.
——. *Last Orders*. London: Picador, 1996.
——. 'Our Nicky's Heart.' *Granta 69: The Assassin* (Spring 2000): 169–78.
——. *The Light of Day*. London: Hamish Hamilton, 2003.

1.2. Criticism and Journalism

Swift, Graham. 'Throwing Off Our Inhibitions.' *The Times*, 5 March 1988: 20.
——. 'Looking for Jiří Wolf.' *Granta 30: New Europe!* (Spring 1990): 9–40.
——. 'I Never Pretended My Novel Owed No Debt to Faulkner.' *The Times*, 10 March 1997. *The Times and The Sunday Times Compact Disc Edition*. Full text, from 1990 onwards. CD-ROM.
——. 'Fishing, Writing and Ted.' *Granta 65: London: The Lives of the City* (Spring 1999): 345–51.
——. 'My Canterbury Tale.' *The Observer*, 6 January 2002. 17 June 2002 <http://www.guardian.co.uk/Archive/Article/0,4273,4329880,00.html>.

1.3. Interviews

Bernard, Catherine. 'An Interview with Graham Swift.' *Contemporary Literature* 38.2 (1996): 216–31.

Bernard, Catherine, and Gilles Menegaldo. Interview with Graham Swift. *Graham Swift ou le temps du récit.* Ed. Michel Morel. Paris: Ed. Messene, 1996. 9–18.

Birnbaum, Robert. Interview with Graham Swift. *Identity Theory*, 2 July 2003. 13 July 2003 <http://www.identitytheory.com/interviews/birnbaum114.html>.

D'hoker, Elke. 'Vanuit de duisternis.' Interview with Graham Swift. *De Financieel-Economische Tijd – Tijd Cultuur*, 18 December 2002: 23.

Hemmerechts, Kristien. 'Verwarring is de essentie van het leven.' Interview with Graham Swift. *De Standaard der Letteren*, 12 December 2002: 4–5.

Porée, Marc. 'Entretien avec Graham Swift.' *La quinzaine littéraire* 621 (1993): 10–11.

Profumo, David. 'The Attraction of the Pessimistic View.' Interview with Graham Swift. *The Sunday Times*, 6 March 1988: G9.

——. Interview with Graham Swift. ICA *Guardian* Conversation. 1988. Writers Talk: Ideas of Our Time. *The Roland Collection of Films & Videos on Art.* 25 July 2000 <http://www.roland-collection/rolandcollection/preview/W82.ram>.

Quinn, Anthony. 'Voice of the People Graham Swift Has Gone from the "Sublime to the Gorblimey" with His New Novel. He Tells Anthony Quinn Why.' Interview with Graham Swift. *The Observer*, 14 January 1996: 16. *Northern Light Special Collection.* 25 July 2000 <http://library.northernlight.com/MB19990930010757300.html>.

Rosenberg, Scott. 'Glowing in the Ashes.' Interview with Graham Swift. *Salon*, 6 May 1996. 1 June 2003 <http://www.salon.com/weekly/swift960506.html>.

Smith, Amanda. 'Graham Swift: The British Novelist Grapples with the Ambiguities of Knowledge and the Secrets of the Past.' Interview with Graham Swift. *Publishers Weekly*, 17 February 1992: 43–44. *Literature Resource Center.* Gale Group Databases. Universiteitsbibliotheek K. U. Leuven, Leuven. 8 May 2001 <http://www.infotrac.galegroup.com/>.

Vásquez, Juan Gabriel. 'Graham Swift y el sentido de la historia: Una entrevista.' *Cuadernos Hispanoamericanos*, February 2003: 99–110.

Vianu, Lidia. 'I Hope I Write with My Soul First and My Mind Second.' Interview with Graham Swift. *România Literarà*, 21–27 February 2001. 10 June 2003 <http://lidiavianu.scriptmania.com/graham_swift.htm>.

2. Secondary Sources

Abrams, M. H., et al., eds. *The Norton Anthology of English Literature.* 6th ed. Vol. 2. New York: Norton, 1993.

Arendt, Hannah. *Eichmann in Jerusalem: A Report on the Banality of Evil.* Revised and enlarged ed. Harmondsworth: Penguin, 1984.

Armstrong, Nancy. *Fiction in the Age of Photography: The Legacy of British Realism.* Cambridge, MA: Harvard University Press, 2002.

Attridge, Derek. 'Innovation, Literature, Ethics: Relating to the Other.' *PMLA* 114.1 (1999): 20–31.

——. 'Literary Form and the Demand of Politics: Otherness in J. M. Coetzee's *Age of Iron*.' *Aesthetics and Ideology*. Ed. George Levine. New Brunswick: Rutgers University Press, 1994. 243–63.

Aulich, James. 'Introduction.' *Framing the Falklands War: Nationhood, Culture, Identity*. Ed. James Aulich. Buckingham: Open University Press, 1992. 1–12.

Banville, John. 'That's Life!' Review of *Last Orders*, by Graham Swift. *The New York Review of Books*, 4 April 1996: 8. *Northern Light Special Collection*. 25 July 2000 <http://library.northernlight.com/SL19980508050010016.html>.

Barthes, Roland. *Camera Lucida: Reflections on Photography*. Trans. Richard Howard. London: Fontana, 1984.

Belau, Linda. 'Trauma and the Material Signifier.' *Postmodern Culture* 11.2 (2001). 22 February 2001 <http://jefferson.village.virginia.edu/pmc/current.issue/11.2belau.html>.

Benhabib, Seyla. 'Arendt's *Eichmann in Jerusalem*.' *The Cambridge Companion to Hannah Arendt*. Ed. Dana Villa. Cambridge: Cambridge University Press, 2000. 65–85.

Bennetts, Melissa. 'A Journey in Memory of an Old Friend.' Review of *Last Orders*, by Graham Swift. *The Christian Science Monitor*, 27 February 1997: B1. *Academic Search Elite*. EBSCOhost. Universiteitsbibliotheek K. U. Leuven, Leuven. 9 November 2000 <http://search.epnet.com/>.

Bényei, Tamás. 'The Novels of Graham Swift: Family Photos.' *Contemporary British Fiction*. Ed. Richard J. Lane, Rod Mengham, and Philip Tew. Cambridge: Polity Press, 2003. 40–55.

Bernard, Catherine. 'Dismembering/Remembering Mimesis: Martin Amis, Graham Swift.' *British Postmodern Fiction*. Ed. Theo D'haen and Hans Bertens. Amsterdam: Rodopi, 1993. 121–44.

——. *Graham Swift: La parole chronique*. Univers anglo-américain. Nancy: Presses universitaires de Nancy, 1991.

Bhattacharya, Soumya. 'Murder He Wrote.' Review of *The Light of Day*, by Graham Swift. *Hindustan Times*. 14 April 2003 <http://www.htcricket.com/news/181_228783,0011000400070001.htm>.

The Bible: King James Version. Oxford Text Archive. 22 June 2003 <http://ota.ahds.ac.uk/>.

Birkerts, Sven. 'Chains of Love.' Review of *The Light of Day*, by Graham Swift. *Book Magazine*, May/June 2003. 29 April 2003 <http://www.bookmagazine.com/issue28/sbirkerts.shtml>.

Blanchot, Maurice. 'After the Fact.' *The Station Hill Blanchot Reader: Fiction and Literary Essays*. Trans. Lydia Davis, Paul Auster, and Robert Lamberton. Ed. George Quasha. Barrytown: Station Hill, 1999. 487–95.

——. 'Literature and the Right to Death.' Trans. Lydia Davis. *The Work of Fire*. Stanford: Stanford University Press, 1995. 300–44.

——. *The Space of Literature*. Trans. Ann Smock. Lincoln: University of Nebraska Press, 1982.

——. *The Writing of the Disaster/L'écriture du désastre*. Trans. Ann Smock. Lincoln: University of Nebraska Press, 1986.

Botting, Fred. *Sex, Machines and Navels: Fiction, Fantasy and History in the Future Present*. Manchester: Manchester University Press, 1999.

Boughner, Sheila Rae. *Ethics at the Edge of Sense*. Dissertation. State University of New York, 1996. Ann Arbor: UMI, 2000.

Bouniot, Sophie. 'La solution finale: L'ordinaire monstrueux.' Interview with Rony Brauman. *L'humanité*, 5 June 1999. 16 October 2002 <http://www.humanite.presse.fr/journal/1999/1999–06/1999–06–05/1999–06–05–023.html>.

Bradshaw, Peter. 'Through a Beer Glass Nostalgically.' Review of *Last Orders*, dir. Fred Schepisi. *The Guardian Weekly*, 17–23 January 2002: 19.

Brauman, Rony, and Eyal Sivan. *Éloge de la désobéissance*. Manifestes. N.p.: Le Pommier, 1999.

Brewer, John, and Stella Tillyard. 'History and Telling Stories: Graham Swift's *Waterland*.' *History Today* 35 (January 1985): 49–51.

Buell, Lawrence. 'Introduction: In Pursuit of Ethics.' *PMLA* 114.1 (1999): 7–19.

Burns, E. Jane. 'Courtly Love: Who Needs It? Recent Feminist Work in the Medieval French Tradition.' *Signs: Journal of Women in Culture and Society* 27.1 (2001): 23–57.

Camus, Albert. *The Rebel*. Trans. Anthony Bower. London: Hamish Hamilton, 1960.

Caruth, Cathy, ed. *Trauma: Explorations in Memory*. Baltimore: Johns Hopkins University Press, 1995.

Caruth, Cathy. *Unclaimed Experience: Trauma, Narrative, and History*. Baltimore: Johns Hopkins University Press, 1996.

Cavell, Stanley. *In Quest of the Ordinary: Lines of Skepticism and Romanticism*. Chicago: University of Chicago Press, 1988.

Celyn-Jones, Russell. 'Locked Up in Its Own Subtlety.' Review of *The Light of Day*, by Graham Swift. *The Times*, 5 March 2003. 13 March 2003 <http://www.timesonline.co.uk/article/0,,923–599309,00.html>.

Coe, Jonathan. 'Jagged Edges.' Review of *Out of this World*, by Graham Swift. *The Guardian*, 11 March 1988. 22 August 2002 <http://books.guardian.co.uk/reviews/generalfiction/0,6121,98881,00.html>.

Cooper, Pamela. *Graham Swift's* Last Orders*: A Reader's Guide*. Continuum Contemporaries. New York: Continuum, 2002.

——. 'Imperial Topographies: The Spaces of History in *Waterland*.' *Modern Fiction Studies* 42.2 (1996): 371–96.

Critchley, Simon. *Very Little…Almost Nothing: Death, Philosophy, Literature*. London: Routledge, 1997.

Davies, Tony. *Humanism*. New Critical Idiom. London: Routledge, 1997.

Decoste, Damon Marcel. 'Question and Apocalypse: The Endlessness of *Historia* in Graham Swift's *Waterland*.' *Contemporary Literature* 43.2 (2002): 377–99.

de Graef, Ortwin. 'Suffering, Sympathy, Circulation: Smith, Wordsworth, Coetzee (But There's a Dog).' *EJES: European Journal of English Studies* 7.3 (2003): 311–31.

de Graef, Ortwin, Vivian Liska, and Katrien Vloeberghs. 'Introduction: The Instance of Trauma.' *EJES: European Journal of English Studies* 7.3 (2003): 247–55.

de Man, Paul. *The Rhetoric of Romanticism.* New York: Columbia University Press, 1984.

Derrida, Jacques. 'Faith and Knowledge: The Two Sources of "Religion" at the Limits of Reason Alone.' *Religion.* Ed. Jacques Derrida and Gianni Vattimo. Cambridge: Polity Press, 1998. 1–78.

——. *The Gift of Death.* Trans. David Wills. Chicago: University of Chicago Press, 1995.

——. 'Given Time: The Time of the King.' Trans. Peggy Kamuf. *Critical Inquiry* 18 (Winter 1992): 161–87.

——. *The Other Heading: Reflections on Today's Europe.* Trans. Pascale-Anne Brault and Michael B. Naas. Bloomington: Indiana University Press, 1992.

——. *Specters of Marx: The State of the Debt, the Work of Mourning, and the New International.* Trans. Peggy Kamuf. New York: Routledge, 1994.

——. 'Violence and Metaphysics: An Essay on the Thought of Emmanuel Levinas.' *Writing and Difference.* Trans. Alan Bass. Chicago: University of Chicago Press, 1978. 79–153.

de Vries, Hent. *Philosophy and the Turn to Religion.* Baltimore: Johns Hopkins University Press, 1999.

Dobbins, Austin C., and Roy W. Battenhouse. 'Jessica's Morals: A Theological View.' *Shakespeare Studies* 9 (1976): 107–20.

Duchêne, Anne. 'By the Grace of the Teller.' Review of *Out of this World*, by Graham Swift. *The Times Literary Supplement*, 17 November 1988: 275.

During, Lisabeth. 'The Concept of Dread: Sympathy and Ethics in *Daniel Deronda.*' *Renegotiating Ethics in Literature, Philosophy, and Theory.* Ed. Jane Adamson, Richard Freadman, and David Parker. Cambridge: Cambridge University Press, 1998. 65–83.

Eaglestone, Robert. *Ethical Criticism: Reading after Levinas.* Edinburgh: Edinburgh University Press, 1997.

Edkins, Jenny. 'Trauma, Memory and Sovereign Power.' Paper presented on the panel 'Mediating Internationals' at the International Studies Association 42nd Annual Convention, Chicago, Illinois, 20–24 February 2001. 15 December 2002 <http://www.isanet.org/archive/edkins1.doc>.

Eliot, T. S. *The Waste Land.* Abrams et al. 2146–60.

Ewans, Michael. 'Patterns of Tragedy in Sophokles and Shakespeare.' *Tragedy and the Tragic: Greek Theatre and Beyond.* Ed. M. S. Silk. Oxford: Clarendon, 1996. 438–57.

Farrell, Kirby. *Post-Traumatic Culture: Injury and Interpretation in the Nineties.* Baltimore: Johns Hopkins University Press, 1998.

Felman, Shoshana, and Dori Laub, M. D. *Testimony: Crises of Witnessing in Literature, Psychoanalysis, and History.* New York: Routledge, 1992.

Flint, Kate. 'Looking Backward? The Relevance of Britishness.' *Unity in Diversity*

Revisited? British Literature and Culture in the 1990s. Ed. Barbara Korte and Klaus Peter Müller. Tübingen: Günter Narr Verlag, 1998. 35–50.

Freud, Sigmund. 'Mourning and Melancholia.' *The Standard Edition of the Complete Psychological Works of Sigmund Freud.* Trans. James Strachey. Vol. 14. London: Hogarth, 1978. 243–58.

Frow, John. 'Parallel Texts and a Fictional Life.' *The Times*, 15 March 1997. *The Times and The Sunday Times Compact Disc Edition.* Full text, from 1990 onwards. CD-ROM.

Gallix, François. *Graham Swift: Écrire l'imagination.* Pessac: Presses universitaires de Bordeaux, 2003.

Gasché, Rodolphe. 'The Felicities of Paradox: Blanchot on the Null-Space of Literature.' *Maurice Blanchot: The Demand of Writing.* Ed. Carolyn Bailey Gill. London: Routledge, 1996. 34–69.

Gasiorek, Andrzej. *Post-War British Fiction: Realism and After.* London: Edward Arnold, 1995.

Gibson, Andrew. *Postmodernity, Ethics and the Novel.* London: Routledge, 1999.

Gorra, Michael. 'When Life Closes In.' Review of *The Sweet Shop Owner*, by Graham Swift. *The New York Times Book Review*, 23 June 1985: 11.

'Graham Swift.' *eDionysus.* 17 June 2002 <http://literature.edionysus.com/biography/s/swiftg.html>.

Gramsci, Antonio. *Selections from the Prison Notebooks.* Ed. and trans. Quintin Hoare and Geoffrey Nowell Smith. London: Lawrence & Wishart, 1971.

Greengrass, Paul. 'Foreword.' *Framing the Falklands War: Nationhood, Culture, Identity.* Ed. James Aulich. Buckingham: Open University Press, 1992. ix–x.

Harpham, Geoffrey Galt. 'Ethics and Literary Criticism.' *The Cambridge History of Literary Criticism, Volume 9: Twentieth-Century Historical, Philosophical and Psychological Perspectives.* Ed. Christa Knellwolf and Christopher Norris. Cambridge: Cambridge University Press, 2001. 371–85.

——. *Getting It Right: Language, Literature, and Ethics.* Chicago: University of Chicago Press, 1992.

——. *Shadows of Ethics: Criticism and the Just Society.* Durham: Duke University Press, 1999.

Harries, Martin. *Scare Quotes from Shakespeare: Marx, Keynes, and the Language of Reenchantment.* Stanford: Stanford University Press, 2000.

Harris, MacDonald. 'Love among the Ichthyosaurs.' Review of *Ever After*, by Graham Swift. *The New York Times Book Review*, 29 March 1992: 211.

Hartman, Geoffrey H. 'On Traumatic Knowledge and Literary Studies.' *New Literary History* 26.3 (1995): 537–63.

Hartung-Brückner, Heike. '(Re)constructions of History and (De)constructions of "Englishness."' Part 3 of 'History and "Englishness" in Graham Swift's *Last Orders.*' *Postimperial and Postcolonial Literature in English.* 15 July 2003 <http://www.victorianweb.org/post/uk/gswift/lastorders/hhb3.html>.

Herman, Judith. *Trauma and Recovery: The Aftermath of Violence – from Domestic Abuse to Political Terror.* New York: Basic Books, 1992.

Hickman, Alan Forrest. *'Wedded to the World': Natural and Artificial History in the*

Novels of Graham Swift. Dissertation. University of Arkansas, 1990. Ann Arbor: UMI, 2000.

Higdon, David Leon. 'Double Closures in Postmodern British Fiction: The Example of Graham Swift.' *Critical Survey* 3.1 (1991): 88–95. *Literature Resource Center*. Gale Group Databases. Universiteitsbibliotheek K. U. Leuven, Leuven. 8 May 2001 <http://www.infotrac.galegroup.com/>.

——. '"Unconfessed Confessions": The Narrators of Graham Swift and Julian Barnes.' *The British and Irish Novel since 1960*. Ed. James Acheson. Houndmills: Macmillan, 1991. 174–91.

Holmes, Frederick M. 'The Representation of History as Plastic: The Search for the Real Thing in Graham Swift's *Ever After*.' *ARIEL* 27.3 (1996): 25–43.

Hutcheon, Linda. *A Poetics of Postmodernism: History, Theory, Fiction*. New York: Routledge, 1988.

——. *The Politics of Postmodernism*. London: Routledge, 1989.

Ingelbien, Raphaël. '"England and Nowhere": Contestations of Englishness in Philip Larkin and Graham Swift.' *English* 48 (Spring 1999): 33–48.

Irish, Robert K. '"Let Me Tell You": About Desire and Narrativity in Graham Swift's *Waterland*.' *Modern Fiction Studies* 44.4 (Winter 1998): 917–34.

Jacobmeyer, Hannah. 'Graham Swift, *Ever After*: A Study in Intertextuality.' *EESE* (1998). 2 April 2002 <http://webdoc.gwdg.de/edoc/ia/eese/artic98/jacobm/8_98.html>.

Jameson, Fredric. *The Political Unconscious: Narrative as a Socially Symbolic Act*. Ithaca: Cornell University Press, 1982.

Janik, Del Ivan. 'History and the "Here and Now": The Novels of Graham Swift.' *Twentieth Century Literature* 35.1 (Spring 1989): 74–88.

——. 'No End of History: Evidence from the Contemporary English Novel.' *Twentieth Century Literature* 41.2 (1995): 160–89. *Northern Light Special Collection*. 25 July 2000 <http://library.northernlight.com/LW19971006230003220.html>.

Kaczvinsky, Donald P. '"For One Thing, There Are the Gaps": History in Graham Swift's *Shuttlecock*.' *Critique: Studies in Contemporary Fiction* 40.1 (1998): 3–14.

Keats, John. Letter to George and Thomas Keats, December 21, 27 (?), 1817. Abrams et al. 830–31.

——. Letter to Richard Woodhouse, October 27, 1818. Abrams et al. 836–37.

Kitto, H. D. F. *Form and Meaning in Drama: A Study of Six Greek Plays and of Hamlet*. 2nd ed. London: Methuen, 1964.

LaCapra, Dominick. *History and Memory after Auschwitz*. Ithaca: Cornell University Press, 1998.

——. *Representing the Holocaust: History, Theory, Trauma*. Ithaca: Cornell University Press, 1994.

——. *Writing History, Writing Trauma*. Baltimore: Johns Hopkins University Press, 2001.

Landow, George P. 'History, His Story, and Stories in Graham Swift's *Waterland*.' *Studies in the Literary Imagination* 23.2 (1990): 197–211.

Last Orders. By Graham Swift. Screenplay by Fred Schepisi. Dir. Fred Schepisi.

Perf. Michael Caine, Bob Hoskins, Tom Courtenay, David Hemmings, Ray Winstone, and Helen Mirren. Sony Pictures Classics/Metrodome Distribution, 2001.

Lecercle, Jean-Jacques. 'Répétition, remémoration, perlaboration dans *Waterland*.' Morel 39–48.

Lee, Alison. *Realism and Power: Postmodern British Fiction*. London: Routledge, 1990.

Lee, Hermione. 'Shutter and Lens.' Review of *Out of this World*, by Graham Swift. *The Observer*, 13 March 1988: 43. *Literature Resource Center*. Gale Group Databases. Universiteitsbibliotheek K. U. Leuven, Leuven. 10 July 2003 <http://www.infotrac.galegroup.com/>.

Le Guin, Ursula: 'Victorian Secrets. "Ever After" by Graham Swift.' Review of *Ever After*, by Graham Swift. *The Washington Post*, 22 March 1992: 6.

Leigh, Nigel. 'A Limited Engagement: Falklands Fictions and the English Novel.' *Framing the Falklands War: Nationhood, Culture, Identity*. Ed. James Aulich. Buckingham: Open University Press, 1992. 117–28.

Lentricchia, Frank, and Thomas McLaughlin, eds. *Critical Terms for Literary Study*. Chicago: Chicago University Press, 1990.

——. *Critical Terms for Literary Study*. 2nd ed. Chicago: Chicago University Press, 1995.

Levenson, M. 'Sons and Fathers.' Review of *Ever After*, by Graham Swift. *The New Republic*, 22 June 1992: 38–40. *Academic Search Elite*. EBSCOhost. Universiteitsbibliotheek K. U. Leuven, Leuven. 9 November 2000 <http://search.epnet.com/>.

Lévinas, Emmanuel. *Autrement qu'être ou au-delà de l'essence*. Le Livre de Poche. N.p.: Kluwer Academic, [1996].

Lewis, C. S. *The Allegory of Love: A Study in Medieval Tradition*. London: Oxford University Press, 1936.

Leys, Ruth. *Trauma: A Genealogy*. Chicago: University of Chicago Press, 2000.

Lord, Geoffrey W. 'Graham Swift.' *Post-War Literatures in English: A Lexicon of Contemporary Authors*. Ed. Hans Bertens et al. Groningen: Wolters Noordhoff, 1995. 1–11, A-1, B-1.

——. 'Mystery and History, Discovery and Recovery in Thomas Pynchon's *The Crying of Lot 49* and Graham Swift's *Waterland*.' *Neophilologus* 81.1 (1997): 145–63.

Machado, Antonio. *Poesías completas*. 9th ed. Madrid: Espasa Calpe, 1962.

Malcolm, David. *Understanding Graham Swift*. Understanding Contemporary British Literature. Columbia: University of South Carolina Press, 2003.

Marsden, John Lloyd. *After Modernism: Representations of the Past in the Novels of Graham Swift*. Dissertation. Ohio University, 1996. Ann Arbor: UMI, 2000.

——. 'After Modernism: Representations of the Past in the Novels of Graham Swift.' Unpublished manuscript, [1997]. Revised version of Marsden, John Lloyd. *After Modernism: Representations of the Past in the Novels of Graham Swift*. Dissertation. Ohio University, 1996. Ann Arbor: UMI, 2000.

Marx, Karl. *The Eighteenth Brumaire of Louis Bonaparte*. *Marx/Engels Internet*

Archive. 1999. 13 July 2003 <http://www.marxists.org/archive/marx/works/1852/18th-brumaire/index.htm>.

McKinney, Ronald H. 'The Greening of Postmodernism: Graham Swift's *Waterland*.' *New Literary History* 28 (1997): 821–32.

Mecklenburg, Susanne. *Martin Amis und Graham Swift: Erfolg durch bodenlosen Moralismus im zeitgenössischen britischen Roman*. Heidelberg: Universitätsverlag C. Winter, 2000.

Millar, Stuart. 'Literati Back "Plot-Lifter" Swift.' *The Guardian*, 10 March 1997: 3.

Milne, Kirsty. 'Static Pools.' Review of *Ever After*, by Graham Swift. *The New Statesman*, 21 February 1992: 40.

Miquel, Catherine. 'Immortal Longings: La mort en représentation dans l'oeuvre de Graham Swift.' *Études Britanniques Contemporaines* 17 (1999): 131–48.

Moi, Toril. *Sexual/Textual Politics: Feminist Literary Theory*. London: Routledge, 1995.

Morel, Michel, ed. *Graham Swift ou le temps du récit*. Paris: Ed. Messene, 1996.

——. '*Last Orders*: Le récit orphelin.' Morel 71–84.

——. '*Out of this World*: Le romancier, pourvoyeur d'images malgré lui.' Morel 19–27.

Moretti, Franco. *The Way of the World: The* Bildungsroman *in European Culture*. London: Verso, 1987.

Moss, Stephen. 'A Classic Reworked in an Original Way.' *The Guardian*, 10 March 1997: 3.

Murphy, Sean P. 'In the Middle of Nowhere: The Interpellative Force of Experimental Narrative Structure in Graham Swift's *Waterland*.' *Studies in the Humanities* 23.1 (1996): 70–83.

Murray, Ian. 'Booker Winner Denies Plot "Theft."' *The Times*, 10 March 1997. *The Times and The Sunday Times Compact Disc Edition*. Full text, from 1990 onwards. CD-ROM.

Norton, Cherry. 'Swift's Booker Winner "Borrowed" from Faulkner's Masterpiece.' *The Sunday Times*, 9 March 1997. *The Times and The Sunday Times Compact Disc Edition*. Full text, from 1990 onwards. CD-ROM.

Nünning, Ansgar. *Von historischer Fiktion zu historiographischer Metafiktion, Band 2: Erscheinungsformen und Entwicklungstendenzen des historischen Romans in England seit 1950*. Trier: Wissenschaftlicher Verlag Trier, 1995.

Nussbaum, Martha C. 'Exactly and Responsibly: A Defense of Ethical Criticism.' *Philosophy and Literature* 22.2 (1998): 343–65.

——. *Love's Knowledge: Essays on Philosophy and Literature*. Oxford: Oxford University Press, 1990.

——. *Poetic Justice: The Literary Imagination and Public Life*. Boston: Beacon Press, 1995.

O'Donnell, Patrick. 'Masterplots II: *Shuttlecock*.' *The Salem Press*, 1 January 1987. *Northern Light Special Collection*. 25 July 2000 <http://library.northernlight.com/DG19980107030007306.html>.

O'Mahony, John. 'Triumph of the Common Man.' *The Guardian*, 1 March 2003.

10 March 2003 <http://books.guardian.co.uk/review/story/0,12084,904399,00.html>.

Parini, Jay. 'Canterbury Tale.' Review of *Last Orders*, by Graham Swift. *The New York Times Book Review*, 5 May 1996: 13.

Parker, David. 'Introduction: The Turn to Ethics in the 1990s.' *Renegotiating Ethics in Literature, Philosophy, and Theory*. Ed. Jane Adamson, Richard Freadman, and David Parker. Cambridge: Cambridge University Press, 1998. 1–17.

Parrinder, Patrick. 'Verbing a Noun.' Review of *Out of this World*, by Graham Swift, *Three Farmers on their Way to a Dance*, by Richard Powers, *The March Fence*, by Matthew York, and *What is the Matter with Mary Jane?*, by Daisy Waugh. *The London Review of Books*, 17 March 1988: 17.

Paul, Anthony. 'Gesprekken bij de laatste as.' Review of *Last Orders*, by Graham Swift. *Vrij Nederland*, 23 March 1996. *Literaire Knipselkrant* 08.96.03.071.01.2/01 Gesprekken/Paul.

Pavey, Ruth. 'Heart of Bermondsey.' Review of *Last Orders*, by Graham Swift. *The New Statesman & Society*, 19 January 1996: 37. *Academic Search Elite*. EBSCOhost. Universiteitsbibliotheek K. U. Leuven, Leuven. 9 November 2000 <http://search.epnet.com/>.

Picot, Jean-Louis. '*Waterland*: La machine à remonter le temps.' Morel 29–38.

Poole, Adrian. 'Graham Swift and the Mourning After.' *An Introduction to Contemporary Fiction: International Writing in English since 1970*. Ed. Rod Mengham. Cambridge: Polity Press, 1999. 150–67.

——. 'Hurry Up Please It's Time.' Review of *Last Orders*, by Graham Swift. *The Guardian*, 12 January 1996. 1 June 2003 <http://books.guardian.co.uk/reviews/generalfiction/0,6121,98886,00.html>.

Porée, Marc. 'Au non dit du père et du fils.' Review of *L'affaire Shuttlecock*, by Graham Swift. *La quinzaine littéraire* 607 (1992): 20–21.

——. 'Quelques clefs pour l'imaginaire Swiftien.' Morel 49–69.

Posner, Richard. 'Against Ethical Criticism.' *Philosophy and Literature* 21.1 (1997): 1–27.

Prince, Gerald Joseph. *Métaphysique et technique dans l'oeuvre romanesque de Sartre*. Genève: Librairie Droz, 1968.

Pritchard, William H. 'Tradition and Some Individual Talents.' *The Hudson Review* 45.3 (Autumn 1992): 481–90.

Redfield, Marc. *Phantom Formations: Aesthetic Ideology and the Bildungsroman*. Ithaca: Cornell University Press, 1996.

Reynolds, Oliver. 'On the Old Kent Road.' Review of *Last Orders*, by Graham Swift. *The Times Literary Supplement*, 19 January 1996: 25.

Reynolds, Paul. 'Mrs Simpson's Secret Lover Revealed.' *BBC News Online*, 30 January 2003. 8 May 2003 <http://news.bbc.co.uk/1/hi/uk/2706889.stm>.

Rorty, Richard. *Contingency, Irony, and Solidarity*. Cambridge: Cambridge University Press, 1989.

Rosenshield, Gary. 'Deconstructing the Christian Merchant: Antonio and *The Merchant of Venice*.' *Shofar: An Interdisciplinary Journal of Jewish Studies* 20.2 (Winter 2002): 28–51.

Roth, Michael. 'History, Memory, Trauma: Problems in Representing the Extreme.' Research Libraries Group, 1999 Annual Membership Meeting. 15 May 2003 <http://www.rlg.org/annmtg/roth99.html>.

Ruskin, John. 'Of the Pathetic Fallacy.' Abrams et al. 1278–79.

Sacks, Peter M. *The English Elegy: Studies in the Genre from Spenser to Yeats.* Baltimore: Johns Hopkins University Press, 1985.

Sartre, Jean-Paul. 'M. François Mauriac et la liberté.' *Situations I: Essais critiques.* [Paris]: Gallimard, 1947. 33–52.

Schad, John. 'The End of the End of History: Graham Swift's *Waterland*.' *Modern Fiction Studies* 38.4 (1992): 911–25.

Schiller, Friedrich. *On the Aesthetic Education of Man in a Series of Letters.* Ed. and trans. Elizabeth M. Wilkinson and L. A. Willoughby. Oxford: Clarendon Press, 1967.

Shakespeare, William. *Hamlet.* Ed. Harold Jenkins. London: Methuen, 1982.

——. *The Merchant of Venice. The Complete Works.* By William Shakespeare. Ed. Stanley Wells and Gary Taylor. Oxford: Oxford University Press, 1988. 425–51.

Smethurst, Paul. *The Postmodern Chronotope: Reading Space and Time in Contemporary Fiction.* Postmodern Studies. Amsterdam: GA, 2000.

Sontag, Susan. *On Photography.* New York: Farrar, Straus and Giroux, 1978.

Spiering, Menno Ewout. *Englishness: Foreigners and Images of National Identity in Postwar Literature.* Amsterdam: Rodopi, 1993.

Stow, Simon. 'Unbecoming Virulence: The Politics of the Ethical Criticism Debate.' *Philosophy and Literature* 24 (2000): 185–96.

Tal, Kalí. *Worlds of Hurt: Reading the Literatures of Trauma.* Cambridge: Cambridge University Press, 1996.

Taylor, D. J. 'South London Reveries.' Review of *The Light of Day*, by Graham Swift. *The Times Literary Supplement*, 28 February 2003: 21–22.

Terada, Rei. *Feeling in Theory: Emotion after the 'Death of the Subject.'* Cambridge, MA: Harvard University Press, 2001.

Todd, Richard. 'Narrative Trickery and Performative Historiography: Fictional Representation of National Identity in Graham Swift, Peter Carey, and Mordecai Richler.' *Magical Realism: Theory, History, Community.* Ed. Lois Parkinson Zamora and Wendy B. Faris. Durham: Duke University Press, 1995. 305–28.

Tredell, Nicolas. 'Graham Swift.' *Dictionary of Literary Biography, Volume 194: British Novelists since 1960, Second Series.* Ed. Merrit Moseley. Gale Group, 1998. 262–69. *Literature Resource Center.* Gale Group Databases. Universiteitsbibliotheek K. U. Leuven, Leuven. 8 May 2001 <http://www.infotrac.galegroup.com/>.

Trumpener, Katie. 'The Time of the Gypsies: A "People without History" in the Narratives of the West.' *Critical Inquiry* 18 (Summer 1992): 843–84.

van Alphen, Ernst. *Caught by History: Holocaust Effects in Contemporary Art, Literature, and Theory.* Stanford: Stanford University Press, 1997.

——. 'The Performativity of Histories: Graham Swift's *Waterland* as a Theory of History.' *The Point of Theory: Practices of Cultural Analysis.* Ed. Mieke Bal and Inge E. Boer. Amsterdam: Amsterdam University Press, 1994. 202–10.

van der Kolk, Bessel A., and Onno van der Hart. 'The Intrusive Past: The Flexibility of Memory and the Engraving of Trauma.' Caruth 158–82.

Wall, Stephen. 'Self-Slaughters.' Review of *Ever After*, by Graham Swift. *The London Review of Books*, 12 March 1992: 26. *Literature Resource Center*. Gale Group Databases. Universiteitsbibliotheek K. U. Leuven, Leuven. 22 March 2002 <http://www.infotrac.galegroup.com/>.

Waterland. By Graham Swift. Screenplay by Peter Prince. Dir. Stephen Gyllenhaal. Perf. Jeremy Irons, Sinéad Cusack, and Ethan Hawke. Fine Line Features, 1992.

Wells, Lynn. *Allegories of Telling: Self-Referential Narrative in Contemporary British Fiction*. Costerus New Series. Amsterdam: Rodopi, 2003.

Wesseling, Elisabeth. *Writing History as a Prophet: Postmodern Innovations of the Historical Novel*. Amsterdam: John Benjamins, 1991.

Westphal, Bertrand. 'Le complexe de Schéhérazade: Temps et histoire chez Graham Swift.' *Études anglaises* 49 (1996): 52–64.

Wheeler, Wendy. 'After Grief? What Kinds of Inhuman Selves?' *New Formations* 25 (Summer 1995): 77–95.

——. 'Graham Swift.' *Postmodernism: The Key Figures*. Ed. Hans Bertens and Joseph Natoli. Malden, MA: Blackwell, 2002. 297–301.

——. 'In the Middle of Ordinary Things: Rites, Procedures and (Last) Orders.' *New Formations* 34 (Summer 1998): 129–51.

——. 'Melancholic Modernity and Contemporary Grief: The Novels of Graham Swift.' *Literature and the Contemporary: Fictions and Theories of the Present*. Ed. Roger Luckhurst and Peter Marks. Harlow: Pearson, 1999. 63–79.

——. *A New Modernity? Change in Science, Literature and Politics*. London: Lawrence & Wishart, 1999.

——. 'Swift, Graham.' *The Literary Encyclopedia and Literary Dictionary*. Ed. Robert Clark et al. 21 May 2003 <http://www.litencyc.com/php/speople.php?rec=true&UID=5071>.

Wheeler, Wendy Jayne. *From the Sublime to the Domestic: Postmodernism and the Novels of Graham Swift and Peter Ackroyd*. Dissertation. University of Sussex, 1994. Boston Spa: British Library Document Supply Centre (British Thesis Service), 2002.

White, David A. 'On Bridging the Gulf between Nature and Morality in the *Critique of Judgment*.' *Journal of Aesthetics & Art Criticism* 38.2 (1979): 179–88.

Widdowson, Peter. 'The Novels of Graham Swift.' *Literature in Context*. Ed. Rick Rylance and Judy Simons. Houndmills: Palgrave, 2001. 209–24.

Williams, Garrath. 'Kant and the Question of Meaning.' *Philosophical Forum* 30.2 (1999): 115–31.

Winnberg, Jakob. *An Aesthetics of Vulnerability: The Sentimentum and the Novels of Graham Swift*. Gothenburg Studies in English. Gothenburg: Gothenburg University Press, 2003.

Žižek, Slavoj. *The Sublime Object of Ideology*. London: Verso, 1989.

Zumthor, Paul. 'An Overview: Why the Troubadours?' *A Handbook of the Troubadours*. Ed. F. R. P. Akehurst and Judith M. Davis. Berkeley: University of California Press, 1995, 11–18.

Index